Be In The Number

Pochettino's final season through the voices of Tottenham Hotspur Supporters' Clubs around the world

By Carl Jones

To my beautiful family for allowing me to plan our lives around
Tottenham Hotspur Football Club.

To Dad, for letting me tag along to Meadow Lane on that dreadful
night in 1994

"It is better to fail aiming high than to succeed aiming low. And we of Spurs have set our sights very high, so high in fact that even failure will have in it an echo of glory."

BILL NICHOLSON

"If you don't win anything, you have had a bad season."

ALSO BILL NICHOLSON

"This is my club, my one and only club."

LEDLEY KING

CONTENTS

Introduction   vii

AUGUST

1   Que Sera, Sera – *Yorkshire Spurs*   1

SEPTEMBER

2   Lost. At Sea. – *LA Spurs*   16

OCTOBER

3   Things Look A Little Messi – *Lebanon Spurs*   33

NOVEMBER

4   A Game of Two Halves – *Sweden Spurs*   46

5   It Could Have Been Six or Seven – *Kiwi Spurs*   57

DECEMBER

6   Derby Day – *Ghana Spurs*   71

7   A Nou Hope – *Iceland Spurs*   82

8   Twelve Goals of Christmas – *Las Vegas Spurs*   95

JANUARY

9   Nkoudou to the Rescue – *Malaysia Spurs*   106

FEBRUARY

10   From Borussia With Love – *Germany Spurs*   128

MARCH

11   Hugo's Glove - *OzSpurs*   142

APRIL

12   Finally Home – *Hong Kong Spurs*   160

13   VAR, my Lord – *Norway Spurs*   175

14   One Hell of a Hangover – *Spurs Canada*   190

MAY

15   One Moura Game – *Punjabi Spurs*   201

JUNE

16   Don't Concede Early   218

Madrid 2019:

Supporters from around the world share their experience

2018/19 Results and Table

The Humble One

INTRODUCTION

As you read this, the 2018/19 season will be but a memory. Tottenham Hotspur Football Club will have a brand-new home. For better or for worse, I could be about to record their unexpected but momentous first title triumph for over half a century. Perhaps it will be their marginally more unexpected first relegation from the top flight since 1977. Or, most probably, something in between.

As I write this, the 2018 World Cup in Russia is currently in full swing. England are about to head into a quarter final against Sweden, odds-on to reach the last-four. Love Island is on the telly every night and this green and pleasant land is a little bit browner than usual as we bask in one of the hottest summers in living memory. The hosepipes are banned, Brexit is being ballsed, wildfires are raging across the grasslands of northern Britain, but football appears to be coming home and that, quite frankly, is all that anyone seems to really care about.

Leading the charge for both the Golden Boot and football's grandest prize is Harry Kane, backed by a merry band of Tottenham teammates who braved and beat the dreaded penalty curse just a few nights ago. This is Gareth's team, but the spirit of Poch burns brightly among England's four Lions. And, let's face it, we can make a decent claim for Kyle Walker too.

In this increasingly global game, fans around the world are becoming accustomed to what Spurs fans have known for a year or two now. While Eriksen, Son, Vertonghen and even Kieran Trippier gain new plaudits as talismen for their respective nations, the brightest new talent in world football and heir to the Ballon d'Or is one of our own.

Another noticeable trend in this World Cup more than any

that preceded it is the number of overseas fans across social media sharing in the success of Tottenham's contingent. With Belgium marching on, France looking strong and South Korea, Colombia and Denmark all joining England in looking to Spurs players to lead the way, the online forums remain abuzz even in the close season. Meanwhile, Tottenham fans around the globe express concern over split loyalties watching so many of their boys progressing through to the knockout stages – not least the good people of Sweden, a fellow surprise package in the last-eight, who stand in England's way for a first semi-final since 1990.

Tottenham's increased profile on the world stage is no accident, of course; nor is it quite as romantic as it might appear on the face of it either. Years of overseas tours in locations including Asia, where the popularity of the Premier League has grown exponentially, and more recently North America - perhaps football's final frontier for the growth that the National American Soccer League of the 1970's and Diana Ross's missed penalty in 1994 didn't quite deliver - have long made commercial sense for English football's most established brands.

It wasn't always this way. Currently in my early thirties, I'm the first of a generation that cannot consciously remember a time before the razzamatazz of the Premier League. Its all-conquering exposure was a slower burn, however – and while overseas players became more commonplace on our shores, it would take a little longer for English football's rebranded top flight to compete with Italian, Spanish and even German club football both on and off the field. A lack of marketability combined with technology was holding the English game back overseas. It's a subject I consider myself a specialist in having pleaded with my own parents to ensure Spurs matches were planned into every summer holiday as a teen and subjecting my own young family to the same rigour several decades later.

During the Easter holidays of 1995, I went on an aeroplane for the first time. While that Portuguese holiday is most fondly remembered for my mum sleeping in the bath after a heavy night on the Tia Maria and my dad's wide selection of bum bag, socks and sandals combinations on the various VHS recordings of us murdering karaoke in the hotel bar, I remember it for something else.

On Sunday the 9th of April 1995, I spent the best part of an afternoon frantically chasing my Dad from tavern to saloon in search of a TV showing Everton versus Spurs in the FA Cup Semi Final. By the time we'd eventually found a shabby looking building with a huge satellite that looked more capable of receiving alien contact than Super Sunday, we were already two goals down. A 4-1 battering ended our hopes of domestic silverware.

A few years later, I went cross-Atlantic for the first time. At least in the Algarve you could pick up a Sunday paper a little later in the day if you couldn't watch the game on Saturday. In Florida, the Sunday paper was a couple of days behind. The memory of my 13-year-old self, poring over every result with wide eyes and a large glass of Sunny Delight on the Tuesday morning that followed is one that remains oddly sentimental, especially now I'm a father and my own son is developing a similar addiction to the game.

'Dad!' I cried from the breakfast counter of the holiday home that was three times bigger than our own. 'Man United beat Forest 8-1! Solskjaer scored four of them in the last twenty minutes!' The recollection of that record scoreline makes the date easy to pinpoint; I had to look up who Spurs played that same afternoon just now. I'm not sure how that goalless draw with Coventry City slipped from my memory.

Fast forward another decade and the internet had revolutionised access to football. While you might reasonably expect to find lovers of the game huddled around a screen during any World Cup since the inception of the television regardless of where you were on the planet, it would be of equally little surprise to find a hardcore gaggle of present-day fans glued to a live stream of a Premier League match in the most unlikely of places today.

I first experienced this in February 2011 while on holiday in New York. On a freezing Saturday morning, my wife and I found shelter in an Irish bar called Flannery's for breakfast. The location was no accident. With a little research, I had located the Big Apple's dedicated Spurs supporters' club. And dedicated truly was the word – displayed around the bar were shirts, scarves and various other framed paraphernalia from seasons and matches of yesteryear. Inside, a small handful of tourists and a large gathering of locals cheered like they were in the ground. It was a morning of camaraderie, Guinness, a 2-1 win over Bolton and, perhaps most pleasingly of all, the featured match from St James' Park seeing Newcastle United come back from four goals down to salvage a point against Arsenal.

Oh, and the rest of the visit to Manhattan was also fun. I'm available for presenting duties on Holiday if they bring it back and Judith Chalmers doesn't fancy digging her sarong out.

My next venture into the world of the supporters' club came last season in October 2017. Giving up my season ticket to my Dad so he could take my son down to Wembley, I would instead be watching one of Tottenham's season defining games in the The Greyhound Bar and Grill on the outskirts of Los Angeles. What was truly the holiday of a lifetime would, of course, be punctuated with a very early alarm on the Sunday to experience the match with the LA supporters' club. Wherever I am and whatever the time difference, I'll almost always find a way to watch Spurs.

There are times when this ever-connected world is unwelcome, though. Following the pain of our unexpected and ultimately fruitless title battle with Leicester City in 2016, the solace of being abroad for the dead rubber of a final game of the season at St James' Park might once have been welcome. I made a conscious effort to avoid keeping an eye on the score as I enjoyed a birthday trip to Barcelona. As the tapas and afternoon wine glasses were cleared away, I glanced at my phone to see the runners-up spot had been conceded to our good friends and neighbours following a 5-1 defeat. Spoilt the rest of the afternoon. Sometimes it's just not worth punishing yourself.

If my experience in Manhattan's miniature White Hart Lane had been a blueprint for the explosion of satellite gatherings that was beginning to pick up pace around the globe, LA was the model of things to come. The Greyhound is an innocuous looking bar that lives and breathes Spurs. More than a hundred fans gathered and sang from start to finish as Liverpool were dismantled in devastating fashion. I stepped outside to call my dad at the interval to share the incredulity at our first half performance and speak to my son.

'I can't hear you very well,' he bellowed down the phone as I fanned myself in the early-morning heat. 'But we're playing bloody brilliantly. We're just getting a hot chocolate, it's freezing here.'

As I sat with Dad and watched the closing moments of the 2017/18 season unfold in the ding-dong 5-4 win against Leicester City, my eyes focused in on a familiar sight flashing around the electronic hoardings of Wembley. While we began to reflect on a bittersweet but largely successful season in our temporary home, the names of each and every official Tottenham Hotspur supporters' club displayed beneath the Club Wembley tier as they had done so often during the season.

I thought back to the small handful of friends I made in LA and their end of season party. I wondered what might be happening in the bars of Auckland, Reykjavik, Sydney and Oslo as we trudged back to the car recounting an extraordinary ninety minutes. I marvelled at the thought of Spurs fans in Sweden, Lebanon, Ghana and Malaysia heading back home in their replica shirts. And then, in that very moment, I decided to write a book about them.

This book is intended as a memoir – a time capsule of sorts - that records the progress of a transitional season back across North London from HA9 to N17. A literary season ticket on tour across the globe.

Within these pages are the stories of Tottenham diehards like me who plan their lives, their holidays and even their careers around the boys from White Hart Lane. They go to extraordinary lengths to see their team in action, be it in a bar halfway around the world in the middle of the night or by saving up every penny with the goal of savouring that walk down the High Road once again; or perhaps even for the very first time.

Some have never sung the names of their heroes from the Park Lane. Others grew up there and moved away. Whatever their story, one thing unites all of them: Tottenham Hotspur Football Club.

At this stage, a gentle warning: this book is unashamedly about Spurs so if that sort of thing makes you queasy, you might want to put it down now. But it's also about the obsession of fandom and the intangible, immeasurable dedication between supporter and football club that's universal. This is my Club, my one and only Club and I know I'm not alone.

Come 3pm on a Saturday, 7am on a Sunday or 3am on a weekday Wednesday, it doesn't matter who you are or where you come from. You can Be In That Number.

AUGUST

1
QUE SERA, SERA
YORKSHIRE SPURS

It's hard to explain how the summer still seemed to drag after the ticker tape was cleared away in Moscow. Memories of the tournament-free summers of my youth, waiting for the fixture lists to be released without a Spurs game on the horizon to look forward to, were agony as a kid. With Gareth Southgate's men extending interest for an extra fortnight and a truly memorable tournament capped off with a Tottenham captain lifting the trophy, there was little reason for those few short weeks to toil like they did. And while there were no knighthoods mooted at the time of writing, no fewer than nine of Pochettino's men extended their involvement until the very final few days with five English, three Belgian and one victorious Frenchman delaying their holidays until the very last moment.

Closer to home, what remained of Tottenham's squad gathered at the state-of-the-art training centre in Enfield. With a growing list of suggested outgoings before the transfer window slammed shut on the eve of the new season, the rumour mill was suspiciously quiet on incoming acquisitions. As Europa League-bound Burnley finally put pen to paper on their first signing of the summer, focus fell on Spurs who became the only side, not only in the English top flight but also of the twenty-five teams already guaranteed a spot in the Champions League group stages, to have failed to add to their squad. Anxious anticipation for a marquee signing to mark the new stadium move grew, while the fanbase began to fracture over the necessity of such an addition.

In one camp, the strong argument that the squad needed no

further improvement given that it possessed the group of players with more World Cup minutes under their belts than any team on the planet. How can you strengthen that? On the other - a camp I leaned towards - the very same argument that our squad possessed the group of players with more World Cup minutes under their belts than anyone else. We needed a few reinforcements to mitigate against the wantaways, maintain a high energy pressing game for the whole season and perhaps have a bit more game changing quality on the bench. More than that, though, with the most expensive season tickets in the land and one bumper TV deal after another, why not splash out on a few new additions? In fairness, the mortgage on the new place was perhaps a sufficiently sobering reason.

'You need to be confident and trust in the people that you have, and the way we work,' said Pochettino in the week before the transfer window closed. 'But of course, football is about adding more quality every season like different clubs, our contenders, are doing. If we cannot do that, we need to be creative and of course the help of our younger players would be amazing. We are working so hard, but we still are like we were on the first day of the transfer window, with no signings.'

In the end, the window would close with only one new arrival. On the 8th of August, Harry Kane tweeted an image of his newborn second child Vivienne Jane Kane. 'She is beautiful,' replied Gabby Logan, adding that 'this means you already scored in August.' While Gabby's grasp of procreation appears sketchy to say the least, I can confirm from personal experience that he's unlikely to score again until at least Christmas.

The lack of actual signings triggered the predictable flurry of headlines, late-night panel discussions and people shouting on phone-ins that would only be partially be quelled by a hard-fought 1-0 win at St James' Park in the new season's opener. For every considered take that the settled squad of seasoned campaigners gave Spurs an advantage over their competitors, there was the opposing view that a lack of ambition in the transfer market at a time when the club were showing unprecedented ambition off the pitch was a missed opportunity that was unlikely to present itself again. While rival fans mocked Spurs for claiming the 'net spend trophy', the figures were undeniable; in four years at Tottenham, across eight transfer windows, Mauricio Pochettino had spent just £29m more than he'd recouped – the equivalent of one Moussa Sissoko, minus postage and packaging.

Fixture release day had been relatively kind to Spurs, with the opening day trip to Newcastle followed by the visit of newly promoted Fulham. Last season, in my 33rd year on the planet, I became the proud owner of a Tottenham Hotspur season ticket. As a 10-year-old, I'd begged my Dad to take me to White Hart Lane every Saturday for years. Unfortunately, due to the obligation of running a family business combined with the 300-mile return journey from Chesterfield, such a commitment wasn't possible. Instead, we'd go to every away game north of Watford that didn't fall during opening hours. For a while in my early teens, I'd visited Villa Park, Elland Road, Hillsborough and Filbert Street more often than White Hart Lane itself. Those rare trips down, though, were truly something special.

My first ever Spurs game was a League Cup tie at Notts County. A memorable night for me turned into a forgettable one for the club, as a 3-0 defeat saw the end of Ossie Ardiles' reign. I can't remember a great deal about the match itself other than the barrage of abuse that rained down from the stands towards the dugout. I've been back to Meadow Lane in a work capacity on several occasions since – unsurprisingly, it's an evening that's much more fondly remembered on the banks of the Trent even a quarter of a century on.

My first game at White Hart Lane was a more memorable affair. An early season victory over Sheffield Wednesday relieved the pressure on Gerry Francis in 1997/98 but he wouldn't last a great deal longer. I can still almost point to the seat I sat in when images of the beautiful old stadium are broadcast. It still feels strange referring to it in the past tense. I wonder when that will change.

A driving license meant my trips to the Lane became more frequent in my late teens, as did the away days. I stood through Grimsby away in the League Cup and watched Darren Bent gloat as he threatened to derail our top four bid with a brace at the Stadium of Light. I was in the away end a few months later when Peter Crouch headed Spurs into the Champions League before we very nearly screwed it up against Young Boys. I was up in the gods at the San Siro when Heurelho Gomes trudged off the field and Samuel Eto'o slotted Inter Milan into a 2-0 lead after just 12 minutes and my old Blackberry battery died from the incoming messages of support and derision. I had to wait until I got back to the hotel to charge it and received the barrage of banter that preceded Gareth Bale announcing himself onto the world scene with THAT hat-trick.

A season ticket, though, had never really seemed to be in my grasp. The prospect of moving from Derbyshire to London was something I'd toyed with for a few years in my early 20s. I joined the waiting list for a while but came back off it when a career, then a family, then the unexpected twist of a reasonably successful side career as a stand-up comedian meant weekends would be spent on stages scattered across the country. When the increased capacity of our temporary home offered the chance of a ticket to every home game, I found myself looking at my own son and remembering how I'd longed to spend my Saturdays watching Spurs at his age. The opportunity might not come around again. We were on our way to Wembley.

One man who knows all about such excursions is Paul Pavlou, or Pav to his mates, the 39-year-old London born Chairman of Yorkshire Spurs. It's not just around the globe that Tottenham supporters' clubs have sprung up in the past few years. With our relative recent success fuelling the growth of a national fanbase as well as an international one, such regionally dispersed UK collectives have been forming just as quickly as they have overseas. With no representation in North East Derbyshire, Yorkshire Spurs are my 'locals'.

'Yorkshire Spurs was set up about a year ago,' he tells me. 'This time last year it was just a Facebook page. A good friend called Alex set it up and it became official, but I don't think he realised how time consuming it was. Alex stepped down and after a quick chat with another friend called Ro (Huntriss), we decided to keep the momentum going as we could see it was just on the verge of doing alright. Without that conversation, it would have probably remained as a Facebook group full of banter and local fans talking football.

'We did a few small group trips down to Wembley. Our first was the Stoke game last season and there were only about 15 of us. By the end of the season, it was about 50 or 60 people, so it's grown a lot. People are seeing the trips on social media and the club promote it too. We get a few emails a week from people that want to sign up.'

It seems like the perfect network of enthusiasts across the world. If supporting a football club is the ultimate sign of consumer dedication, these brand advocates are actively bringing together other diehards in geographically dispersed areas to share the product with – and, better still from a commercial point of view, it's all voluntary. While Paul recognises how little he gains from the business model by comparison to the club, he's keen to point out the role comes with a few perks.

He continues: 'The club have done stuff for me. Last Christmas, Pochettino and Daniel Levy did a Q&A for about 50 people and I was invited to that and had a kick about with a couple of first team players for a training experience just before the season finished. You don't know when you're going to get them; you'll just get a phone call asking if you can make it down to the training. That's not costing them anything but it's just a thank you for your hard work.'

As we chat ahead of the second game of the fledgling season, the two subjects that have dominated all conversation about Spurs going into the weekend have been the stadium delay and the lack of incoming transfers. Paul is quite relaxed about the whole situation.

'I'm not shocked,' he says calmly on the news that the stadium will now be delayed for at least several more games beyond the first scheduled home tie against Fulham. 'It looked like it wasn't going to be ready in a couple of weeks but I'm just looking at the bigger picture really. In a month or two or three we are going to have one of the best stadiums in the world and it's going to be there forever and it's still in the heart of Tottenham isn't it? So that doesn't really bother me too much. It's a shame not to get in there but it's just like waiting a bit longer for Christmas!'

Unlike the average kid at Christmas, who might be prone to tantrums upon discovering no sparkling new signings are waiting under the tree, Paul is also all about the deferred gratification of retaining what still looks like the strongest Spurs XI in living memory.

'I'm just too positive,' he laughs, reflecting on the strong opinions of both sides of the argument. 'I'm just a positive person! I'm just happy we've kept everyone together. It would be great to have a marquee signing I suppose but realistically it's never happened. We don't do that, do we? So, they are not going to change.

'Everyone was saying about this £150m war chest. We've not spent that ever, so I didn't think we were going to change this summer. I'm just happy we've kept Toby (Alderweireld) and hopefully he pulls his weight and buys into it all. The way we buy people and the way we spend, it's hard to get someone that improves the first XI.

'And it's hard to get squad members that are happy to sit on the bench and be squad members for a price the club are gonna pay. Poch is quite a loyal person, isn't he? This whole thing with Grealish,' he continues, in reference to the continual links with the young Aston Villa midfielder over the summer that eventually came to nothing. 'I think being such a loyal person, if he thinks Winks is going to come back in and do a job then there is no reason to buy someone in that position. People have forgotten about Winks, but he did really well last season when he actually played. So, if he bought someone in that position, it's a kick in the teeth for Winks.'

Paul's positivity is contagious as he points out a fact that's hard to deny: 'Going back four or five years, a couple of the players would have left, wouldn't they? There is quite a lot of negativity about with what's going on, but I just try and be positive. There is no point being negative about things.' You can't argue with that.

Despite being the Chairman of Yorkshire Spurs, Paul began life much closer to White Hart Lane than his current residence in Leeds, where he arrived at the beginning of a University degree more than two decades ago and has remained ever since.

He says: 'I worked in the club shop for a bit of pocket money going through college. I also did a bit of stewarding. When I was growing up, I wasn't really interested in anything else. I was wondering what I should do to get me through college and then it dawned on me: I'll work at Tottenham.

'Most of the members are Yorkshire born and bred. There are a couple of them that have moved up from London but a lot of them are born and raised in Yorkshire and perhaps their dad was from London and they moved up and they are second generation Spurs fans. It's a mixture, really.

'We've got one member called Jimmy Dimmock. His uncle scored the winner for Tottenham in the 1921 cup final. Jimmy must be in his 80's now. He remembers playing with a tin can on the streets of Edmonton with his uncle. He's an interesting guy.'

Since becoming Chairman of Yorkshire Spurs, Paul has come across several other supporters' clubs while on his travels. It's something he's already done some research into ahead of the coming months as well – with an upcoming trip to New York clashing with a glamour tie against Manchester City, there's the added anxiety that the visit of the reigning champions is presently being mooted as the first game at the new stadium. The second and third home games of the season against Liverpool and Cardiff City respectively have now officially been moved to Wembley.

'It's a bit surprising isn't it?' ponders Paul on the explosion of our international fanbase. 'One of our members went to New York supporters' club last season for the Arsenal game at half seven in the morning and there are 300 people in there. I'm 40 in December and when I used to go between 16 and 25, I used to sit in the south lower and it was all just guys from north London. But now it's worldwide. It's absolutely gone nuts, it's totally changed.

'I go away a few times a year and I always try and track down the local supporters' club and catch a game with them. Last year I went to Malta and ended up watching the game with them. There were only about 20 people there, but I ended up meeting up with some guys from Glasgow Spurs. I was chatting to them and they'd done the same thing. It's a really good networking thing for us.'

And what about Maltese, Glaswegian or New Yorker Spurs fans making the return journey to Leeds, Doncaster and Barnsley?

'No one really comes to us but if you're going to places like LA or any holiday destination, it's great. There's an application going in for Las Vegas Spurs. That would be quite a cool one. It's a good way of making a fan base bigger. You've got all these chairmen around the world doing it for free and we're promoting it and bringing people together. It's just a really good idea.'

Bringing people together is exactly what Yorkshire Spurs has done. From a small handful of fans dispersed across the region, membership has ballooned to an impressive 160 members. While the lively Facebook group remains a pillar of the community, live events have also been hugely successful – and Paul has ambitious plans for the future.

'Last year we had Ossie Ardiles come up and do a Q&A. I paid him to come up and sold a few tickets, we broke even, and it was a brilliant night. We had Paul Stewart up last month for another Q&A. We are going to do a couple more probably towards the back end of Christmas and end of this season. It's good fun.

'Last season - and I think we were one of the first clubs to do it - we started a podcast. We have done a supporters' club 5-aside tournament in Leeds where we had seven or eight supporters' clubs from around the country come as we are quite central to the UK and that went down quite well.

'Football is such an international language. If you meet a Spurs fan, whoever or wherever they are, it's just an instant bond isn't it? A couple of these members I've only known for a year or so, but I feel like I've known them for ten years because we've been socialising and doing our trips and you've got so much in common. It's a really good way of meeting new people.'

Despite the lengthy commute, that provided its own personal challenges during busy parts of last season for me by car, Paul and his fellow members generally rely on trains out of Leeds and Doncaster to reach Wembley. The juggling of fixture changes combined with the sheer effort and expense of getting to every home game means the occasional trip is forsaken – but they're the minority.

Paul continues: 'I'm self-employed, so apart from keeping the wife happy with all the travelling, it's quite flexible. A lot of our members are employed people but they're quite good at working their rotas around Tottenham!

'It was quicker to get to Dortmund than Wembley though and it's cheaper sometimes. One of our guys is always having nightmares on the train. After the Dortmund game last season, he missed the last train back to Leeds and had to sleep at King's Cross until the first train at six or seven in the morning. Then he went straight to work. He's always getting reminded about that one.'

Paul won't be making the trip to Wembley for Fulham, as is rumoured to be the case for quite a few on Saturday. He's very clear that it's in no way a protest, however – just the simple balance of family with Spurs.

'I'll be keeping an eye on my phone on Saturday. I think we should have it in the bag hopefully. I've heard it's not going to be well attended but I don't know if that's just a rumour. By January or February, everyone will have forgotten about it. It's long term, not short term. I'd rather move into the stadium when it's totally finished. You can't rush things like this too much, can you?'

Paul's patience is shared by many. While the ambition to return to White Hart Lane after just one season away was admirable, there is a mixture of frustration from season tickets holders and sympathy that it was clearly an unrealistic goal driven by commercial interest, even by Daniel Levy's standards. Let us not forget this is a man who once tripled his money selling Kevin Wimmer.

Our chat ends with Paul kindly putting me on the guest list for a collective of Spurs fans who gather at the Novotel on Wembley Way. Organised by another official supporters' club, the Punjabi Spurs, who memorably organised Bhangra dancing to Chas and Dave by way of half-time entertainment during one game last season, it's exclusively for members who meet in a large conference room with its own small private bar. It will be my first official perk having joined.

'What do you think then, Jacob?' enquires my dad, a man with the credentials to have launched Yorkshire Spurs from his Barnsley home at any time since 1967 had he had the foresight, to my 9-year-old son halfway along our journey to Wembley. 'Easy win today or what?'

'Errrrmmm…' he replies thoughtfully, looking up from his tablet from the back of the car for the first time since junction 29 of the M1. '3-1' he offers. 'I think 3-1 as well,' I chime in.

'I think it will be four or five,' replies his grandad. 'And Harry Kane to break his goalscoring duck in August.' It's our first Spurs game as a threesome since the night we beat Real Madrid and there's an air of early season confidence mixed with an admirable fuel efficiency in the Jones family Kia on a warm and muggy late summer's afternoon.

Despite this, the familiar sight of the towering arch on the walk from our industrial estate parking space of choice invokes a reminder of where the new campaign *should* be starting. While the anxiety of last season's shaky start at Wembley was soon replaced with the reassurance of several long unbeaten runs, the novelty was wearing off long before Pochettino's men had successfully acclimatised to their new surrounds. The homesickness was palpable in that final game against Leicester – and while news of one more game was just about palatable with most fans, the general mood around confirmation of the extended stay matches the overcast sky in North London.

A long queue snakes from the bar in the Novotel where some of Paul's members will congregate before this afternoon's match. There's no sign of any Yorkshire Spurs scarves amongst the throng but a corridor leading upstairs attracts a regular stream away from the ground floor crowd. After lingering around for a few minutes, I check with the front desk and confirm my hunch as the receptionist points me in the direction of the elevators. There, a club within a club exists.

Inside, more than a hundred fans attempt to enjoy the entertainment provided by Cardiff and Newcastle in the lunchtime kick-off. 'Bloody hell,' says one fan as he reaches his group with a pint of Heineken in a plastic cup and gestures towards his surroundings. 'I can't believe we're back here.'

We enter Wembley through the familiar entrance by the Bobby Moore statue, absorbing the team news as we head towards unfamiliar seats close to where our season tickets had been. The lively Lucas Moura, frequently cited as being 'like a new signing' by anyone keen to defend the transfer window, is named in the starting XI, as is Toby Alderweireld in a three-man defence. A pre-match presentation celebrates both Harry Kane's Golden Boot and Hugo Lloris' triumphant return as a World Cup winner by a famous face who knows all about that sort of thing. Ossie Ardiles, the man whose managerial reign ended the night my love affair with Tottenham Hotspur began, is kept busy these days as a Club ambassador.

Fulham's travelling contingent appear to be enjoying themselves in the early stages of the game. Despite an opening day defeat, their surprise promotion here in the play-off final despite playing much of the game with ten men remains fresh in the memory. They're a welcome addition to the Premier League, bringing an attractive brand of pacey, attacking football that will provide a decent test this afternoon. Craven Cottage, with its middle-class food stalls and leafy suburban surrounds on the banks of the Thames is undoubtedly up there with my favourite away days too.

A dominant early start is familiar at Wembley, especially in the 3-5-2 formation with wingbacks Pochettino has opted for today. With the back three defending a high line and halting the progress of Fulham's potent looking forwards, Spurs repeatedly look to get the ball out to Kieran Trippier on the right-hand side to whip the crosses in. It's a game plan Fulham look prepared for and, barring a contentious Harry Kane penalty shout that's waved away, are more than capable of repelling.

'Can you do the Delebration, Grandad?' enquires Jacob, referring to the viral nature of our number twenty's newly trademarked pose before a ball had been kicked. He demonstrates for my sexagenarian (that's what they're called, look it up) father who attempts to replicate it with such difficulty that it appears to momentarily alert a nearby steward in anticipation of a medical emergency.

Another Trippier cross leads to the opening goal on the stroke of half-time as a weak defensive clearance falls beautifully to Lucas Moura. We're right behind it as the little Brazilian whips the ball around the reach of Marcus Bettinelli and in off the far post before wheeling away to celebrate. I have a tendency of instinctively picking my son up when we score, something which dates back to the first games I ever took him to when he wouldn't be able to see the pitch after the whole stand had risen to its feet. He's a little taller now, and more than a little heavier. I quietly ponder to myself when I'll do that for the last time as we settle back into our seats. Perhaps neither of us will know or remember until long after it happens, like me and my own father. Hopefully it's before my back gives out and at least by the time he's reached his mid-twenties.

We bump into a few mates from the surrounding seats of our season ticket last year in the queue for coffees who embrace us like long lost relatives. It's a phenomenon I've read about in other books, most notably John Crace's brilliant *Vertigo*, about the trials and tribulations of following Tottenham. While our bond was understandably not quite as strong after just one season at Wembley, it's a reminder of the simple kinship that sharing the experience of supporting your side can bring – this being the very essence of becoming part of a supporters' club, I suppose. I hugged at least two of them while caught up in the moment on the unforgettable night we beat Real Madrid tighter than I have any distant relative at a family gathering.

Fulham come out swinging in the second half and a shot cannoning off the post proves to be the warning of what's to come as Alexander Mitrovic's unorthodox header to draw the visitors level drains away some of the patience our first half dominance has earned. An early tactical switch sees Davinson Sanchez spared for Erik Lamela who looks even livelier than usual in a cameo role. With Heung-Min Son released for Asian Games duty in a bid to relinquish the necessity to fulfil national duty in South Korea, the Argentine clearly sniffs an opportunity having finally returned to full fitness and put pen to paper on a new deal.

A freekick around 25 yards out offers the chance to retake the lead in the 74th minute. For once, it's not Christian Eriksen stepping up or even Harry Kane on guest duty. Kieran Trippier stands confidently over the ball, weighing up the defensive wall before bending an inch-perfect delivery over them and into the corner. It's practically a replay of his heroics in Russia and, as he wheels away, the 58,000 in attendance are instantly delivered a month back in time to the glorious moment when football coming home seemed little more than an inevitability.

Erik Lamela's driving run at the heart of the Fulham defence a few minutes later sees him execute a perfectly timed ball to release Harry Kane who shows composure to check back in onto his right foot and calmly slot beyond the Fulham goalkeeper. The game is won; Spurs maintain their early 100% record.

'Me and Dad got it right, Grandad. You were

wrong!' Jacob teases on the walk back to the car.

'I said we'd win by a few goals and Harry Kane scores in August!' he replies. 'Still wrong though, weren't you?' comes the smart-arse response from his grandson.

With the Jones score prediction league off to a successful start, and the newborn Premier League table looking healthy with Spurs sitting just ahead of Bournemouth at the summit ahead of the evening kick-off, there's even an Arsenal defeat to listen to on the long journey back to Chesterfield, even if it is to Chelsea.

'Sounds like I missed a cracker,' says Paul via text message. 'I'll be there for the Liverpool game if you fancy a beer.' If the atmosphere in the Novotel was uncharacteristically reserved for Fulham, the yearning for home by Liverpool will surely be palpable.

In the week that follows, our official club membership packs arrive in the post. Among the various goodies in the commemorative tin is a blank key bearing the Spurs emblem. The accompanying letter explains that it's meant to 'signify the unlocking of the doors to our new home'.

For now, at least, it remains uncut.

The Yorkshire Spurs gang head off on another 'away day'.

SEPTEMBER

2
LOST. AT SEA.
LA SPURS

Earlier this year, I made a rather unfortunate detour across France. How the detour came about and who was to blame is up to you to decide.

It occurred on Saturday 26th May, the day when Liverpool and Real Madrid would contest the Champions League Final. This would also be the day that, after a hectic few months of work, I would be spending a well-earned week away on a campsite in Brittany with my family.

Having travelled down to Folkestone the night before, we set off for France on Saturday morning. With a 7-hour journey ahead of us, and all driving duties in mainland Europe falling to me, we hit the road early with one goal in mind: arrive at the campsite in time for the Champions League Final.

After an early pit stop for fuel and a slightly soggy service station jambon et emmantal triple shortly after arriving on French soil, we made the unanimous decision to plough on and reach Camping L'Atlantique without stopping again. While en route, we invented a game where everyone in turn picked a favourite song which we then streamed on my iPhone. Jones FM-ily we called it, playing an eclectic mix from Disney, Oasis, Chas & Dave, Arctic Monkeys, Johnny Cash, tunes from various musicals, the theme from Jurassic Park and The Wheels on the Bus. It really killed the time and we're hoping to go for an official license in the near future to give BBC Radio 2 a run for their money.

To play this game, my wife Lynsey had to swap phones

midway through the journey for streaming purposes. It was at this point that she made a fateful announcement.

'Oooh, good news kids,' she said, turning to our patient but severely bored offspring in the back of the car. 'Mum's phone gets us there five minutes quicker than Dad's phone!'

'Are you sure you've got the right place?' I enquired, a moment I might implore you to consider as circumstantial evidence when coming to a decision later. 'Yes,' she replied, in a response that would immediately rule herself out of the position of Traffic and Travel Reporter once that commercial radio license does eventually come through.

It was at this point in the movie of our lives where there might be a record scratch and a freeze frame, as this is probably the bit where you become aware of what was painfully obvious to anyone except us as we continued on our merry road singing Ossie's Dream and commenting on how well the kids were coping with the long journey. I say 'you' would become aware quite pointedly – I'd probably miss it the second time around as well. I'm not the most observant – something of a disadvantage for an observational comedian. I can still remember wondering why everyone was gasping in the cinema at the big reveal in The Sixth Sense as the film's revelation sailed over my head and into the rows behind. Consequently, I still haven't gone back to re-watch it since out of spite.

On eventually reaching the campsite with an hour to go before the football began, the main reception was closed. Not an issue according to a lady behind the bar who spoke as much English as we did French – something of an occupational hazard when working the summer season at an international holiday camp, I suppose, but we shared enough vocabulary to get by. We ordered a few drinks and began to unwind after counting down every hour of the journey since Calais.

It was at this point that a small, nagging doubt began to appear in the back of my mind. Something didn't seem quite right. As we waited for a receptionist that would never arrive to confirm a booking we'd never made, a quick glance at our geolocation on

Google Maps confirmed it - we'd gone too far down the coast. We were at the wrong campsite. Disaster. No wonder they didn't know who the hell we were and hadn't spoken English since 1983. Still, it didn't look too far on the map at first glance, at least. I recalculated to the correct final destination and took a deep breath...

THREE HOURS FORTY-NINE MINUTES WRONG. 336 KILOMETRES WRONG. APPROXIMATELY THE DISTANCE FROM WHITE HART LANE TO OLD TRAFFORD WRONG.

It's in these moments you discover whether you truly love someone. As the Champions League theme tune began to play behind us on a screen the size of a two-storey house, we took a deep breath, returned our glasses to the bar and got back into the car.

Two movies, two more jambon et emmantal sandwiches, a broken signal for the Champions League Final commentary and quite a lot of Mummy and Daddy 'quiet time' later, we arrived at the correct campsite at 11.30pm.

'Are you there yet?' enquired my dad on the phone as we unpacked the car in the dead of night. 'You did what?' he replied incredulously as I recounted our day. 'You won't have seen what Bale did then? Probably the best goal I've ever seen,' he added, helpfully. I would eventually see our former number 11's wonder strike with a warm beer from the travel bag just after midnight.

With this experience fresh in the mind, it was with trepidation that we returned to France for the final week of the school summer holidays. Spurs would be facing Watford midway through our break on the back of a stunning 3-0 victory at Old Trafford that had continued a 100% record and left an enraged Jose Mourinho departing a press conference while ranting about 'respect' like a livid, Portuguese Ali G impersonator.

Having successfully negotiated arrival at the correct campsite a few days before – an achievement not to be sniffed at based on previous experience - I parked myself on a stool in the campsite bar to see the final half hour of Arsenal's unconvincing but effective overturning of Cardiff City in the afternoon's early kick-off. Then, just as the teams began warming up on the Vicarage Road pitch, calamity struck. Our previously trusty barkeep waved his dodgy remote control and Sky Sports was switched over to an unfamiliar looking venue with unusual goalposts.

'It's the All-Ireland Final mate,' he said in a not particularly sympathetic tone as he clocked my incredulity. 'We've got more in who want to watch that than the football.' I began a mental referendum of the bar — a few disinterested holidaymakers nursing an expensive pint of lager, a few more glued to the Formula 1 and half a dozen folk in unfamiliar replica shirts immediately intoxicated by the football-cum-rugby on offer. At that very moment, with my unfortunate luck around watching eagerly anticipated (by me, at least) matches abroad looking set to continue, a man and his son walked in wearing Watford shirts.

This was no time for tribalism. They were my ticket and, along with a couple more blokes who appeared to be as non-plussed by the experience of this newly discovered sport but who had begun seeking advice on how to bet on it from more knowledgeable punters around them anyway, the balance had finally been tipped.

'You after the Watford vs Spurs game as well, mate?' I asked, raising a mock eyebrow at the big screen above the bar.

'Well, I was pal,' came the response in an accent I couldn't immediately place. 'But to be honest, I'd probably rather watch this!' That's right, reader: I'd found the only Irish Watford fan in Brittany.

After watching Spurs toil into a one-goal lead in the first half on my daughter's tiny pink Kindle screen, the channel was eventually switched over in time for the second half. 'See you later mate,' said my new Irish friend who had gratefully been glancing at the match over my shoulder while largely engrossed in Dublin's victory over Tyrone. My disbelief that he would depart so early into the second half was only compounded when Watford went on to overturn a worryingly soft looking Spurs. Two well-taken set-pieces would confound the odds and extend their own 100% start to the season. I blanked the Watford fan for the rest of the week.

You might have ascertained by now that I really do love a holiday. It's worth clarifying that it's by no means a jet set lifestyle that I lead. I can get by with a battered car and a slightly tatty winter coat entering its third campaign if it means I can put a bit aside each month to go somewhere nice. There aren't many requirements of a trip – a comfy bed, private en suite facilities, inputting the correct details into the SatNav. That sort of thing.

One such trip that had long been on the bucket list was Los Angeles. The Golden State probably isn't the most original of dream destinations, but you don't get a 2:1 in Film and Television Studies without harbouring a yearning to visit Tinseltown for the best part of your life. Despite that, very few things come between me watching Spurs and so, at the break of dawn on the Sunday morning of our trip, sandwiched between a Saturday night sunset stroll along Santa Monica pier and an afternoon Warner Brothers Studio Tour, we'd landed at The Greyhound for breakfast with a side order of one of Tottenham's most memorable displays of recent years as they played a much-fancied Liverpool side off the Wembley pitch.

'I think I was there for that game,' Rolfe Jones, co-founder of LA Spurs tells me in a well-spoken voice with just a hint of a North American twang. 'I make about two thirds of the games because I have a young daughter, so it doesn't always work out time wise.'

Refreshed from Brittany, I'm back on home soil for our chat ahead of the highly anticipated rematch between Jurgen Klopp's Liverpool and Pochettino's Spurs that had served up two of the Premier League's most memorable matches of the 2017/18 season. With the kids bedded down, I head to what I affectionately refer to as my 'home office' but which is little more than a storage space for unused gym equipment and other things we've hoarded surrounding a desk crammed into the corner.

Our anticipated phone conversation begins with an unexpected video call request. 'You get to see what I look like,' he explains from his stationary vehicle as the image buffers during his lunchtime break between meetings. 'That's my Tottenham badge there,' he adds, pointing to the cockerel pin on the breast pocket of his smart business suit. 'I always have Tottenham stuff on!'

As I speedily readjust my appearance to meet the unexpected visual aspect of the interview, I glance around the array of DVDs, unpacked boxes from a house move five years earlier and a child's bike before showing Rolfe the images of White Hart Lane that adorn my office walls and a cardboard framed picture of ten FA Cup Final programme covers from 1901 onwards that my wife bought me for Christmas.

'That's great,' says Rolfe politely as he strains his eyes towards the phone screen. 'I have the '61 Cup Final programme and the '81 and '82 programmes as well because I went to them,' he adds, accidentally trumping my miniature replicas.

Rolfe can be forgiven for having a slightly more impressive range of memorabilia. Having first been to watch Spurs in May 1974, coincidentally also against Liverpool, this Scottish-born ex-pat became hooked from the age of eight-years-old. His Tottenham origin story isn't a regular one, however, considering his introduction to the boys from White Hart Lane came about from his schoolteacher.

'His name was Andrew Silcox and he was a huge football fanatic, especially Tottenham. His subjects were history and geography, but football was his passion. Any chance we got, he'd talk about the great history of Tottenham in the Sixties and how he had a signature of Jimmy Greaves. One day, when the girls had gone off to domestic science, he went around the whole classroom and asked every boy who their team was. I liked football but I hadn't really decided on a team. My dad had some leanings to Chelsea and liked the game, but he wasn't a firm fan of any team. Some boys said Newcastle or Liverpool and he goes to me 'what about you?' and I said, 'I'm Tottenham, sir'. He said, 'good man', tapped me on the shoulder and said, 'you made the right choice there'.'

What was perhaps an instinctive childlike reaction to impress a teacher would become a major turning point in the life of young Rolfe and set him on course to become a key figure in Tottenham's impressive growth on the West Coast of the United States. First, though, he'd need catch the bug for himself.

He continues: 'It was a choice I have never regretted and has led me on an incredible journey to where I am now, sending the occasional email to Daniel Levy, being recognized for being a co-founder of the LA Spurs and subsequently seeing Spurs play all over the world.'

As we return to the classroom of the early-Seventies, Mr Silcox would have another telling involvement in the path that young Rolfe would take.

'I'm not sure exactly how long it was after that, but he said he wanted to take a couple of lads to a game. It was Spurs v Liverpool and he took this other lad called Simon who was a Liverpool fan and he offered to take me. My dad was traveling in the States at the time, so my mum called him at some expense to ask if it was OK for me to go to the game. My father responded that it was fine as long as I didn't go on the terraces.'

Rolfe's father's warning reminds me of a few of the stories my dad told from the same era. As a burly teenager, he'd found himself being momentarily crushed against a barrier. Long before the horrors of the 1980s, it was acknowledged that the largely unrestricted world of football stadia was potentially dangerous. While hindsight should be weighted with the significant changes to public health and safety culture at sporting events over the last five decades, it's pertinent to remember that, even then, the football terrace still wasn't considered a safe place for women or children.

'We sat in the Paxton Road end and it had the old wooden seats,' Rolfe continues. 'It was integrated so there were Liverpool fans right around us. Everyone was friendly, sharing their chocolates and sweets. We went on the turnstiles on Worcester Road and I remember how tiny it was even as a young lad. I remember the whole experience; it was an evening game in the summer, but the lights were on. We were under the cover of the roof so when the ball went up in the air out of view, it seemed like forever.

'Spurs scored first but I didn't see it. The crowd went ballistic and I just remember the roar. I didn't know what had happened; I had no idea how excited everyone would be when Spurs scored. Liverpool had just won the FA Cup a week or so earlier. This was a catch-up game for the season, I think, because a match had been cancelled due to the UEFA Cup. The ticket I had, which I still have, said February. It cost £1. The teacher told my mum it was 60p, so my mother made me give another 40p from my pocket money which I thought was a bit much!'

Rolfe's first Tottenham experience had been an intoxicating one. On a late May evening under the floodlights, a lifelong love affair had been born. For anyone lucky enough to have experienced White Hart Lane on nights like that, it's not difficult to see why.

Rolfe would move away from London to the East Midlands where many of his classmates supported Nottingham Forest or Derby County. With Spurs on the decline, culminating in their relegation in 1977, remaining true to Tottenham might have been tricky for a fickler teenager. Not Rolfe, however, who would be rewarded for his loyalty by the double cup winning side of the early 1980s.

'That magical period in the early 80s was incredible,' he continues, as he recalls missing both the '81 and '82 Cup Finals but having tickets for both replays as Spurs would defeat Manchester City and Queens Park Rangers respectively, both at the second time of asking, to retain the FA Cup.

'We did that two years in a row opposite the Royal Box on the benches that were there. To see Tottenham play at Wembley was like a World Cup Final. There wasn't a lot of football on TV back then. There was Match of the Day, but you didn't know who would be on. You'd often get the paper on Monday at school and read what went on unless you went to the match. It was a different world. Going to a cup final was like being close to God, and two years in a row was incredible.

'The experience of the first one when Ricky Villa scored his goal,' he says, drifting off momentarily at the memory – 'the crowd was shouting for him to pass the ball with Archibald free on the right-hand side. He didn't, and the rest is history. I'd never seen anything like it and that is still the greatest FA Cup goal.'

Rolfe would move to the U.S. a few years later. An offer to play football – or soccer, as he admirably refrains from defaulting to despite three and a half decades across the pond – at a small college in Texas would eventually see him go on to play semi-professionally in the Californian Pacific League; but he always remained in touch with Tottenham's results no matter how difficult.

'I came to the USA in 1983, thinking that I would have to give up much of my love of Spurs as there was no televised coverage at all in those days,' he recalls. 'At first, I wasn't getting any information unless my mum or dad would write to me until, by accident, I was looking in the Dallas Morning News and I just happened to catch a list of the old First Division results. No table or anything, just the results. I would wait up until two or three in the morning every Sunday and keep up with Spurs that way - no write ups or anything else. I was the first person to get it and I'd look at the results, so I at least knew if Tottenham had won or lost. There was no football on American TV at all.

'Towards the late 80s they showed the World Cup on TV and I remember trying to watch the '87 FA Cup Final. I didn't manage it but went to the pub and asked what happened. I thought Spurs would have won and couldn't believe it. I was devastated – Spurs had lost to Coventry.'

To this date, it's the only FA Cup Final that Spurs have ever lost, a record they've staunchly defended by losing all eight semis they've been in since 1993. By 1991, however, things were slowly beginning to change.

'I found out there was a place I could go to through the friend of a co-worker. We went to a place called The Ship in Orange County and that was the first live football game other than a

World Cup that I saw in the States. Little did I realise that was the last time Spurs would be in an FA Cup Final – we'd been in five prior to that in a relatively short period of time. I remember that game well, with it being Gazza's last match. Things were changing in the States and they were getting matches via satellite, but you didn't know what the match would be necessarily. They also had summary programmes midweek, so you were starting to get more coverage.'

The advent of the internet would change things dramatically as the 90s continued and the polished rebrand of the old First Division to the Premiership helped the English game reach a new fanbase. Rolfe's annual trips home would always include attending Tottenham matches, from the drab defeats of that era through to the 1999 League Cup Final and Allan Nielsen's last-minute Wembley winner. Around this time, his experience of supporting Spurs from across the Atlantic was about to be enhanced by the introduction of another Spurs fan who, coincidentally, I also happened to meet on my visit to The Greyhound.

Rolfe continues: 'I met up with this chap, Graeme Rudge – crazy Graeme,' he laughs. It's an affectionate nickname that I need little explanation for having spent just a few minutes chatting to him over breakfast last autumn.

'It was quite an experience,' Rolfe continues. 'I didn't know how to take him at first. His first question to me was to ask how many times I had been arrested watching Spurs. I told him I hadn't. He told me that I couldn't be a *real* Spurs fan then, as he'd been arrested three times. Quite a different approach! Graeme is in England right now. He's going to be going to go to the match at Wembley. He would of course have been going to the match at the new White Hart Lane, but he still kept his travel plans.'

While Graeme and Rolfe might not have made the likeliest pairing, their ambition to unite other Spurs fans in Los Angeles united them. Starting out as just two, they vowed to collect the email address of every Spurs fan they came across to add to an email web-ring that would grow over the next few years until, in

2005, alongside fellow co-founders Jason Maxwell and Kate Sukham, Rolfe's fledgling collective finally became official.

'I got the rights to the LA Spurs domain name and we got the website up – this was before Facebook. Tottenham noticed us and Paul Barber, who was the Executive Director, made a trip to Los Angeles and met a few of us. By that time, we were starting to become fairly established and on the map.

'Originally we were going around to different pubs every week and we'd rotate so we could spread the word. People who may have been casual followers or who didn't know about LA Spurs realised there was a group that met every game and we did that for a few years. It was decided we needed a regular base which was The King's Head – not a bad place to start but the biggest problem was that we were always vying space with other clubs. If Man United were playing, we'd get squeezed out. I hated that.'

An approach from The Greyhound to become the new base of LA Spurs was accepted, as it offered an upgrade in size along with close links to public transport and the freeway, but Rolfe admits the continued growth means they might yet one day even outgrow that.

'I think it's our fourth season there and some matches are wristbands only. We don't charge for memberships although we accept donations. The only way we make any money is through the sale of merchandise, t-shirts, scarves and hats. We don't have a membership and that way anyone can join whatever their financial situation is. We didn't want anyone to feel prohibited or that they weren't welcome.

'It's been quite a journey but when we started, we probably had sometimes two or three people watching a game. Now if we have less than forty or fifty, we think it's a poor turn out! The big games we have two hundred or so – we have to limit the amount of people allowed in. When we played the League Cup finals, they were turning people away at the door, it was jam-packed. Arsenal, Man United, Chelsea – some of those games, you'll fill the place and it will be hard to move.

'The one moment I really reflected on was the League Cup

final in 2014. I stood in the corner – you could barely move - and I looked at this crowd and thought 'wow!'. Who could've imagined that when I first came to the United States, thinking that I might not see another Spurs game on TV for quite a long time, that this is what it had become?'

Rolfe is quick to defer some of the credit, however, and is hugely complimentary of his fellow Board members and the work that they've put in to continue to grow the Club. While some members have left, moving away over the years, they've always been replaced with eager fresh blood. Furthermore, the vision of those around him has helped LA Spurs capitalise on their standing in the U.S. when Tottenham have come to town.

'We started our group at the right time,' he explains. 'There were a lot of factors that came together and were fortuitous for us to have the success that we've had. That doesn't take away the drive and the effort that everyone had in the beginning to make it work. You can watch every Premier League game on TV every week so that helps a lot. Our membership base is getting on for two thousand - we're the largest Tottenham club in the States,' he adds with a noticeable frisson of pride.

'2018 has been a big year for us. Tottenham played in two locations in southern California, which I doubt will happen again. Pasadena was mobbed by Tottenham fans after the game. I live in Pasadena and I never thought I'd see the whole town in the blue and white of Tottenham Hotspur and playing against Barcelona at one of the iconic stadiums of the world.'

From humble beginnings on an expedition with his school teacher to a cross-Atlantic migration that left Rolfe wondering if he'd ever see Spurs again, this unorthodox route to co-founding the biggest supporters' club in the States has also seen Rolfe land himself on first name terms with the Chairman and a Spurs legend or two; something he is understandably proud of.

He continues: 'We have a tremendously good relationship with Daniel Levy and his team. He was very gracious and four of us met with him and his team for over an hour. It was quite an experience. That is one area I will take credit for because I met him at the British Consulate. We were guests of Galaxy rather than Spurs, ironically, and I got to meet with him briefly and chat. We were there to promote the English/U. S relationship and friendship through sport. I wrote to him a few times and he wrote back, which really impressed me. It was a wonderful afternoon and I thought he'd give us ten minutes because he's pretty busy, but he spent over an hour with us. I really respected that.

'We asked very big picture questions and I asked if he was trying to make Tottenham Hotspur the best team in the world. He said "well, best is a bit of an operative term, but we certainly want to be up there with the elite" - and they are with the best stadium, the best training ground. I think they're certainly going to be one of the top five in the world. To his credit and his patience, that's what he and Joe Lewis have done. They've taken a midtable team and made them into a world brand which is what Real Madrid is, Manchester United is.

'I believe Tottenham Hotspur is going to be what Manchester United was. And that's not to say Manchester United isn't still one of the big names, but the financial underpinnings and what they're doing at Spurs is positioning it to be mentioned in the same breath and competing with those elite clubs.'

Big predictions – outlandish, perhaps, just a few short years ago - but ones that feel increasingly realistic to anyone following the progress of Spurs in the last few years.

As the thorny issue of the stadium comes up and given Rolfe's facetime with the men at the very top, it's an opportunity I can't miss to gauge his thoughts.

'I would like them to get the stadium properly ready,' he says after a considered pause. 'What happens, of course, in any large or even small building project is delays but it's most important to have it properly safe and functioning for the future home of Tottenham Hotspur. Probably the time frame was just a bit too ambitious for England, and maybe for anywhere else. I'm not too upset about it but admittedly I'm halfway around the world, so it doesn't have the same impact. But it's gonna be a fantastic place so let's make sure it's correct.'

One permanent home that remains ready for a Spurs match, whatever the time, is The Greyhound. The impressive win at Manchester United was a Monday lunchtime kick-off for the hardcore, who pulled sickies galore to witness a memorable weekday afternoon. While numbers were justifiably down compared to the regular attendance, it was still an impressive turnout.

'We had very good support for that – about 90-plus,' Rolfe tells me. 'Because it's Man United and our first big game of the season, I think a lot of people took the time off or had doctor's appointments of various sorts because it was such a critical early match. The Liverpool game kicks off at 4.30am, so I'll roll out of bed about 4 and get down to the pub and watch the game. Some people stay up all night, there are a variety of different approaches. Some people stay at the bars until 2 in the morning then hang outside and come back in. It just depends on where you are and what your plans are for the night before.

'It's gonna be a tough game for Spurs but if the stars align then I think we can win 2-1. I don't think we're going to have a blow out like we did last season, that was an unusual occurrence.'

And will it be back to bed for Rolfe, win, lose or draw? 'Unfortunately, I normally have to keep myself going through the whole day. There's no way around it because when I get back, my daughter is up. Off we go, I've just got to grin and bear it! The early games are the ones I like because I don't have to interrupt anything. The later ones I have to negotiate coming and going, so in one sense I prefer those because it doesn't have any impact on anyone else except me trying to stay awake.'

As we end our chat, Rolfe has a final anecdote about the opportunities that involvement with LA Spurs has offered him. While playing in the inaugural Tottenham Hotspur Supporters' Challenge Cup in Denver, his victorious team received a trophy from Spurs legend Ledley King. 'This is the closest I'll ever got to winning the F.A. Cup,' quipped Rolfe. 'Me too,' came the characteristically dry response from the former Tottenham captain.

Unfortunately, there'll be little to celebrate getting out of bed for when the match arrives. A lacklustre display from Spurs much more akin to the Watford defeat than the barnstorming performance at Old Trafford sees Liverpool take a two-goal lead that could have been more had it not been for Michel Vorm, deputising for the conveniently injured Hugo Lloris just a few days after a court appearance for a drink driving offence. There are unconfirmed rumours abound that he's been discreetly suspended by the Club.

'Spurs will thank their lucky stars,' says Gary Neville in co-commentary during added time. 'They could have had a real mauling.'

Then, out of nothing, substitute Erik Lamela controls a deep ball from a corner and volleys in from a tight angle to give Spurs a lifeline. Seconds after the restart, the Argentinian wins a freekick from Virgil Van Dijk that eventually leads to a chance for Heung-Min Son to rescue a point. When the returning Korean creates space for a chance and cuts inside, he appears to be upended by Sadio Mané for what would have been another dramatic late penalty against the Merseysiders and perhaps the most undeserved draw in football history. As it is, the referee waves away the appeals and Liverpool hang on for a deserved three points.

'One of the worst Spurs performances I have seen in quite a while,' is Rolfe's assessment. 'Not a bad crowd at The Greyhound for a 4.30am kick-off though, 65 or so. Graeme and a few others who were at the game were very sad that it was such a poor performance. I wish I had stayed in bed.'

Poch showed his characteristic diplomacy post-match, refusing to blame the players, playing down the difference between the Manchester United and Watford results and talking about how much season there was still left to play. Where it would be played remained a mystery; but thanks to Rolfe and his team, one permanent home of Spurs, for the foreseeable future at least, could always be found in LA: The Greyhound on North Figueroa, just off the 110 freeway.

Rolfe on a recent visit to the Tottenham Hotspur Stadium, pictured in the dugout with his father.

OCTOBER

3
THINGS LOOK A LITTLE MESSI
LEBANON SPURS

The term 'international comedian' hasn't always been considered a compliment on the UK circuit. Earning your stripes in the diminishing number of rough and tumble comedy clubs and touring the length and breadth of the country's art centres and sports clubs is where kudos has usually been earned and lost; the concept of entertaining the masses on the cruise ships was left to the variety acts of yesteryear, earning their crust keeping the blue rinse brigade from nodding off between ports (of either kind) and a round of bingo.

The demographic of comedy audiences and cruise enthusiasts has changed of late. While it's not uncommon to see an 80-year-old in a UK comedy audience these days, it's even less unusual to find an 18-year-old on a cruise ship. Combine the two on a P&O ferry, book a curly haired Tottenham Hotspur supporter to entertain them and set them off on a short excursion to Amsterdam as part of the Hull Comedy Festival and you've got yourself a marriage made in heaven.

My brief is to entertain the good folk on this short haul booze cruise in return for a moderate fee, floating bed and board, plus a complimentary excursion to the Dutch capital. Night one goes well, with a strong opening performance in one theatre leading on to a second performance where some of the transitional crowd in attendance watched me just half an hour earlier. Thinking on my feet, I manage to dig enough material out to win over this very definition of a captive audience before retiring to our cabin for the night content with my evening's shift.

I say 'our', because I'm sharing with my funny friend and colleague Patrick. The combination of a snoring bunkmate and the 6am call from the most seductive sounding captain on the seven seas leaves me so exhausted that I begin to question my own emotional stability; I'm genuinely holding back tears absorbing even the most underwhelming Banksy in the museum quarter. I then return to the ship to deliver ten more minutes of pure comedic gold to the same audience as the previous evening, before pleading with each of them not to dare consider returning for my gig on the terra firma of Hull the following night. I return to the cabin to somehow find my body rejects the sleep I so desperately need for a second consecutive night.

As I'd made my way through border control on the outward journey to the Netherlands, I was more than a little tired to begin with. Just over 12 hours earlier I'd been in the unfamiliar vantage point of Wembley's upper tier marvelling at the sheer quality on show as Lionel Messi and his band of merry men carved their way through the Tottenham backline in the first game at Wembley in almost a month since that humbling against Liverpool.

The Monday after that match, Spurs put out a tweet showing an American couple who got engaged in the unfinished stadium. Predictably, it turns into something of a PR own goal.

'Finally, a match at the new White Hart Lane' says one reply. 'They'll be divorced by the time it opens,' says another.

The intervening period, left free of home games in a doomed attempt to allow time for the new ground to be completed, sees a dominant performance at the San Siro in the opening Champions League group game as Spurs take a one-goal lead. Worryingly, they somehow relinquish this completely in the final five minutes to lose 2-1. Grateful of the new 6pm kick-off slot, introduced to further the appeal of the Champions League in other continents by offering more convenient kick-off times, my son Jacob watches every minute, even if he regrets my detailed retelling of my one and only visit to the famous old stadium.

'Is this what is was like watching Spurs when we were rubbish, Dad?' he queries innocently as the final whistle blows. 'Sort of,' I reply, realising how spoilt he is at risk of becoming when a narrow defeat in a very tricky opening Champions League game counts as 'rubbish'. There's no denying the result exposes a soft underbelly that has rarely been seen during the Pochettino era, however; or 'Spursy' as it's often lazily labelled.

Another unusual occurrence would be the gaffer losing his temper in the Milan media room when asked questions about the decision to leave Toby and Trippier at home. While Sanchez struggled, Aurier had been a contender for man of the match and Mauricio was keen to remind the travelling press pack of the necessity to respect his players and his right to utilise his whole squad while juggling so many matches on the back of a busy summer and international calendar.

A win at Brighton, despite another late scare with an Anthony Knockaert goal conceded, sees Harry Kane rain more shots on target in 90 minutes than he had for the opening games of the season combined, converting a penalty in the process as his trademark sharpness looked to be returning. And, while no-one would claim the team was firing on all cylinders just yet, the stubborn grinding out of results through the combined rotation of Son, Moura and Lamela looked to be working a treat.

A 'home' draw in the third round of the Carabao Cup presented a new issue for the delayed stadium project, with the short notice on Wembley availability meaning the fixture would have to be fulfilled at Stadium MK. Once mooted as a possible short-term host venue before the national stadium had been secured for 2017/2018, it only added to the homesickness being felt throughout a frustrated fanbase. Paulo Gazzaniga, deputising for the still absent Lloris, would play a starring role in keeping Spurs in the game before making vital saves in the penalty shootout. Returning hero Dele Alli fired Spurs into the last-16 from the spot.

One place the stadium project had run to time and budget was the release of the new FIFA 19. Often a much-cherished gift from Father Christmas in our household, he delivered a little earlier than usual this year on the basis that we couldn't quite wait until December 25th. It was small comfort for the average Spurs fan desperate to sample the real thing but, with the stunning 4K graphics easy to mistake for the true surroundings of a real football match, it offered a virtual glimpse of what was to come for me and my son.

The visit of Barcelona was a relatively downbeat affair despite the capacity Wembley crowd. Unlike Real Madrid in the previous campaign, when the lingering melancholy that such a mouth-watering fixture wouldn't be taking place at White Hart Lane was quashed by the team delivering a night to remember, this felt a little different.

A clever marketing campaign plastered around London advertising the new Tottenham Stadium as 'the only place to see Champions League football' in the capital had been a great side swipe at Chelsea and Arsenal's Europa League involvement but threatened to backfire if the delays continued. In fact, as some media outlets reported, should Spurs be eliminated before they'd moved into the new ground then they might even be eligible for a fine under false advertising. As the Catalans raced into a 95-second lead after Philippe Coutinho's composed finish capitalised on a horrendous misjudgement from the returning Lloris, it was beginning to look increasingly likely.

Back at Wembley with my son and dad, there was a feeling of resignation from us too as we'd not been quick enough to seal our regular seats and instead found ourselves high up in the upper tier where the playing contingent on the pitch far below appear to be the size of Subbuteo players. While Messi looked to be so mobile he almost glided, it seemed a wasted vantage point to at least try and enjoy one of the greatest players of all time in the flesh as he threatened to demolish Spurs singlehandedly before a late rally made a game of it. One chap seated beside me spent much of the game inexplicably recording clips on a small digital camera from on high, presumably with a view to putting BT Sport out of business when he uploaded them to YouTube later.

After the magical Messi ball that had created Coutinho's opener, Ivan Rakitić added a second on the volley before the little Argentinian almost added a third just a minute after the break; only the post saved Tottenham's blushes. Harry Kane's individual brilliance halved the deficit for just a few minutes until Messi restored the two-goal lead after converting a flowing Barcelona move. Erik Lamela's deflected shot brought Spurs back into the game midway through the second half but there were audible groans in Wembley as the goal threat of Heung Min Son was replaced with Moussa Sissoko. A half-chance that was skied high into the upper tier by the Frenchman would have done little to improve his fragile confidence soon after. Messi completed the win in the final minute of the game.

One international Spurs fan for whom the Barcelona game had provided welcome respite from studying was 20-year-old Anthony El Chaer, Chairman of Lebanon Spurs. Having supported Spurs since he was just 10-years-old, he went on to establish the official supporters' club as a teenager after searching the internet for other fans in his homeland. He was unable to share the experience of Wednesday evening with this network of friends, however; university revision saw to that.

'It was actually before one of my major passing exams so I couldn't go and join the them,' he tells me as I nail caffeine to ward off the fatigue-induced hallucinations that are beginning to kick in three days after the match and just a few hours after arriving back home from Amsterdam. 'I was super sad. I ended up watching it with my girlfriend at home – it was frustrating. I am in the Lebanese American University and study Industrial Engineering. I have a lot of maths and engineering courses that require a lot of studying and preparation. It actually happened that all of my exams were over the last seven days or so - it was not a very entertaining week!'

I begin to tell Anthony the story of my own dissertation year in 2006. I vividly recall saving my essay, on floppy disk, before heading to the living room five minutes before kick-off to watch Tottenham's last ever visit to Highbury. As the season came to a climax, Martin Jol's hugely improved Lilywhites had closed the gap to Wenger's underachieving Gooners, with the match offering an opportunity to gain vital ground on their own turf and give realistic hope of finishing above our bitter rivals for the first time in over a decade. A 1-1 draw was a fair result, and a favourable one for Spurs, on an afternoon best remembered for Jol and Wenger going nose-to-nose on the touchline. I'd gone back to my studies a few minutes after full-time, such were the demands of impending deadlines, unaware that a dodgy lasagne would soon break my heart.

In a country where you'd be more likely to spot the replica shirts of many of Europe's heavyweights, including Barcelona, Anthony's dedication to wearing Tottenham's colours wherever he goes is admirable – even if it does occasionally attract unwanted attention.

'The day of the Barcelona game I went to university with my Spurs shirt on and everyone said to me 'it's gonna be your game, you will win against Barcelona' and I said not to have too high hopes and just to watch and enjoy the game. And since everyone has seen me since the game, it was terrible because even my teachers have been talking to me saying 'you could see even after one minute and thirty seconds that Tottenham would lose'…it wasn't very enjoyable the day after!'

A replica shirt isn't the only clue Anthony wears to represent his dedication to North London. Inked into his skin, just below his rib cage, is the famous cockerel crest. It's as painful looking as it is impressive.

'That's actually one of the reasons behind my tattoo,' he continues, after we discuss his determination to still wear his Spurs shirt to university the day after the Barca defeat. 'Wherever I go, it's engrained on my skin. You tattoo something that means something to you that you'd never let go of and that's Tottenham. Tottenham is way more than a club; Tottenham is a way of life. For me, Tottenham have changed so much in my life. It made me want to give the club a lifetime commitment, so the tattoo is a lifetime commitment to them.

'I got it done three years ago when I was 17 or 18. I was actually passing by the tattoo shop. I stopped, and I thought about the love I have for the club, which is indescribable. I thought: it's time to make a lifetime commitment. So, I went on Google search. I actually wanted 'To Dare is to Do' but then I found the 1983 logo and I took a part of it and tattooed it.'

Anthony's reasons for choosing Spurs are romantic. Aged just ten, he watched the League Cup Final against Chelsea and fell headfirst. He might well have been a Chelsea fan, like so many others in his peer group, had it not been for a twist of fate.

He explains: 'Let me tell you something about Lebanon. We don't really have the football mentality. In England, at eight-years-old, you go watch games. Here it's not very common, so I had to make a big effort to see a game or support a team. Before the 2008 final I supported one player, not a team, and it was Michael Ballack. I watched the 2006 World Cup and he was the captain of Germany. I decided to follow this player, but I wasn't really into Chelsea - thank God I wasn't! It was easy to start watching another team as I didn't have anything stopping me. So, I decided to watch that game and I fell in love directly.

'I grew up playing football. It might not have been the main sport here in Lebanon, but I grew up playing as a centre back. I had Michael Dawson as a big inspiration. I liked his mentality and the way he was a very good captain. I liked the combination of him and King.'

Anthony recounts the story like a lovestruck teenager. Given Chelsea might have been the easier option for a glory hunting fan, his conviction that he was almost waiting to discover Tottenham instead is endearing. He's also quite clear that he hasn't allowed his university career to hinder his relationship with Tottenham either. Like a lovelorn schoolboy, he's keen to share an anecdote where Spurs came before an important university exam. It was the second leg of the Champions League knockout tie against Juventus at Wembley last year – a match I'm unsure I've recovered from emotionally myself having been in the stands.

'I can easily remember the game. It was one of my major course exams – advanced maths,' he begins. Sadly, no advanced maths was needed for the aggregate score as Spurs gave up a promising first leg away draw to miss out on a place in the Champions League last eight. 'It happens that we sometimes have evening exams at 8pm. There was a time conflict and I gave the game the priority. I had to then fake an illness in order to get the make-up exam so I didn't fail.'

As a seemingly studious individual, that Anthony's sacrifice wasn't rewarded with a place in the quarter finals seems cruel. I relive the moment I watched Sanchez being sent the wrong way from high up behind the goal as Dybala ran through and slotted the decisive goal beyond Hugo Lloris. Despite me generally having an excellent and extremely useful skill of almost instantly forgetting the finer details of matches we've lost, that one still lingers.

'I am your complete opposite!' exclaims Anthony, as I describe my fortunate ailment that's helped numb the pain of almost a quarter century of misery. 'When I am sad, I remember. When I'm happy, I am just enjoying the moment. When I am sad, like in that moment, I cannot forget the step that Dybala did to score.' Unfortunately, on this occasion, neither can I. It's at this moment that our conversation takes an unexpected and amusing turn.

'After every game like the Barcelona or Juventus game, I have to refill the house with plates,' he tells me quite matter-of-factly. 'I throw plates at the wall or the floor,' he continues, non-plussed, like this is the most natural confession in the world. When I enquire as to what this means exactly, it turns out it's exactly as it says on the tin. If times are stressful on a matchday in the El Chaer household, the crockery is in for it.

'It's an extra cost to the family,' he continues. 'You pay the ticket price, I pay the plate price. When things go bad, it depends what is in front of me. I hope my girlfriend will never be in front of me because there won't be any difference between her or the wall.'

While I can't compete with plate smashing, I do sympathise

with the emotional release. During our first ever Champions League campaign, a moment I felt like I'd waited for my entire life, I'd watch games while clutching a sofa pillow. With my infant son asleep upstairs, exploding with elation or frustration wasn't an option, but neither was keeping it in. It can't be healthy to absorb all that elation or anger inside of you, after all.

When he wasn't down the Lebanese Ikea refilling the cupboards, Anthony was busy recruiting his compatriots to join him in making his supporters' club official. In the beginning, it was far from easy.

'I actually started really alone,' he tells me. 'Spurs fans were few and far between, but gems are hard to find, right? And then, through social media, I started to get to know other people. By posting on the internet, others got in touch saying they didn't know there were other fans in Lebanon. I started the efforts to meet others in 2014, so now it's four years, soon to be five years. It has been impossible to get everyone together – in England you have public transport like trains and buses. Here we don't have public transportation so either you have your own car or it's really hard to try to join everyone together.'

That hasn't stopped his efforts of bringing all Lebanese Spurs fans into one place, though. 'The most I managed to gather together was around 15. There were also three or four English people who joined us for last season's game against Liverpool. I guess some people come to Lebanon and want to watch a game, so we make more effort. There is no correlation on age; we have a 12-year-old kid and a 50-year-old – one member is the statistician of the group. If there is a conversation about older players, he always brings up the 70s and 80s. He is very knowledgeable about all of this.'

One additional Spurs fan Anthony recruited also bears the brunt of his academic side.

'My girlfriend is now addicted to Tottenham having never been interested before,' he laughs. 'We act as if we are in the stadium while watching the game: when we hear chants being sung for example, we sing with them. She has weekly exams about the players, the coach, everything. I prepare the exams and she has to pass them!' I laugh along but I think he might just be serious.

When Anthony and I first made contact before the season began, he'd confidently predicted 2nd place in the table, behind Manchester City, for the upcoming campaign. While the first few weeks of the season appeared to back up his confidence, recent results had been less encouraging. I'm eager to find out if his optimism was still intact.

'I feel less comfortable about 2nd to be honest because of the transfer activity of our rivals and our own transfer activity. Sometimes I feel like Pochettino in his press conference tries to speak as positively as possible, but I feel that deep down it is bothering him with the players and transfer activity. Sometimes he mentions the game schedule and these things give me less confidence about finishing second. But we are Tottenham, you don't know. We win at Old Trafford on Monday and lose at Watford a few days later. At the same time, it's exciting and devastating, you can't predict. You really can't explain what is happening!' There's certainly wisdom in these words.

Of the players Anthony would have liked to see return in the transfer window, one stands out above all others. While most fans longed for the return of Gareth Bale, Anthony holds the talismanic Welsh wizard in particularly high esteem; almost the highest of all, in fact.

'I am a religious person,' he begins after a pregnant pause as he considers my query as to what Bale means to him. 'I believe in Jesus Christ and after Jesus Christ is the saviour, Gareth Bale. He was the saviour whenever we needed him, he was there. The goal against West Ham where he got knocked down, stood up and scored the goal. Any time we needed a goal, he was there. Fake it to the left and boom. That's what I loved about him. He was able to change a game whenever he wanted. And I guess we miss this type of player now. I see a Gareth Bale in Lucas Moura, I hope I'm right, but I see this.'

Turning our attention to the afternoon's game against Cardiff,

Anthony assures me he won't miss a minute of the action. 'I watch every game on the sports channel,' he tells me. 'I have the whole package. Every game is shown live so I miss zero games. I'll be at home this afternoon. As a Spurs fan, I always say there's no such thing as an easy game. I think that we're going to win but I think that we face problems with low tempo during the mid-game. I hope I'm wrong because the most important part of the game is right before and after half-time. I predict that Spurs will win 2-0.'

Finally, after half an hour chatting in his charming company, I enquire about his plans to visit England. From everything he's said so far, the prospect of watching a Spurs game in the flesh appears to be something he might fantasise about each night while sweeping up shards of crockery. How long will it be before he samples the atmosphere inside the new stadium?

'I should be in England in about three years for my Masters,' he says, a little breathlessly. 'I really want to do something related to football. I have visited England – I never watched a game, but I went to White Hart Lane and did the stadium tour. I hoped to return this December, but it won't happen now because of the stadium delay.' While images of the pitch being laid earlier this week were circulated, the latest updates coming out of the club suggest the festive games appear to be out of reach for the opening game.

Before our chat ends, Anthony has a generous offer to extend to Spurs fans around the globe who might visit his beautiful homeland. 'Whoever comes to Lebanon or wants to visit shouldn't hesitate to talk to us. We can make sure that they stay in a good hotel to make it easier to plan being here and watching a game with us. Come here and don't worry about anything!' It's an offer I hope to take him up on one day soon.

A much-needed afternoon nap later and I'm able to catch a stream for the match before heading back to Hull. While it's unlikely there is much plate-smashing going on in Lebanon, it's a tedious affair with Eric Dier's early goal and Joe Ralls' dismissal just after the hour mark keeping Cardiff at arm's length.

Despite unceremoniously holding the ball in the corner for the closing minutes of the match against the ten men of the division's basement club, Spurs move up to 3rd above Chelsea and within a point of the summit before the remainder of the weekend's games. Cardiff, meanwhile, remain bottom with just two points from their opening eight games – a brief that would present familiar challenge for a certain Mr Henry James Redknapp if ever there was one.

Despite the equivalent of one combined night's sleep across 72 hours, the gig proves to be one of my best of the year. Every joke lands, every audience interaction is a joy and there is even an unlikely sight on the front row that convinces me I might still be hallucinating. Despite my pleas onboard the P&O ferry, one couple who saw me perform three times in the space of 24 hours are back for more and appear to still be chuckling along.

'I can't believe you're here,' I say to them as we have our photo taken at the end of the night. 'This has never happened before,' I add with incredulity, while beginning to wonder if I'm inadvertently being groomed for a threesome. My growing fears (well...) are somewhat averted by the bloke's next line, however. While there appear to be no plans to take me home tonight, it appears I've acquired new friends.

'See you tomorrow,' he says.

Anthony shows off his tattoo with pride.

NOVEMBER

4
A GAME OF TWO HALVES
SWEDEN SPURS

Saturday 27th of October would be a day that would be remembered for the worst of reasons. Following the afternoon's late kick-off between Leicester and Cardiff on BT Sport, a helicopter carrying five people including Leicester City owner Vichai Srivaddhanaprabha took off from the centre circle of the King Power Stadium. It crashed in the car park of a nearby industrial unit less than a minute later. Nobody survived.

The day had already begun with the deeply worrying news that Spurs legend Glenn Hoddle had collapsed just a few minutes after the morning's football show finished its broadcast. With updates sketchy and vague, fans were left helpless at the outlook of 'God', as he was nicknamed during his playing days at White Hart Lane. Tottenham's early season title promise would receive a blow following a narrow 1-0 defeat to Manchester City in the Monday night game at Wembley, but it was an evening when the football on the field seemed to pale into insignificance considering the weekend's terrible news.

It had been a breathless month of football during a revitalised international break with the inaugural UEFA Nations League seeing England recapture the imagination of the country with an impressive 3-2 win thanks to a hat-trick from their captain.

'Kane masterclass downs Spain' cried the headlines, while the Sky Sports narrative was even more bombastic given they owned the broadcast rights.

'They'll be remembered as the boys from Seville!' gushed Martin Tyler with trademark hyperbole as the post-match interviews focus on the narrative that a glorified friendly somehow surpasses the achievements of the summer in the same way an insecure new boyfriend might seek assurances that an ex-boyfriend is out of the picture.

Another win at West Ham had made it seven wins from nine but it still wasn't enough to even hold onto a top four place by the time Arsenal had defeated Leicester on Monday night to move back above Spurs on goal difference. It's an unwelcome sight after consistently being above Arsenal in the pecking order for a solid two years, barring alphabetical order. The only side flagging in the breathless contest between the big six is Jose Mourinho's Manchester United, who find themselves distinctly midtable with just fourteen points from their opening nine games after defeat at Stamford Bridge.

After seemingly beginning to rediscover some of the World Cup-winning form that had recently escaped him in such dramatic fashion with a match-winning performance at the London Stadium, a rush of blood from Hugo Lloris was compounded by a rare mistake from Toby Alderweireld in Eindhoven that left Tottenham's Champions League qualification hopes in the balance. After turning a comfortable looking six points into just one in the closing stages of both of their opening away assignments, with a visit to the Nou Camp in an attempt to avenge the Wembley defeat still to come, even the Europa League parachute place wasn't looking promising.

With the confirmation that all remaining home league games in 2018 would be played at Wembley, frustration among the fanbase was beginning to grow with some supporters even vowing to stay away until a return to White Hart Lane was initiated. It looked ready for football on the regular updates posted across various channels, but further safety checks had been delayed or postponed leaving a confirmed date for the opening game impossible to predict.

After a calamitous few months that involved getting sacked by his national side and then Real Madrid following a 5-1 defeat in El Clásico, Julen Lopetegui's departure from the Real Madrid hotseat meant the long-term future of Mauricio Pochettino became another source of constant anxiety. Showing increasing flair for a colourful metaphor in his second language, Poch offered the following observation on the continued interest of Madrid and others in his services.

'It is like you are with your girlfriend or wife and you are holding hands, walking down Oxford Street,' he said. 'But because you are so handsome, another woman is looking at you. But your wife is so proud and, rather than worrying, she is so happy to be with you and falls more in love with you.'

For anyone struggling to follow the thread, he quickly returned to more straightforward, reassuring ground on the progress being made in N17.

'We are very close to creating, in terms of facilities, one of the best clubs in the world,' he said. 'Of course, everything comes with a cost. Sometimes to win titles today is difficult, for many reasons that you and our fans know very well. But sometimes patience is short, and frustration is there. I think we are so close to reaching the last level, but we need to have that patience that makes us stronger.

'When I arrived at Tottenham the first video that Daniel [Levy] showed me had a message: 'When we are talking about Tottenham Hotspur, we are talking about the glory.' I want to feel the glory with Tottenham. I think when I watch video from the 1960s, it's very emotional and I think it would be fantastic to deliver that moment again for our fans. But first, we need to finish the stadium, move in, make home.'

Amen to that.

Off the field, a new contract for Dele Alli was exactly the kind of news needed to brighten up fans with only Alderweireld, Vertonghen and Eriksen of the squad's main spine not committed until at least 2021.

On the pitch, the disappointing defeat to Manchester City leaves Spurs languishing behind the leaders. With a tricky looking trip to Wolves to follow, I chat with Sverker Otterström, the 47-year-old Chairman of Sweden Spurs. We've exchanged emails about Tottenham before our chat where he listed Glenn Hoddle as his favourite to ever pull on the famous white jersey. The worrying news over his health is a natural starting point for our chat.

'I first started supporting Spurs in the early 80s when Swedish TV broadcast one match every Saturday. Glenn Hoddle was my hero - anyone who saw him play would know why,' he swoons. 'His view of the game and his long passes make him immortal in my view.' Timely words as the news slowly begins to seep out that Hoddle is recovering slowly.

'Of course, it was bad news to hear,' he says. 'At first, I didn't know what the problem was, I just heard that he collapsed in the TV studio and there was no further information. But he is out of intensive care and talking to his family. I hope he will pull through.'

There's a tinge of disappointment in his voice when we discuss the Manchester City match as we reflect on the missed opportunity to catapult ourselves into the mix. 'I saw the game at home,' he says. 'In the first half, they could do whatever they wanted! It was scary sometimes because in the first 30 minutes or so, we didn't have anything. The second half, I think a lot of things changed. It was maybe one of our better games this year and when Alli and Eriksen came on, it was a totally different match. One of my favourite players is Lamela – he got a lot of stick in his first three years, but I really liked him from the start. He moves in a special way, like he's floating or gliding around the pitch, and he can also be a pain in the backside for opponents,' he adds, showing admirable knowledge of derriere-based idioms.

Overall, though, he's pleased with the durability of the present-day team compared to the teams of old, even when not playing well against a side with City's fire power. It's a point that had been made by Gary Neville in the media, claiming that Spurs had always been 'spineless' during his lifetime, leading to an unseemly tit-for-tat with Harry Redknapp. Sverker tends to agree, however.

'We battle now. They used to say 'hey, it's only Tottenham'

but they can't do that anymore.'

The upcoming fixture at Molineux is a fitting one to speak to Sverker about. After their formation in 2004, the founding members of Sweden Spurs made a trip to the UK to see a 5-2 win over Wolves at White Hart Lane in a game where Robbie Keane scored a hat-trick against his first professional side but refused to celebrate.

'About twenty members went on this trip and began to explore the idea of setting up a supporters' club that winter,' Sverker explains. 'The following summer, Spurs signed Erik Edman which saw a spike in media interest here coupled with fine co-operation between us and the club. Then we had a dream start. Tottenham spent a week training in the Swedish coastal town of Kungsbacka with three training matches on Swedish soil in pre-season. Hundreds of Spurs fans visited these matches and the foundation was built for the current supporters' club membership base.' It turned out to be another commercial masterstroke in boosting Tottenham's Scandinavian fanbase.

'I first became involved in 2010,' Sverker continues, 'when we had a golf tournament and I made contact to play. I have been involved with the Board for five or six years, handling tickets and questions from our members. I have an ordinary day job and the Chairmanship is totally voluntary.

'A lot of my time is spent in relation to questions from members regarding tickets. Now I am also the Chairman, every year, we are sending out a member pack just like Spurs do. There's a member card, a flag that we have produced – it's a lot of work getting local merchandise for our members. And of course, I have contact with the Club.'

His duties sound familiar. With the added distance requiring an extra logistical issue, most visits orchestrated by the supporters' club involve group trips that Sverker oversees.

'We usually have two members trips every year, one in Spring and one in the Fall,' he continues. 'When it was White Hart Lane, there was between sixty and one hundred people on those trips. In those days, it wasn't as easy to get tickets in another way as everyone came to us and then we got tickets. Nowadays, at Wembley of course, everyone can get tickets and people are used to travelling by themselves. We have a lot of season ticket holders in Sweden, so people are going to almost every game. Nowadays, not many buy tickets through us, they buy directly and have season tickets.'

The commute from Scandinavia makes my own return journey from Derbyshire look positively tame. It makes perfect sense that the boom of budget airlines has made season ticket holders overseas a reality, though.

'There are a lot of flights of course and it is quite cheap as well,' Sverker explains. 'If you go with the likes of Ryanair, you can get return flights for around £30 so it's cheaper than the ticket for a game! If we are playing in Tottenham, Stansted is a very good place to fly into. You fly into Stockholm – well, it's one hour away from Stockholm. They call it Stockholm South! It's double the distance from London to Stansted but the flight is just two hours and 15 minutes.'

And what about the extreme lengths Sverker has personally gone to for a game?

'For one North London Derby, I got up at 3.30am to drive an hour to the airport and catch the morning flight to Stansted. It was the lunchtime kick-off and we won 2-1! I was in the Shelf End and they celebrated both goals just underneath where we were sitting. I was able to catch the 6pm flight to Stockholm and got home just before midnight.'

Much like my own long return trips to Spurs, the adrenaline of a win is enough to get you home. 'It's a pretty long journey if we don't win!' he laughs.

Sverker's discovery of Sweden Spurs in his early forties was welcome after a lifetime following Tottenham's fortunes in near solitary confinement.

'At first, I knew of maybe one other Spurs supporter through school and my football team,' he recalls. 'Everyone else supported either United or Liverpool, because Liverpool was big back then because they had Glenn Hysén, the Swedish defender, who played for Liverpool when they won all the titles. It wasn't really until I discovered the Swedish supporter organisation in 2010 through the chatroom on the website that I started to realise that it's not only me that supports Tottenham! Before, I was in my own bubble. Before the internet, you can only find out the results from the newspaper to see if Tottenham had won – and they didn't win that often back in those days! We also had one televised game every Saturday, but you might only see Tottenham twice or three times across a whole season.

'I hooked up with someone on that first golf day that went to Inter Milan and then I joined a couple of members' trips, maybe four or five of those, before I got more involved in arranging them as well. My first ever trip to White Hart Lane was in 2006 against Man City when we won 2-1 – before the oil money. I arranged it through work. I got offered a paid trip from my boss at the time and he asked me what I wanted to do. I told him I wanted to go and watch Tottenham!' What a great boss. They clearly do have work/life balance sussed in Sweden.

Sverker namechecks the only Scandinavian on show that day in Teemu Tainio. While the combative Finnish midfielder wasn't Swedish, there is a hint of pride in this recollection. A few years had passed since the last Swedish international to play for Spurs, 57-time capped Erik Edman who was fondly remembered for scoring a belter at Anfield in front of the Kop but little else during his time at White Hart Lane, had left the club. He wasn't the only Swedish Spur though, as Sverker reminds me.

'We had a guy called Oscar Jansson, but he only played with the Academy and perhaps a few friendlies. He will be our guest at our annual members meeting next Saturday. We have our meeting of course, where we select the board for next year – the boring stuff! Then we have Oscar for a Q&A and then we watch the game against Crystal Palace. Oscar still plays in the Swedish First Division.'

The Scandinavian connection is an important one to Sverker, with Spurs predictably offering a further opportunity for friendship with their neighbours.

'We have a great connection with the Norwegian club because we meet up a lot in London,' he tells me. 'They have a really huge fanbase of around 5,500 members. We did a Legends night with Norwegian Spurs last October in connection with the Liverpool game so we had Ossie Ardiles, Micky Hazard and Steve Archibald so that was a great night. I always want the club to help us more though, including holding better events for international fans. It is good already, but it could always be better.'

After discovering Sweden Spurs, Sverker's rise to a senior role in the organisation means he's played his part in considerably increasing their membership – even if Sweden's greatest ever player moving to these shores stunted their efforts for a while.

'When I joined the Board four or five years ago, we had 1100 members. Now it is 1750. We have increased by 100 to 150 every year. I suppose it's because of Tottenham performing better of course, and that people are finding us on the internet. Due to the geography of Sweden, it's difficult for everyone to get together regularly, but members get together in pockets around the country.

'It's quite easy to watch a Spurs game in a Swedish bar. Your 3 o'clock games can't be broadcast in the UK but in Sweden for the past couple of years our broadcasters can show every game at 3pm. Only one match will be on TV, but others will be on internet channels. In the last couple of years, they have only been able to show one match at 3 o'clock but usually the big games are moved to other times so those games are on anyway.

'We had problems the season before last when Zlatan was playing for United because if they played on a Saturday and both Tottenham and United were playing, they always showed United because of Zlatan.'

And have Swedish football fans turned their attention to the MLS now the mercurial talisman is in North America? He lets out a sigh.

'The mainstream media do it, but I don't do it. I would have loved to have seen him in a Tottenham shirt though.'

At this point, I risk opening an old wound. When I first contacted Sverker, the World Cup was in full flow and England vs Sweden was on the horizon. How did it feel to see so many of the players he cheered on every weekend line up against his home nation in such an important match?

'I hoped for Sweden to win but it was very strange, especially when you have that amount of Tottenham players for England,' Sverker reflects. 'You don't want them to pick up an injury while playing for England, but I think you won fair and square. No hard feelings! For Tottenham of course it was bad as we had nine players in the semi-finals and they only had five days pre-season. Kane was fantastic though. At least he didn't have to take corners this time.'

Back to Spurs, and Sverker is pragmatic about the season so far. While he might have liked to see a few new recruits, he is confident in the squad that remains until the January transfer window opens at least.

'In relation to the transfer window, I must say I'm surprised. I thought we would bring in a couple of big signings, although that is not like Tottenham under Levy. But I'm not that disappointed. OK, we didn't sign anyone, but we didn't lose anyone either. There was talk about Toby going – it was a great relief that he stayed. If we look at it, Lamela was injured almost the whole of last season so it's almost like a new player. Winks is like a new player that we didn't have last season so I'm not that disappointed. I understand people want new signings, big signings, but we have proven ourselves that it's not always good.

'We have bought players for a lot of money that have not performed. At the start of the season we didn't play well. We picked up points but not with the style of play that we're used to, attacking all the time. It just felt like the match never started without our usual tempo – like machinery without oil. But I think we've seen that in the last couple of games; and Eriksen and Alli make a huge impact now that they are back. I think when we don't have Eriksen, Kane comes deeper down the pitch to collect the ball rather than being up front to score.'

Like so many Tottenham diehards, Sverker's dedication to the cause doesn't go unnoticed by those who care about him. Those semi-regular cross-continental dashes are par for the course if you're married to the Chairman of Sweden Spurs.

'My wife is getting used to it after the 19 years we have been together even though my dedication has increased year after year. All my friends who don't support Spurs – I do have some of those – think I'm a little bit crazy. We don't have kids of our own, but my brother-in-law's first son is two and half years old and already supports Spurs! His little brother was born in August and received his first gifts from me; they were Tottenham related also. My wife was there a couple of weeks ago and they were colouring, and she asked Mason what his favourite colour was, and he replied Tottenham blue. Then I knew my work here was done.'

The Chairman of Sweden Spurs is already indoctrinating the next generation. Even Mason's name is Spurs related.

Finally, I wonder what Sverker's predictions are for the rest of the season. Can Spurs mount a serious challenge?

'I think that we will be in the top four again this season. I would like to think that we can make a run for the title but if you look at what the other teams are doing in the transfer market, it sure looks difficult to stand a chance. But we have a group of players that have been together for a long time. I must say Pochettino is my all-time favourite Spurs manager for the way he has developed this team, so who knows?'

The week gets better with a 3-1 League Cup victory over West Ham meaning Spurs advance to the quarter finals with a visit to the Emirates Stadium on December 19th. It's always nice to call in on your neighbours at Christmas.

To say the game at Molineux was the archetypal game of two halves would be an understatement. First half goals from Lamela, Lucas and Kane put Spurs in a dominant position at the break even though Raul Jimenez's reply for the home side was incorrectly ruled out for offside. Promising youngster Juan Foyth had been handed his Premier League debut after an impressive performance at West Ham and again looked assured in the first half. By the game's conclusion, he had conceded two penalties and given Wolves a route back into a game that they had long looked out of. The look of bewilderment on the Argentinian's face when referee Mike Dean pointed to the spot for a second time made for painful viewing, but Spurs hung on.

Spurs had climbed back into fourth place on the unfamiliar 7.45 Saturday evening kick-off and had advanced into the last eight of the Carabao Cup. Only the Champions League looked out of reach at this stage. A crunch tie at Wembley against PSV Eindhoven would help decide their fate once and for all.

5

IT COULD HAVE BEEN SIX OR SEVEN
KIWI SPURS

A midweek trip to Wembley on a school night is something of a treat for my 9-year-old son. The giddy anticipation of being collected from the school gates to go directly to a match is one I remember clearly from my own childhood, with the promise of sweets, something unhealthy for tea and the heady mix of your heroes lining up under the floodlights being almost too much to bear during times tables. Throw the Champions League theme tune and must-win jeopardy into the mix and he was at the very front of the classroom queue at half past three.

Earlier in the day, Spurs had posted an official video showing the stunning new golden cockerel looking down over the new pitch from on high. A brand-new sky walk, accessible on a special tour that would allow fans to zipwire down to ground level, added another breathtaking detail to allay frustration over the ongoing delay.

Due to the unscheduled nature of Tottenham's extended residence at the national stadium, there was a reduced capacity at Wembley for the visit of the Eredivisie leaders. The Dutch side had arrived in great numbers and were creating a phenomenal atmosphere long before kick-off that was only amplified when Luke de Jong put the visitors into a 2nd minute lead.

What followed was one of the most dominantly fruitless 75 minutes of football the Champions League is ever likely to witness. As Tottenham threw the kitchen sink at PSV, and heading out of the competition, it took the managerial nous of Pochettino and the genius of Harry Kane to continue our involvement. The introduction of Fernando Llorente as a battering ram paid dividends for the 78th minute equaliser, with the big Spaniard's knockdown being despatched by the number 10. With PSV continuing to shut up shop for the draw, Kane struck again from a Ben Davies cross to seal all three points and somehow preserve our chances of qualification. With 30 shots, 16 corners, three times the number of passes and 76% possession, it was the least our dominance had deserved.

FA Cup First Round weekend would offer a new and unexpected vantage point for the new stadium as Haringey Borough – the Isthmian Premier Division side who pride themselves on being the only football club to reside on White Hart Lane itself – were chosen for live coverage on the BBC. Their offer of free season tickets was a far cry from the disgruntlement expressed by those forking out a couple of grand to continue watching Spurs at Wembley and was perhaps a canny gesture to entice a few new faces to their Coles Park home. Either way, shots from the television drones panning out from their tiny ground to show the new stadium against a backdrop of nighttime London was truly an awe-inspiring sight.

Back in a Three Lions shirt, Harry Kane was the saviour again as his late Wembley winner against Croatia lifted England from potential relegation and into the semi-finals of the slightly baffling Nations League. While it had at first seemed like a trumped-up international version of the Peace Cup (a trophy is a trophy, after all), it was hard not to get wrapped up in the excitement as the England captain wheeled away to bury at least some of the disappointment from a bittersweet World Cup summer.

Meanwhile, another Harry had entered the jungle. Former gaffer Mr Redknapp took time out from arguing with Gary Neville to spit semi-masticated fish eyes into a glass before drinking them with Noel Edmonds. A shrewd TV executive had naturally arranged for the septuagenarian to hang out of a car window in the very first task as he dug his hand into a boxful of critters and spent twenty minutes telling a lobster he was close to bringing Niko Kranjcar in on loan.

I'm chatting with Paul Ruscoe, the UK-born Chairman of New Zealand's Kiwi Spurs, ahead of the Chelsea game. Initially, I'd assumed the time difference might make it tricky to arrange a call, but it would appear his international travel schedule is more than a little unpredictable and he's currently back in England. Given the previous evening's television is the current talk of the nation, it's where our conversation begins.

'I haven't seen it actually!' he laughs. 'I heard he was on it but when it comes to reality tv, I stick to Love Island. I think I'm A Celebrity is one step too far for me.'

He's apologetic – unnecessarily so - over the difficulty we've had nailing down an appointment. His slightly unpredictable day job appears to be the main reason.

'It's been one thing after another recently so if we don't have this chat now, we'll probably never have it!' he begins with an accent much closer to White Hart Lane than Wellington. 'My day job is a bit of a myth really - that's what everyone else seems to think - but the reality is that I work in media and advertising. My life priorities involve watching Spurs, mainly. I come and go as I please, taking contracts. I'm currently in the UK for a little bit. I live in this fantasy world where I live to the beat of my own drum, or at least try to. I'm in London for the season and was hoping to be here for the new ground but obviously we're still at Wembley. I'm doing a bit of contract work in London until around about the end of the season.

'I came back to the UK this year to see us in the new stadium. I've now been back three or four months and I've still not seen us in there so yeah, thanks for that Spurs, that's awesome!' he laughs.

Despite his permanent residence being based about as far away from White Hart Lane as you can get, Paul spent his formative years a stone's throw away from the old stadium before gradually moving further away. His story around how he ended up in the southern hemisphere is a particularly colourful one.

'I grew up originally in Tottenham itself,' he continues, 'but most of my teenage years were just a couple of miles up the road in Enfield which is big Tottenham territory. I was on holiday in Las Vegas sat at a blackjack table three sheets to the wind and out of the blue my phone rang from an old boss asking if I wanted to go and work for him again. He claims to this day that he said he was clear and transparent that the job was in New Zealand, but I didn't have any clue at the time. By the time I got back to London there was a contract on my doorstep. I thought I'd check it out and seven years later I'm still there.'

Paul is now based in Oratia, a suburb of west Auckland in the Waitakere Ranges Regional Park. While it certainly sounds more picturesque than Enfield, it did mean keeping up with Spurs was tricky at first.

'It was actually really weird to begin with,' he continues. 'Going back to 2011, in terms of watching games, you'd be lucky to get maybe a third of the games on the telly during the season. There was one TV network that broadcast the Premier League and they would normally pick two or three games a week. At the time we were bang average, going through a lull at the back end of being successful under Redknapp and almost back into the doldrums again with AVB and Tim Sherwood.

'We'd get two or three games a week on the telly and more often than not it wasn't a Spurs game; it was Liverpool or United or dare I say the filth that were on the telly,' he continues, with an affectionate nickname he's monikered for Arsenal. 'It was really tough. You'd have groups of guys desperate to find a stream and texting each other to see who'd got one. We'd be sat up at 3am in our pants waiting for the game to come on and invariably ending up with a very sketchy broadcast that you could barely see. That meant the bleary-eyed Monday mornings were without good cause as you'd have hardly seen any of the game either.'

That all changed for Paul and his Y-front clad contingent when the rights were acquired by an online company to provide any game via an on-demand service. 'We could get that set up in the pub and so, lo and behold, we'd even found a suitable excuse to frequent our local, The Fox, and meet up for games there,' he recalls. 'Ever since then, we've had the fortune of every Spurs game televised irrespective of the time. It was really tough to begin with and it doesn't get any easier when it comes to the time zone but at least we get to watch the games in full glory rather than watching it with lots of pop-up ads for Viagra.' No pun intended, of course.

With a Kiwi collective now growing in Auckland, the seeds were being sown for the revitalisation of foundations that were set before Paul was even born.

'It's another funny one with how it's grown,' he continues. 'I'd broadly say it's a 50/50 mix between locals and ex-pats. It's funny, we've always been a relatively disorganised club. We date back in our original form to the 70s with a bunch of guys who all have unfortunately passed on now. They'd congregate and catch up around games in the garage of a gentleman called Bryan Ruck who died a few years ago. They'd just have a natter about football without having ever seen any of it.

'When I got involved, the organised guys were in a little place called Timaru in the South Island in the arse end of nowhere really. They formed the official Spurs club and they were a small group of guys who'd meet up down the pub every now and then just to talk rather than watch games. We moved the club up to Auckland in 2015 when I began the Chairmanship and took over from those guys.

'We immediately tied it with a pub and a gentleman called Michael who is a big, big, loud man – about 6'5" tall, 6'5" wide – tends to literally force people to come to the pub to watch games. He's a big character in the group and eventually we just started to formalise our catch-ups and organise our meets and we started to grow exponentially from then.'

With New Zealand's vast geography largely spread over the two main islands, it's tricky for the majority of members to come together. There have been a few occasions, however, when that has been achieved.

Paul continues: 'Most of the guys bumped into each other in

Auckland when Spurs played in Sydney in 2015. We went over there and had these Kiwi Spurs t-shirts and there were a few more of us kicking around than we realised. We're all one group, the Kiwi Spurs, but what we do have is our outposts. We have a chapter in Dunedin - there's a guy out there called Wayne who organises regular meet-ups in the boozer. They don't necessarily watch games there as they don't have the volume of people to keep the pubs open at three in the morning. It's the same in Timaru but they're regulars in the ale house down there. There are the guys in Wellington who go down to the Four Kings and they've got a vocal, organised support there. Then there's us in Auckland who are probably the controlling majority due to size. We're all together and many know each other. We do normally meet up once a year and that's at a Legend's Night where I bring someone over for a meal with the guys.'

I put to Paul the notion that this growing global popularity of Premier League teams like Spurs is down to ease of access via the internet – does he agree?

'I totally endorse that,' he says. 'Even in the last couple of years, you wander the streets of Auckland and you've got people wearing Man City shirts, Chelsea shirts, you name it. The Premier League has grown exponentially in the New Zealand market. If you look at the cost to acquire the rights for broadcasters, it's gone through the roof. If you go back to 2011, you and I could have probably bought it. Now, in relative terms, it's serious money.

'In terms of Spurs' popularity in New Zealand, I'd argue we're one of the top two or three organised supporters' groups. I wouldn't say we were one of the biggest. Even now, despite their troubles, United have got a strong following. Then there's Man City and Chelsea because of the sheer commercial giants that they are. In terms of organised support groups, Liverpool are massive in New Zealand, they're unbelievable and so well organised across the country. The other two groups that are well organised are Rangers and Celtic. The Celtic supporters' club even formed their own football club many years ago. They now play in the third tier of New Zealand football, such is their strength.' Maybe Kiwi Spurs FC could be born one day soon.

Thanks to this international network of fans, Paul knows more than a few New Zealand-based Chelsea fans and will be checking in with them over the weekend.

'We have a bit of banter with the Chelsea boys and know them quite well through the cricket tours with the Barmy Army. They used to be quite well-structured, but they've suffered big time over the years and don't really meet for games any more. They only really turn out when we play them!' he teases.

Paul's position as New Zealand Chair came about after years of travelling with work and visiting clubs in other countries as a fan himself before deciding to take the reins of his own supporters' club back 'home'.

'I've been aware of it all for some time,' he says. 'I was in New York in July just after the World Cup and then I was in Los Angeles before that. I've been travelling to watch Spurs for a long time, overseas and quite often on pre-season tours. The first time I realised about the overseas network was in 2010 against San Jose Earthquakes in California under Harry Redknapp. My first encounter was with the San Francisco Spurs and a whole bunch of the LA Spurs guys and they're all good mates of mine now as well.' Including Rolfe?

'Yeah, very interesting bloke! I nickname him Captain Bluetooth cos he wanders around with one of those early-2000 things in his ear. Lovely bloke but he needs to put the Bluetooth away! Don't tell him I said that or he's gonna slap me. But top, top guys, they put on a good show and I always go watch games when I'm there.

'I first encountered New York Spurs last Christmas at Flannery's. Great overseas venue, that is. The guy behind the bar is great, he looks after you. I spend a bit of time in Australia with the OzSpurs as well. Us Kiwi Spurs have a bit of a love/hate relationship with them, but the Sydney Spurs are good lads.'

I'm intrigued by that last statement. Is it a case of the usual national rivalry spilling over into football?

'There's a little bit of competitiveness and a little bit of one-upmanship although they probably wouldn't admit that,' Paul continues. 'Kiwi Spurs have done a lot of work since 2015 raising money for charity, bringing Spurs legends to New Zealand. We'll never see Spurs play in New Zealand so, as a result, we do what we can, and I think a couple of times we've had envious eyes looking at us when Graham Roberts and Clive Allen turn up to shows in New Zealand and bypass the Aussies. But they're a good bunch and they looked after us when we went over for games in Sydney and Melbourne. It's a nice little friendly rivalry, no doubt.'

Despite the points total, Paul's not been too impressed with performances so far, even though he acknowledges that results have been positive. 'This season we've been crap to be honest,' he says frankly. 'We've not played well in any game, we've played well in patches in Europe, but generally we've been utterly shite. And yet, somehow, we find ourselves third in the table and only beaten three times, with two of those in games where you get a free hit against Liverpool and Man City, so you can't be disappointed with that.

'If we'd have got that result against Watford and held out instead of losing, people would be saying we're genuine title challengers without playing well. So, you've got to be relatively comfortable with how we've performed and that's down to the manager and players grinding out results when we don't necessarily deserve them.'

While the ongoing saga of the stadium delay has drawn sympathy for the average match-going supporter from oversea fans, it hasn't affected them too directly by their own admission. That's not the case for Paul who has literally planned his day job around the supposed first season in our new home.

'The stadium is a ball ache generally, but it really is for the fans in particular. Even me, going to every home game and most of the away games, you get to the point where every home game you ask yourself whether it's even worthwhile traipsing down to Wembley and taking two and half hours to get home. It's hard and it's frustrating but it affects the fans more than the players I imagine because they've got jobs to do and they're getting it done.

'I'm in Enfield which is ridiculous. Sometimes you come out of a game in midweek and it might finish at 9.30 or 10 and you get staggered through the process getting to Wembley Park (Tube station). If you're unlucky, you hit every stop signal. Then you've got to get into London and back out again and jump on a bus. It's an absolute nightmare and can take anything from an hour and a half to two and a half depending on public transport. Before I moved away and we were at White Hart Lane, if it got really bad, I could just walk home. I think people are just getting a little bit tired of it. But we're keeping our heads above water in the league and doing alright so what can you say? It's difficult to have too many complaints.'

When back in New Zealand, going to extreme lengths to see matches is a given when the time difference is factored in. With the kick-off time here catapulted half a day into the future in Auckland, there is rarely such a thing as 'convenient' scheduling.

'The kick-offs can be tricky,' admits Paul, 'especially when we were in the Europa League and playing Thursday and then Sunday which is Friday morning and Monday morning. It's 6am on a Monday morning and you've just hammered someone, had your breakfast and you know the bar is open at 8am. Everyone else is taking a cheeky day off and you've got to go to work at nine – do you, or don't you?

'Many times, I've gone to work probably three sheets to the wind and maybe called in an hour late. The most ridiculous thing I've ever done was in 2012. My good friend Trevor from LA Spurs called me up and asked if I was coming over for Spurs versus Galaxy a few weeks before we played them on tour. I told him I couldn't get the time off work and it wasn't gonna happen. Later that night, I was out in Auckland in a little suburb where all the bars are at, three sheets to the wind, which you can probably tell is a bit of a habit,' he laughs. 'He sent me another text to let him know if I'd changed my mind, but I knew there was no chance. Two or three days later I got a credit card statement and I'd got a charge of two and half grand in NZ dollars. I thought that was odd and that my card must have been skimmed; it wasn't skimmed at all, I'd booked flights to see Spurs play the Galaxy.

'If that's not ridiculous enough, I'd only booked myself in for three days, so I flew 12 hours for the game, had a few beers and flew back for work on the Monday. Not the smartest move I've ever made. You go back almost a full day with the time zones, so I was a bit of a mess. It wasn't a pleasant week at work when I got back.'

Paul's love affair with Spurs began in the early-90s when, as a young kid, he'd first visited White Hart Lane.

'I think it must have been 1990 maybe?' Paul says, taking up the tale. 'I'm 35 so I'd have been about seven at the time. I remember this mate of my older brother's would turn up at the door and try and flog my Dad tickets. My dad used to buy 'em and we'd march down to the Lane, we only lived down the road. I remember as a kid really getting into football during that period; the World Cup qualifying campaign and the build-up to Italia '90 was where I really started to get obsessed.

'When I went to my first Spurs game, I found it impossible not to be mesmerised by Paul Gascoigne. Irrespective of what I can really remember of him on the pitch, what I do remember vividly is his attitude in the press and his attitude in the public eye. You couldn't help but be enamoured by him as a young kid watching him do tricks and pull all sorts of funny faces in the media. He was almost like an ideal person as a kid, you're gonna be attracted to people like that.

'And then the World Cup kicked off and obviously Gascoigne and Lineker and a few ex-Spurs players like Chris Waddle featured, it just kicked on from there. I became fascinated with him and obviously living so closely to Tottenham as well, they were the two things that really kicked in. When Gascoigne got injured in the Cup Final and subsequently left without playing another game for us, it was devastatingly sad for a kid that age who'd just become fixated. I remember turning the telly on in the semi-final and watching him belt that one in the top corner against the Arsenal and being over the moon, wanting to replicate that freekick. I could barely kick the ball ten yards!'

That golden spell for both Tottenham and England would be enough to cement a lifelong love affair – and give Paul the endurance for the tougher years ahead, albeit with the occasional superstar still dropping by. Alongside his present-day heroes, his studious side left him with more than a century of players from bygone days to pore over.

'I wanted to pick books up and got fascinated with Glenn Hoddle then. Video footage wasn't as easy to come by at the time, maybe old VHS and so on, but I would read old programmes and my dad used to say I could recite every first-choice goalkeeper Spurs had had since the First World War. I was one of those weird kids!

'My all-time favourite player and when my love was cemented was when we signed Klinsmann. In that 1994 World Cup there were some vivid memories I had and, weirdly as an England fan, I became bizarrely enamoured by the Germans. Even though they were quite a functional team, I still loved Matthäus, but Klinsmann became synonymous with that World Cup. When we signed him off the back of it, I couldn't quite believe it.

'This guy was genuinely world class, not just in my eyes but in the eyes of the footballing public. He was the first one I remember where we were signing a legitimately proven world class player. Like Gascoigne, he had that endearing personality. Stood outside the West Stand as a kid watching the players drive into the ground and seeing this geezer arrive in a battered old VW Beetle - a world superstar! Then he scores his first goal at Sheffield Wednesday and takes the piss out of himself by doing the dive – these people are underrated characters, they're superstars, but they're the real people you don't see in the game anymore that play with a smile on their face and laugh at themselves and still do the business.

'The whole world has gone crazy now in the corporate world with people unable to laugh at themselves; footballers are so sensitive about what they say to the media. But these people, they weren't dry people, these characters who you can adore for reasons beyond football as much as the football themselves.'

We leave our chat there for the time being. There is excitement when the team news is announced as it will be the first time this season that Kane, Alli, Eriksen and Son will start together; but nothing beats the news that Glenn Hoddle is out of hospital and recovering at home where he'll watch his two former sides lock horns. The game itself would provide one of our most memorable London derby performances of recent years.

Dele Alli's 8th minute header from Christian Eriksen's inswinging freekick gets Spurs off to the perfect start before Harry Kane's turn and low shot from outside the box has shades of the career-launching brace he scored against the same opposition on New Year's Day 2015. The pick of the bunch comes from the boot of Heung Min-Son, however. Released down the right flank by Dele Alli, he runs half the length of the pitch to cut inside and slot the ball beyond Kepa. It's a stunning piece of solo brilliance from the South Korean to essentially beat Chelsea's entire backline and goalkeeper by himself. A late consolation from Olivier Giroud is the only blot on a near perfect ninety minutes.

Alan Shearer suggests that 'it could have been six or seven for Spurs' on Match of the Day while Harry Kane tweets: 'What a performance! Enjoy your Saturday night.' With a gig in Mansfield on a full moon to go to, Harry, I can only do my best.

I catch back up with Paul after the game and his celebrations were typically understated with friends on all sides in his adoptive home.

'Oh yeah, I might have sent a few texts out!' he laughs. 'It would have kicked off around 6.30 in the morning over there. Most of the Chelsea boys are over in Sri Lanka with the Barmy Army so as soon as I got home there were texts flying around, taking my photo at Wembley with the score in the background and I think there were a few expletives sent in my direction. I'll have to make sure my house in New Zealand is still standing.

'I don't think I've seen us tear a team like Chelsea apart like that, ever! The last time I saw us put a top team to the sword in that manner was Arsenal in the League Cup semi-final when you'd argue they didn't have their full-strength team out.

'We ripped them (Chelsea) to pieces from the first whistle and I sneakily suspect that the guy next to me was an undercover Chelsea fan. I was doing as much as I could to make it clear that I'd sussed him out and was trying to wind him up as much as I could.'

With the first of a three-part saga in a potentially season-defining week successfully under our belts, Paul is at least making most of the increased game time, even if it does mean the long trek across North London to Wembley more regularly than he'd like.

'I'm not going to Arsenal but I'm going to Inter,' he says of the week ahead. 'I'll be watching on TV on Sunday rather than visiting the stadium of filth. I think we'll beat Inter comfortably but the Arsenal game will be tough. They haven't really blown anyone away yet, everyone has had their chances against Arsenal and not taken them.

'If we can go there on the back of a lot of confidence after a good result against Inter, I think we can go there and get a result. I'm a very optimistic person though – I remember us losing to Real Madrid 4-0 in the first leg a few years ago and convinced myself we'd win the second leg 5-0, so if your next question is whether we'll get beyond Barcelona with ease or not, I think we'll win the Champions League and be crowned the greatest team of all time.'

We joke that I have the editorial power to make him look like Mystic Meg or just remove that sentence, so he's covered either way.

'Mystic Meg or a complete and utter lunatic!' he laughs. Only time will tell.

DECEMBER

6
DERBY DAY
GHANA SPURS

Step two in a week of three parts would be the must-win Champions League tie against Inter Milan. With it effectively being a knockout game for Spurs, playing this match as the filling in a fixture sandwich of Chelsea at home and Arsenal at the Emirates was far from ideal. With confidence high on the back of a truly exceptional performance against the blue corner of West London, though, hope sprang eternal that Pochettino's men had found form just when they needed it.

'Tottenham away' remained a fixture that brought former Inter fullback Maicon out in a cold sweat following the torrid evening he'd received against Gareth Bale on that incredible night at White Hart Lane in 2011. Recreating the same white-hot atmosphere when we needed it most would be tricky at Wembley. Oh, how we longed to be home.

That every meeting between Inter and Spurs before kick-off had ended with a home win, with an aggregate score of 11-11, indicated a growing rivalry spawned between two of European competition's heritage sides since their first meeting in 2010. More pertinently, it suggested Spurs might end the night with their threadbare chances of qualification still intact.

It was a line-up picked to attack, with Toby and Jan partnered at the back and Christian Eriksen rested to eventually provide a match-winning cameo from the bench. Moussa Sissoko's driving runs to turn defence into attack are pivotal again as the revitalised Frenchman, finally beginning to show his international form of Euro 2016, puts in a man of the match performance. It will be one of these runs, so absent in his clumsy, laboured performances of old, that releases the onrushing Dane via Dele Alli, to fire in a precious winner with ten minutes to play. Sissoko's £30 million price tag looks a snip in that moment alone as Spurs climb into the coveted second qualifying berth behind Barcelona with just one match day remaining.

Sissoko's continued improvement leads to the most startling turnaround of a Tottenham player in recent memory; after audible derision from the stands for the best part of two seasons, he would go into the Arsenal game as a key player. Even the club's official social channels share his visit to a local primary school to encourage entries to a Premier League writing stars competition. It's the kind of spotlight he might have been protected from during most of his Spurs career. Now, his resurgence offers a potential opening line for any budding poets; with the most popular new chant on the terraces providing a helping hand:

Wake me up before you go-go; who needs Bale when we've got Sissoko? (repeat)

Fresh with inspiration, I also decided to give it a go...go:

When we signed Sissoko, I first said 'oh no, no'
His form was just so-so and filled me with woe-woe.
But now he's no joke-o; he's better than Coco!
I'm sorry, Sissoko. Don't ever go-go.

Continuing the positive feeling around the club, an announcement about a stadium familiarisation event taking place on December 16th, the day after Burnley at Wembley, is greeted by an eager fanbase as the early Christmas present it appears to be – it feels like a major step forward in setting a date for the opening match. Not all weeks can be perfect though.

I've discovered over the years that the gut feeling you get waking up on North London derby day is usually one to be trusted. From long periods as underdogs to more recent meetings as narrow favourites, the range of emotions usually follow a similar pattern, from the varying expectations of victory to the sickening fear of defeat. With plenty of draws shared in the last couple of decades, these emotions have often been settled with relief mixed with intermittent ecstasy and all-too-occasional despair.

The main talking point pre-match is the decision to start Juan Foyth despite having Toby Alderweireld on the bench. While the young Argentinian had looked impressive in patches, his tendency to make costly errors was a real concern going into a game of this magnitude. Trust in Poch was high, but it was difficult not to wonder whether this game of all games might be a big ask for the 20-year-old, not least on enemy soil.

I would be watching from the comfort of the sofa after facing my own heavyweight clash at a Christmas gig in Hull, narrowly escaping with a victory on away goals. In December on the Humber, that's like winning a Champions League Semi Final. My main duty today will involve providing text updates for my dad who has somehow managed to book a flight to Lanzarote that conflicts directly with kick-off. He would land midway through the first half. The updates from my end went something like this:

2.18pm: Started terribly. Defence all over the place. Vertonghen concedes a penalty with a handball from a corner. Yellow card and 1-0 to them inside 10mins.

2.38pm: Yeeeeeees! Dier! Sparked a brawl. 1-1.

2.41pm: GET IN THERE! Kane penalty. Don't think it was. Who cares! 2-1. We've been awful so far. They should have equalised before half time as well but Lloris kept us in it.

At this point, Dad must have landed. I picture him at the baggage carousel bemoaning how long it's taking and loudly questioning why families of five are huddled around the conveyor belt blocking everyone else out when it's only the bloke with the Hawaiian shirt on who has any intention of lugging the luggage onto the trolley. He replies:

We will shine in the second half. Keep me up to date.

It pains me to say it, but he couldn't be more wrong:

3.17pm: Foyth looks unconvincing and Jan is on a yellow so I would like to see Toby for one of them early in the second to shore us up a bit. Lots of bite and a few brawls. Proper Derby.

3.20pm: Started much better. And now they've equalised. 2-2.

3.32pm: Sonny just had a great chance to put us back in the lead. Could go either way this, 68mins gone.

3.39pm: Losing 3-2. Aubameyang hat-trick deflected off Dier. Mistake from Foyth in the build-up.

3.44pm: 4-2.

3.48pm: Second yellow for Vertonghen. Down to 10. Hope the hotel is nice.

He doesn't reply and I don't expect him to. I can almost hear him telling Mum he's "glad he didn't delay the holiday for that rubbish" from 2,000 miles away. As ever, Poch didn't appreciate post-match querying of the wisdom to start Foyth. It was hard not to question whether Jan's worst performance in memory was linked to being asked to shepherd his new partner into a game that he'd probably have preferred his trusted compatriot alongside him for. The missed opportunity to secure third place in the league table is punished as we drop to fifth behind Arsenal and Chelsea. It's a sucker punch that will continue into the following morning when I arrive to find my desk decorated red by an Arsenal supporting colleague.

At least I have another supporters' club representative to chat to, in this case the delightfully named Eric Matey, the 29-year-old Chairman of Ghana Spurs, who lives in Accra where he works for the Ghanaian DVLA. Every Friday – win, lose or draw, and despite working with a mass of Chelsea, City and Manchester United fans – Eric wears his Tottenham replica shirt to work on dress down Friday.

We first made contact a few months ago and have been in touch via WhatsApp ever since. He's a bright and optimistic Spurs fan who began the season convinced we'd win the league – a lofty ambition but reach for the stars and all that – and still remained convinced the last time we spoke. I'm looking forward to finally chatting to him on the phone, albeit just 24 hours after the defeat at the Emirates.

Our call gets off to an unusual start. An immediate satellite delay on the line combined with an array of loud sound effects that resemble a cross between a network newsflash and a Japanese gameshow provide a distraction. It turns out Eric is stood next to a television which he quickly moves away from.

'Yesterday at Champs Bar we were all really vibing until the second half started,' he tells me excitedly before his voice drops a little: 'and then the chaos was upon us! We took it on the chin. We must accept sometimes that the players were a bit more tired. We beat Chelsea and Inter, and it had been a good week, but it wasn't to be.'

Eric and his fellow members had come together to watch the Chelsea game the week before but were unable to for Inter. Finding a bar showing the match, even in Ghana's capital, can be tricky, especially on Champions League nights when the choice is huge. It's likely to be an issue again in early January with the news hot off the press that we'll face either Tranmere or Southport away in the third round of the FA Cup. Unsurprisingly, they're not teams Eric is too familiar with.

'I think those are a bit of a given, you know? We should be able to go through without even trying. We always do that!' he laughs. It's true that Spurs have successfully avoided embarrassing exits in recent years, notwithstanding significant cup scares against Wycombe, Newport and Sheffield United.

As I shiver in my home office after a sub-zero dog walk, Eric is trying to keep cool in the central African heat. Amid a few technical difficulties with the call, we move on to the foundations of his love for Spurs.

'Why Tottenham for me?' he says, repeating my question. 'I think the story starts in 2006. I was in secondary school...' says Eric, before leaving a tantalising pause for effect. 'I was the Tottenham guy. We all then found each other on Facebook. As Spurs fans, we just look for any group on Facebook and join, we just want to be part of something. We found ourselves on this one group and in the comments section, which I'm a fan of reading, I noticed this comment was from Ghana, that comment was from Ghana. So, I would add them, and we'd network like that. Some were Ghanaians in the UK and some in Africa. We started with six members and now we have 41. But today as I speak to you there can be no more than 100 Tottenham Hotspur fans in Ghana.

'Initially, when Spurs were in Champions League matches and even Premier League matches, Tottenham matches would not be shown. I practically have to pay the charge twice to be able to watch the telecast of the match, just because I want Tottenham Hotspur to be shown on one of the three TVs in the area. A lot of times you go to the pub and nobody in there wants to watch Tottenham. Those guys just make money from people wanting to watch TV, so it was so challenging, trust me.

'People are watching football, but they want to watch teams like Manchester United, Chelsea, Liverpool and City – these are more renowned teams in Ghana. Then there's this odd dude who wants to watch Tottenham Hotspur!' he laughs. I put the image to Eric that as soon as he walks into the bar, they know they'll need to change the channel. He laughs in agreement: 'I order food and I pay twice for the space. It helps when the other members come as well.'

While Tottenham's standing in Ghana might not match some of their rivals, it appears that they're a growing force. Many years of Champions League football, however, plus high-profile African players such as Yaya Touré, Didier Drogba and Eric Djemba-Djemba – how else might you explain Manchester United's presence? - have raised the popularity of the English game across the continent.

'I think it would be huge if a Ghana player played for Tottenham,' Eric ponders thoughtfully. 'But I don't think Tottenham Hotspur needs too much of this,' he adds, in reference to the type of new fan this might bring in. 'We are about people with an in-depth knowledge of football who actually support the team. If you bring in a player to bring in plastic fans, you just get people supporting Tottenham because their countryman plays, so it would be bad in a way. But I would still love to have a Ghanaian play for Tottenham Hotspur.'

Tottenham's lack of marketability in Africa appears to be the combination of a trophyless decade and the absence of high-profile players from the continent. Clearly Adebayor is as popular there as he was here.

'In Ghana, they see us a team that finishes fourth or third,' Eric explains. 'They don't see us as a stable force. We might win today, we might win tomorrow, but we can always lose. I was on TV today,' Eric throws in, casually dropping his broadcasting career into the conversation, 'and they had asked us the last time we were on if we would beat Chelsea. I correctly predicted we would, so I bragged a lot there. I said the same about the Arsenal game and, well…it didn't go well!' he laughs. 'Bad, bad, bad,' he adds.

'We do a lot of radio as well. Noticeably in our group, a lot of Spurs fans in Ghana are radio personalities, some are TV personalities and sports broadcasters. People who have an elite idea about football and understand what it's like to be a Tottenham fan. Ask anyone here and they will tell you it's a lifestyle choice.'

And what of Eric's confidence that we would be challenging

at the top of the league? Until yesterday's result, we had remained on the coattails of the devastating form of Manchester City and Liverpool. How does Eric feel the season will play out from here on in?

'I feel a fully fit Tottenham Hotspur is the best team in the world,' he says confidently. 'Nobody can dispute that. Tottenham beat Real Madrid who went on to complete the treble last season. Sometimes it's not about saying Ronaldo is better than Messi at talent. You clearly know Messi is better at talent. Everyone knows Tottenham Hotspur is well placed to be at the top, but we are in a process at this time and we are trying to respect the process.'

Every now and again, the deafening background noise of a television or a car blasting its horn interrupts our chat. 'I'm just at home,' Eric tells me when I enquire on whether he's at the bar now. 'I'm changing the TV channel.' I endeavour to make the chat more captivating from here on in. Has Eric ever managed to see Spurs in the flesh?

'I've never been to the UK before, but it is a big dream to visit White Hart Lane,' he tells me. 'It's in the pipeline and will hopefully happen in 2020. I should be in a financial position to go to a game. Organising the guys is very tedious though. I have to encourage them to pay fees and come to meetings. Sometimes you must subsidise a lot of things. It is difficult but we get there. You have to be there to encourage them through the hard times. It's just like being a father to a whole lot of grown-ups,' Eric sighs before adding his infectious laugh. I suggest that the mother in this metaphor must be Tottenham.

'At some points we get so emotional,' he continues, running with the theme. 'It's like being in a relationship, you have to work at it. Sometimes you want to kill them! It brings out in you the worst. Sometimes it's beautiful. There is nothing better than seeing them wanting to win, wanting to make things happen and the fight in them. When you see the carelessness sometimes, it hurts, you know? It hurts. You want to see more dedication and them playing at their best. It can be a headache.'

On a lighter note, I ask if Eric has seen news of our former manager taking on the Australian jungle. He seems proud to tell me he's following every update. 'Yes, I am aware of that programme,' he says. 'I did see clips of him and read excerpts from the Daily Mail Online. We don't miss many things like this as we all read a lot. Anything that happens to Tottenham Hotspur, we are aware. It goes to prove the fact that Spurs fans are unique people.'

With plans around each match not always simple to organise, Eric isn't confident of finding anywhere to watch the upcoming Southampton game. Given that he once watched a full match through a gap in a wall because it wasn't showing anywhere else, his spider sense for finding a venue can certainly be trusted.

Eric will instead watch from home where his role as Chairman means he'll be carrying out a hugely beneficial service for his members, as he explains: 'One or two of our guys won't have access to the match. I will watch the match on my phone, and I use the split screen function to provide text commentary – in fact I run commentary regularly for my guys. They follow the commentary and it's as real as watching it,' he adds, modestly. I consider asking if my dad can tap in from the Canary Isles considering he'll almost be as close to Accra as Wembley on Wednesday evening but think better of it.

'They are big fans!' Eric continues. 'They do not always have the same privilege to be able to watch the game. I am a poet, so it makes description exciting for me and good for them. It goes both ways.' I resist sharing my Sissoko effort and instead enquire as to whether Spurs have ever been a muse to Eric's creative side over the years.

'I've never written one about Tottenham,' he laughs. Can I commission one? 'Maybe. We will see. Sometimes as a poet you need motivation, or you write bullshit! Tottenham can help to invoke those emotions and look back on happy memories.'

The game itself would keep Eric busy on the text updates as Spurs cruise to a 3-1 victory that never really sees them get much beyond second gear. It's a strangely muted atmosphere with just over 33,000 – less than capacity at the old White Hart Lane – turning out on a bitterly cold midweek evening.

A dejected travelling fellow Yorkshire Spurs member allows himself a little moan on the long train home. It's understandable given the fixture was classed as a Category B game, making it more expensive than the upcoming match against Burnley. The frustration is simple: why can't the club cut costs considering the continued frustration and inconvenience of Wembley being experienced by match going fans? Even the performance seemed lacklustre in a game where Spurs could have easily scored six or seven but end up sacrificing a clean sheet thanks to a late Charlie Austin consolation.

But enough of all that. The final word goes to Eric, who messaged me a few days later with his first ever poem directly inspired by Tottenham Hotspur Football Club – Spurs' very own poet laureate:

The Lilywhite hearts of honest men hang furthest!
The most rugged soul was mine
till love called!
Spurs was that "girl", She verbed vibes of reality & truth,
Of devotion and that which made my heart loop;

...for Spurs of course, there's more & more, for that which I had sweat
& sought...
.. for this was that sort of love that Romeo thought eschewed flaws!
and to the honest of men that loathed heights and yet had to fall...
Of the parable of football and that small spot that Spurs got!
The respect for the game on and off field;
the philosophy of the most sublime of styles passed-on over time!
Gaffers come and go,
Players grow old
But the support is everlasting!
Amalgamism of the 12th men that clamour thundering decibels,
pierced and ruptured throats chanting love the best ways ever known!
From the arm-chair supporter,

The honest man's love, was all that was and never lost!
Viva Tottenham Hotspur!

Nice one, Eric. It's definitely better than mine.

Ghana Spurs show off an impressive range of replica shirts.

7
A NOU HOPE
ICELAND SPURS

During my university days, I worked weekends at Sheffield's Hallam FM as an assistant producer on the sports show. Hosted by Julian Warren, one of the nicest men in broadcasting and surely Jeff Stelling's long-term replacement at Sky Sports if there's any justice in the world, it was an exhilarating role at the heart of the action every Saturday afternoon.

One pleasure of the job was chatting and socialising with the local commentators, some of whom I'd grown up listening to. Every week, they'd follow the fortunes of the two Sheffield clubs as well as Barnsley, Doncaster and Rotherham. It seemed like my dream job until I tried it once – a 0-0 draw at Hillsborough that was incredibly difficult to summarise once the combined two shots on target had been covered. While I've sometimes allowed myself to wonder what might have been had a 3-3 classic played out before me that afternoon, I've never attempted to sit in the commentator's hot seat since.

The art of the commentator is to make even the drabbest and dourest game entertaining. Like the subtle decision-making of a good referee indicating an advantage, a commentator should add to the experience of watching the game rather than detract from it. Those at the very peak of their powers can even enhance unforgettable moments to the point that their observations become an intrinsic part of the recollection, even for those who witnessed the game first-hand and without benefitting from audio description at the time. Think Brian Moore as Michael Owen broke through Argentina's backline at France '98 or

Martin Tyler's incredulity as Sergio Aguero sealed the title for Manchester City deep into injury time against QPR.

When esteemed football commentator Clive Tyldesley eventually hangs up his microphone, a single phrase is likely to define his career. Like John Motson's breathless exclamation of David Platt's sensational extra time winner against Belgium in 1990 or Barry Davies' complete lack of concern for the whereabouts of the German defence in a crucial Olympic hockey game, Tyldesley's defining moment had come on 26th May 1999 - 'that night in Barcelona.'

As Manchester United entered injury time in the Champions League Final against Bayern Munich, hopes of a historic treble had been all but extinguished by Mario Basler's sixth minute opener. The four minutes that followed would go down in history as one of the greatest comebacks in the modern game. Tyldesley, who described every moment, would invoke the memories of that famous night in his commentaries for the next two decades to the point of parody, but it could never be denied that what happened in that tie, between two sides with such history and in a game of such magnitude at the very summit of club football, made the turnaround all the more astonishing.

The recent history of Tottenham Hotspur hadn't featured too many nights at the Nou Camp. There had been the glorious one at the San Siro, an unforgettable defeat at the San Siro and, more recently, the extremely lackadaisical turnaround at the San Siro. A draw in Turin last year had initially looked good on paper and some of memorable moments had taken place in stadiums outside of Northern Italy, too. There was last season's heroic point at the Santiago Bernabéu, and impressive points won on the road in Twente, Eindhoven and several more outposts across the continent. That was, at least, until Tuesday 11 December 2018 trumped them all.

I've always had a severe soft spot for Barcelona over Real Madrid; the conduct of the latter in player negotiations with Spurs only fuelled that further. I even visited the city for the first time on my stag do in 2015 and, naturally, the stadium tour was a focal point for the trip. As I daydreamed about the names that had hung on those changing rooms pegs and gazed around the empty stands from the touchline, the likelihood of Tottenham going toe-to-toe with this powerhouse of world football seemed like a distant dream even just a few short years ago.

The draw for the 2018/19 Champions League group stages against Barcelona, Inter Milan and PSV Eindhoven had looked unkind on the face of it. Having seen Spurs win their group with a similar draw the previous season, while falling back into the Europa League despite a more favourable assignment the year before, I was more optimistic; we performed better as the underdogs. However, that opening day defeat in Italy followed by the devastating cameo from Messi at Wembley had dampened my enthusiasm somewhat. At that stage, the final group game in one of the ultimate amphitheatres of football was looking decidedly like a dead rubber.

'I nearly got us tickets for the Barca game,' my mate Dan tells me. As younger men, we were part of the same fundraising events team for a big national charity – ironically both recruited by an Arsenal fan who would wear socks with the club emblem on to work – and found solidarity in numbers as Spurs would frustratingly test the reign of their bitter rivals without ever toppling them. We've been away day buddies ever since, with the trip to the San Siro being one of our highlights.

Tonight, we're at Leicester away for the third season in a row. We meet at the usual haunt, a bar near his old university digs, where some of our regular travelling companions are found. The leader of the group is a man I only know by his nickname, "The Oracle", because of his knowledge and attention to detail in organising every away trip for a large contingent of Spurs fans who truly follow the club over land and sea. This week is no different.

'We fly out to Barcelona on Monday morning,' he tells us. I struggle to contain my jealousy. Against all the odds, the win against Inter Milan means Spurs have somehow extended their Champions League campaign to the final round of group matches despite claiming just seven points from a possible fifteen so far.

As we take our seats, we're surrounded by familiar faces. There are several lads who haven't missed a game in years. Another is memorable for trying to force his way through closing doors on the Milan Metro as the train began to move. His leg became momentarily trapped and he was dragged ten yards down the station platform on his back before the train stopped in response to the frantic Italian screaming and pounding of the windows and everyone was forced to alight. Never have I sobered up more quickly than at the prospect of seeing someone decapitated before my eyes. Thankfully, he's at the King Power Stadium and able to recall the event with a smile.

By far the most memorable member of the group is a chap called Tits. How he earned the unfortunate moniker remains a mystery and, in truth, I don't even want to know anymore. Tits is a little over 5ft but makes up for what he lacks in stature through personality. Noticeably, his hairline has diminished considerably over the years, serving as a reminder that we're all a little older than the footloose and fancy-free lads in our 20s and 30s who witnessed Gareth Bale's trajectory receive rocket fuel that night. That the glorious defeat of that evening has been mentioned to varying extents by every supporters' club I've spoken with to date isn't lost on me. Somehow, that night became our twisted version of "that night in Barcelona".

One of my favourite things about Tits is his failure to recollect meeting anyone outside of his immediate group, including me, despite the number of games we've attended together over the years being comfortably into double figures. While alcohol is undoubtedly a factor, it's not the whole story; he just appears to be gloriously unsentimental about anyone and anything that isn't taking place on the pitch every Saturday.

When Dele Alli's far post header hit the back of the net - a 50th goal in lilywhite in an unerring replica of his very first, scored at the same end of the King Power Stadium beyond Kasper Schmeichel to set Spurs on their way to another victory on the road – I found Tits stood next to me and instinctively hugged him. He returned the favour, but soon moved two seats further away following the restart and looking visibly concerned at the over familiarity of a stranger.

'Not yet,' scalds Oracle as members of his party begin a slightly premature chorus of Jingle Bells to the jeering Leicester fans, a collective who remain convinced they're now our rivals following their title winning season. 'Oh, what fun it is to see Tottenham *probably* win away, OH!', they continue, not wishing to upset the bloke who's *probably* got their Nou Camp ticket in his pocket.

Our very own night in Barcelona gets off to an unfortunate start. Kyle Walker-Peters, the promising young fullback standing in for the injured Trippier and Aurier, is caught in possession and punished; French international Ousmane Dembele races down the field to slot the ball beyond Hugo Lloris with composure. With Spurs needing to match the result of Inter's home tie, and despite trailing with fate in their own hands, another early goal for PSV against the Nerazzuri leaves Tottenham improbably still sitting in second place based on their head-to-head record.

Any Spurs fan with a memory dating back to Chelsea vs Bayern will know relying on another team to do the business is far from ideal. So it would prove. When Icardi headed a 73rd minute equaliser for Inter, the signs looked ominous. As Spurs continued to push hard against a weakened Barcelona side, spurning chance after chance, a confident Inter spent a full minute passing the ball between their backline to loud jeers and whistles from the stands; despite a point being enough for them as it stood, the time-wasting tactics were not welcomed by the home fans.

With all attacking options deployed from the bench and Messi's introduction threatening another destructive half hour cameo in relation to our hopes, Spurs broke forward to find Kane on the left wing. His whipped ball was converted by the onrushing Lucas Moura. With five minutes to play, Spurs were back in the driving seat having effectively been headed for the Europa League for an agonising 18 minutes.

I don't really know what happened next. Having been dual screening both matches, I launched an iPhone across my living room and did a lap around the kitchen. Had I been Lebanese, I'm almost certain plates would have been broken. As I'm the son of a Yorkshireman, it's just simply not advisable so close to hosting Christmas Dinner.

The agonising wait for the whistle to blow in the San Siro was worth every second. Despite the latest of last-ditch tackles to prevent an almost certain winner in the 96th minute for Inter, Spurs were in the knockout rounds. 'I'm a PSV fan now,' announced the increasingly dashing Dimitar Berbatov in the BT Sport studio.

After all that excitement, how do you raise yourself for Burnley at a half-empty Wembley? For me, the answer was simple. Despite it being a mercifully rare solo trip, I'd got plans to meet with Birgir Olafsson, Chairman of Iceland Spurs. Formed in 1995 before becoming official with Spurs in 2001, a formidable number of their 400-strong membership regularly travel over for games. This weekend, thirty members have made the journey across for one of their three group trips this season.

Torrential downpours mixed with a biting wind make Wembley an unforgiving place; it surely can't be much colder in Reykjavik this afternoon. Despite a healthier attendance than the 33,000 brave souls who turned out for Southampton, the catering vans outside the national stadium are sparse and quiet as everybody heads for shelter at the earliest opportunity.

Perhaps the lack of a queue and unseasonable weather has convinced some fans to invest in unlikely memorabilia. While the half-and-half scarf is derided by the purist as being the novelty of the tourist, you might possibly make an argument for their place across the mantelpiece on a showpiece occasion like Tuesday night. Burnley at home, however, is quite another matter. Despite this, I spot six lads proudly wearing their white and claret garment after parting with the best part of fifty quid from what was presumably a wet, miserable and disbelieving vendor. Sean

Dyche's face sewn into fabric truly is a sight to behold.

There are a few surprises in the line-up too. Oliver Skipp, impressive in several cameos as a sub, is named in the starting XI for the first time, alongside Moussa Sissoko. There's a trio of fullbacks in defence as Trippier returns to join Danny Rose in bombing down the flanks while Ben Davies is an unlikely replacement for Jan Vertonghen in the middle.

Spurs start sluggishly, and not for the first time after a big match. So often after the euphoria of a midweek result, the hangover kicks in by the weekend. After group stage victories against Dortmund and Real last season, both incredible nights that could only have been improved had they taken place in N17, Pochettino's men laboured to a goalless draw against Swansea and a dour 1-0 win over Crystal Palace. The latter, a freezing midday kick-off on Remembrance Sunday, had been a particularly brutal return to earth that I'd dragged my semi-reluctant offspring out of the house for.

In the row in front of me, a couple with a boy of about twelve or thirteen are excitedly chatting amongst themselves. It appears to be their first ever match and the kid is beaming from ear to ear. I momentarily yearn for the company of my own son, whose busy festive social calendar – a tenth birthday party, specifically - meant he couldn't join me this afternoon.

Burnley look like a side who've come for a point. Much like their visit the previous season, when Chris Wood's injury time equaliser earned them just that to dent the romantic Wembley-based Bank Holiday weekend I was spending with my wife, they sit deep, press well and go long. Skipp in particular appears to be one target for a physical approach but, with a few understandable signs of nerves in the opening ten minutes seeing him dispossessed, he soon settles into his role for an impressive debut.

The away end musters the occasional repetition of their team's name but it's as half-hearted as their allocation is half-filled. For the hardcore who've made the 466-mile round trip despite the proximity to Christmas and a weather warning, there's little for them to enjoy aside from the continued frustration of the home side. A penalty shout for a clumsy tackle on Harry Kane is about as good as it gets for Spurs before two Burnley players are booked for time-wasting around the hour mark. Total football, this is not.

The antidote to the hangover arrives twenty minutes from the end when Christian Eriksen joins the action from the bench. Presumably rested with a Carabao Cup return to the Emirates in midweek, his introduction lifts the crowd and his combination with Harry Kane in the 91st minute sees him seal the three points with a superb finish from close range. It's a repeat of his match-winning performance against Inter Milan and it couldn't be more welcome.

The previously pedestrian custodian of Burnley's goal finds new vigour in the final seconds as he races to retrieve a ball from behind the goal to large cheers. 'Joe Hart, he runs when he wants,' sing the home fans as the excitement of a second vital late goal of the week settles down.

The scene outside Wembley after the final whistle resembles a twisted waterpark. Streams of water run down the main walkways and vehicles rushing out of the main car parks project walls of water that soak the drowned rats racing back towards refuge. I spend half an hour driving the couple of miles out towards Wembley Central after wisely deciding to join the traffic instead of walking there and still beat Birgir to the bar. Mercifully, it's long enough to blast enough hot air into my soaking trainers to regain feeling in my toes.

I feel a little self-conscious on arrival at the Travelodge where the Icelandic chairman and his thirty-strong posse are headed post-match. There's just one couple enjoying a romantic burger in a bun to the soundtrack of Heart FM blasting out Christmas songs from a TV in the corner. Our first-floor vantage point offers the ironic view of an Iceland supermarket for that extra bit of home comfort for visitors from Reykjavik.

I text ahead to check on the beer I've promised him, and he replies requesting a rum and coke – 'time out on the beers', he adds. When he does arrive, he's equally drenched.

'Wow,' he says as he shakes my hand, shakes his coat and gets to work on adding the mixer to his single. It turns out there's not much preparation for the level of winter hitting London today, even when you live just a couple of thousand miles away from the North Pole. 'We had about five days across summer without rain,' the 43-year-old Icelander tells me as conversation predictably begins with the weather. 'Europe was burning but God forgot Iceland. It was horrible. But right now, it's warmer in Iceland than it is here.'

I've discovered throughout writing this book that me knowing a supporters' club is making the trip across to the UK somehow adds an additional anxiety to the game. As a stalemate became increasingly likely, my mind had wandered several times to Birgir and his compatriots sobering up from an ecstatic week away. That was, of course, until Christian Eriksen sent Wembley into delirium and an uninspiring Burnley home pointless.

'The goal has saved the trip,' he admits. 'Last season we visited three times. The first time was Swansea in September when it was 0-0. Today was looking like copy and paste stuff of that. We also beat Stoke 5-1 and then it was Man City.'

We've barely begun our chat when we are joined by Birgir's dad. I enquire as to whether this is the man responsible for his lifelong love of the Lilywhites. Apparently not. 'My oldest brother is a Liverpool fan, my second oldest is Manchester United and my youngest is also a Liverpool fan. He was not brainwashing us.'

'They made up their own minds,' Birgir's dad adds. 'But I was always a Spurs fan – since 1962. I didn't know Tottenham existed. I was invited to a match in Ipswich, the Charity Shield. Tottenham won 5-1 and I was hooked.'

He beams at the recollection of watching Greaves, Blanchflower, Jones, Mackay and White in full flow as a half century love affair was born. Alf Ramsay was Bill Nicholson's adversary on the touchline that afternoon, an additional detail that makes the recollection even more impressive. I get the impression he'd be very happy to recount his own storied history following Spurs, but Birgir points his father in the direction of the rest of their gathering at the other end of the bar in Icelandic and he trundles away to leave us to chat.

The whole group arrived on Friday and are heading back on Monday, with many landing at the hotel and heading straight for the tourist hotspots. Birgir spent time at Wembley Outlet - it's also where his girlfriend and the wife of another member, cold and miserable, headed with five minutes to go before the final whistle. After 85 minutes of misery, they'd have just about heard the victory cheers from the first department store.

'We'll go to Winter Wonderland at Hyde Park tomorrow and then on Monday we're taking a taxi to the new stadium before we head for the airport,' Birgir continues, sipping his rum and coke. 'They are holding the test event there tomorrow for season ticket holders in the ballot - and for people who know the right people!

'It's funny when you think about it. The stadium is ready, but they cannot open it until all these small details are finalised. I heard about when they opened Wembley that they called in all the local boy scouts to flush every toilet at the same time to test the plumbing. It is incredible. Who would think of that? But I suppose these are the things they need to check.'

With January's fixture against Manchester United now also relocated to Wembley - 'you're only announcing that because we're still happy after last night' came one reply on Twitter following the point at the Nou Camp - eyes were already being cast to February's fixtures and beyond with a potentially crucial 17-day gap between the visit of Mourinho's men and a midweek fixture hosting Watford.

It's causing more than a few logistical issues in Reykjavik, too, as Birgir explains. 'I have a booked flight for the North London derby with a hotel in Stratford and here. This trip was booked before we knew if it would be Wembley or the new stadium. Normally we have our second trip in December after visiting in September or October and then March or April. When we left this hotel last time, we arranged flowers and pictures with all of the staff here, thinking it would be our last visit,' he says, gesturing towards a smiling barman called Mohamed who confirms this with a nod as he pulls another pint for Birgir.

'We'd originally planned for Cardiff but wanted to delay for the new stadium. I chose Burnley as the only other option was Southampton in the midweek which is not good for us. Coming on a Tuesday, leaving on a Thursday; it's two nights and three days of work. I booked twenty hotel rooms in Stratford and cancelled them three weeks later.'

It's a huge amount of admin for Birgir, but it's something he clearly relishes. Shortly after taking over seven years ago, his first major change was to cut ties with the booking agent adding a healthy premium onto their package deals and book them himself. It was a move that reduced the cost per person by around £200 each, he estimates, and it is a saving that's clearly helping to lubricate the bar tab.

Conversation turns to the World Cup – and in turn, Iceland's incredible victory to eliminate England from Euro 2016 and end Roy Hodgson's tenure as manager. 'You remember that?' Birgir teases. 'It was well deserved as well. I used to live in St Albans for four years and I enjoyed sending a few text messages to my friends in the UK. Even one year later I sent them a message to mark the anniversary. The population of Iceland is similar to Coventry,' he beams. 'So, England lost to Coventry,' he adds, keen to hammer the point home. 'When Iceland came back after the quarter finals, 70,000 people came to town to welcome them home. It was incredible.'

Birgir spent two weeks in France during those glorious group stages for his home country, securing tickets for the opening draw against Portugal in St Etienne and the 1-1 stalemate against Hungary in Marseille. However, he's keen to point out that he'd booked the trip before Iceland even qualified, such was the confidence in his national side. I swiftly move the conversation back to club football – and, specifically, Barca.

'I watched it at my flat,' he tells me. 'I didn't expect anything. We were so up against the wall and it didn't really matter that we got a draw because had Inter won then it wouldn't have been enough. To get through with eight points and negative goal difference is quite amazing. The draw for the last-16 is going to be on Monday and it all depends on where the game is gonna be. For us, as a supporters' club, we don't get any away tickets so it doesn't matter who we play against as it will go to the season tickets and I respect that. Even though we come from Iceland, we are there with passion. But you know how it is in many stadiums around England now filling up with tourists taking pictures.'

The intonation of Birgir's statement is clear – while he and his compatriots might not exactly be locals, they are not to be considered tourists either. These are die-hard, match going fans who are just as frustrated by the delayed return to White Hart Lane as everyone else.

'Wembley last season was much better than this season,' he continues. 'People knew we were there for one season, so they were in for it. Now? They're fed up. When I order tickets for Champions League games, I tell people to book a hotel near Wembley because after a game it is horrible to get home. That's why we stay here. It takes us half an hour to go to Oxford Street but after a game – OK, maybe today it was raining like the end of the world – but it's nice to be able to walk back. Try getting on the train after the game! For a midweek game against Southampton? There is no wonder the attendance is low.'

As we continue to chat, more and more members filter in and show interest in my involvement with Birgir. And then, with remarkable timing given the line of questioning, his girlfriend enters the bar.

'I have mentioned to my girlfriend that if we get married, I would like her to walk into the church to When the Spurs Go Marching In.' He throws his arms up into the air as he re-enacts the moment in his mind's eye. She throws her head back with laughter – it's clearly something she hasn't disregarded completely.

Despite Birgir's hugely enjoyable company, it's soon time for me to leave. He's a raconteur who is becoming even more entertaining as the drinks arrive on tap and he has one more revelation before I go that further reaffirms his Spurs credentials.

'Me, my Dad and my brothers were at White Hart Lane when Helder Postiga scored!' he tells me, wild-eyed. 'And they even made a t-shirt – it said I was there when Helder Postiga scored! – I think it was January 2004. He scored against England as well when they lost on penalties, like always!' he adds, unable to resist a poke at the national side of his former home.

'This is a little bit wet – but it's going to dry,' Birgir says, as he interrupts his own diversion to generously push his bobble hat, personalised with Iceland Spurs, towards me. He pulls another from his pocket before disappearing to his room to bring two scarves back for my children. 'I've got lots. It helps spread the word,' he adds, before seeing me out so he can enjoy a cigarette with his beer under the cold and rainy skies of North London. It's certainly an upgrade on a Sean Dyche scarf.

It's been a successful trip for the Icelandic contingent. But rather than end on Burnley, let us savour Barcelona again for a moment as these occasions don't come around every day.

The very concept of magical European nights under the floodlights was born at stadiums like White Hart Lane. There haven't been quite so many in the modern era for younger fans to enjoy, but for those of us who have had the memories of Parks' winning save in '84 or Mullery's winner in '72 passed down to us, it can feel like we were. For the lucky few who were there, they leave an indelible mark. On Tuesday night, the travelling Tottenham brigade sat high up in the mild Catalonian breeze witnessed another; our very own "special night in Barcelona."

I just hope Tits can remember it.

8
TWELVE GOALS OF CHRISTMAS
LAS VEGAS SPURS

When it comes to early Christmas presents, you can keep your latest games console and leave the plasma telly in the box. I don't need chocolates or the latest films on DVD. For your average Tottenham fan, there is little that can bring Christmas cheer in quite the same way a North London Derby win might; and, by coincidence, that's exactly what Spurs delivered.

With Champions League knockout football to look forward to in the new year and a favourable FA Cup Third Round draw to come, a visit to the Emirates Stadium offered the chance to extend involvement in our most realistic hope in the hunt for silverware. It would also be the chance to avenge the league defeat a fortnight earlier and provide festive redemption for Mauricio Pochettino's men, with a legitimate goal of the season contender for Dele Alli sealing a Carabao Cup semi-final spot.

Harry Kane's control, turn and lofted pass from Gazzaniga's clearance would drop perfectly into the path of his England teammate who effortlessly brought the ball under his spell before lifting it over the head of the advancing Petr Cech with impudence. It was a stunning finish to cement a dominant display; and while disappointment at the way a lead had been vanquished in the Premier League tie remained fresh, the days when visits to our North London neighbours struck fear into Spurs hearts were long gone.

The next league assignment would be the tricky looking visit to Goodison Park to face Everton. Falling on my son's 10th birthday, it would mean a compromise being reached to factor in

Laser Quest and a family meal while avoiding the score to watch the recording later. It would be a birthday treat to savour for a boy who rightly moans at the proximity of his arrival to Christianity's main man.

'Yes! That's the one I wanted!' exclaimed Jacob on opening his replica kit and turning it around to see the name on the back. I'd discreetly enquired around his favourite player several times in the weeks running up to December and, despite perhaps more obvious candidates, including Harry Kane MBE as announced in the New Year's Honours list, Lucas Moura had won through every time.

Theo Walcott's opener was a shaky start but the preferred attacking quartet of Kane, Son, Alli and Eriksen would combine with a goal each between the 27th and 48th minutes to blow away the blue half of Merseyside and put a devastating Tottenham out of sight. Ex-Spur Gylfi Sigurdsson offered hope of a comeback in the 51st minute before Son and Kane added a fifth and sixth respectively to record a hugely impressive away win. Happy Birthday, Jacob.

The win left Spurs in third position on Christmas Day, six points behind leaders Liverpool and five points ahead of both Chelsea and Arsenal. The gap to faltering Manchester United was a colossal thirteen points, suggesting the top four places would be occupied by the runaway pack of five rather than the predicted six.

The negotiations for a Boxing Day trip to Wembley for the Bournemouth match didn't end well for the Jones boys in the end. A 5-0 demolition that included a goalscoring start for Lucas Moura and another brace for Heung Min-Son was enough to make the cold turkey sandwiches taste a little sweeter, at least, especially with Arsenal dropping points at Brighton and perhaps more pertinently Manchester City's defeat at Leicester meaning Spurs climbed into second. While nobody had expected to finish 2018 still lodging at Wembley, the lofty league position combined with the best first half to a season in the Premier League era was a welcome remedy.

Instead, my evenings in the disorientating period between Christmas and New Year had been dominated by Netflix and, specifically, the recently launched series of Sunderland 'Til I Die. Just 18 months previous, I'd taken Jacob to his first ever away game at the Stadium of Light, a drab 0-0 draw most likely to be remembered for the unfortunate injury to Danny Rose that would keep him out for the best part of a year. Since then, the Black Cats had been in freefall and found themselves in the depths of League One. Broadcasting a documentary about their demise on a global streaming platform was certainly an unorthodox way to win an international fanbase compared to Tottenham's strategy, but it proved to be a hugely entertaining accompaniment to late night mince pies and cream all the same. What price might Spurs be tempted to open their doors to a camera crew, I wonder…

There comes a moment during the festivities each Christmas when the fun must stop, though. It might be the first tentative step back onto the weighing scales, the last of the Bailey's running dry or your six-year-old daughter singing the one chorus she knows from The Greatest Showman AGAIN when it strikes you; the excess must come to an end and a return to reality is imminent.

However extravagant or restrained the festive period had been, Spurs fans around the globe had been treated to an additional portion of decadence. After those 11 goals in four days that saw Spurs gain further ground on the chasing pack and leapfrog the faltering reigning champions at the halfway stage of the season, the visit of Wolverhampton Wanderers to Wembley would form the acid test − or reflux, if you did overindulge on the trifle − as to whether that return to reality would arrive on the pitch before 2018 was out.

My belated Christmas chat is with Charles Packard, Vice President of the newly formed Las Vegas Spurs. We're speaking on the 27th of December in the barren period between Christmas and New Year where nobody quite knows what day it is. Football can at least provide a crutch to get a handle on where Saturdays fall in the calendar and that's exactly where our conversation begins.

'Good weekend for us,' he smiles from his desk at Desert Pines Golf Club where he is the resident Professional as well as General Manager. 'I was away for the last two matches, but I streamed both. To score eleven goals in two matches is pretty insane. We have players that are injured to come back and we're still playing well although we'll lose Son in a couple of weeks. That could be devastating in many ways because he creates so many chances and brings energy to the team.'

Charles's enthusiasm is contagious from the beginning of our chat. There is plenty to be enthusiastic about, after all, as well as naively fresh optimism at the prospect of the January transfer window creaking back open in the days to come.

'I would say we need some defensive players,' is Charles's assessment. 'Toby is hurt, Jan is hurt. But signing Eriksen up long term would be the priority. The one key aspect of the team that hasn't been signed – that's what we need to do. The elephant in the room is the one nobody wants to talk about though,' he adds, on the rumours that Mauricio Pochettino could yet be tempted away. 'That person is the key to keeping the whole squad intact,' he continues.

'I think if we can win a title or a couple of cups, I think that will definitely change any decision to leave. I think the stadium move will change the perception in the club, not just in the Premier League but also worldwide. When people see the stadium, as beautiful as it looks from what I've seen, players will want to play there.'

Charles knows all about moving into a brighter and better home. Having started life on America's east coast, he's slowly made his way across the country towards the warmer climes of the west.

'I was born in Baltimore and then lived in Northern Carolina, Georgia,' he says. 'I wasn't a big fan of Georgia; too southern and hillbilly for me at the time! Then we moved out to the west coast and Laguna Hills on the beach in southern California. I've been moving further inland since my childhood. Vegas is home for me, the weather is great, there are lots of activities to do. We don't have hurricane or earthquakes that either coast has to deal with. I love it here.

'I manage Desert Pines Golf Club in downtown Las Vegas so I'm the Pro and the General Manager. It's pretty affordable compared to some of the golf clubs in town that charge $500 a round in the summer. A lot of people come into town for the holidays and it's going to be a busy New Year's Eve for us. It's not a particularly busy time for us as it's the winter. It does snow here maybe twice a year, believe it or not. People assume it's hot because it's the desert, but it does get down to freezing. March through to June and then September, October and November are our busiest times - the weather is fantastic! I've been here for 23 years now so I'm used to the heat now if you remain hydrated. The problem is people consume the beer and liquor while they're here but that's OK. That's what Vegas is for.'

Having spent his entire life in the States, Charles's Tottenham origin story is an intriguing one. Unlike Rolfe Jones, his LA equivalent some 270 miles southwest, he didn't bring a love for the Lilywhites across the Atlantic with him. Instead, it was a trip in the opposite direction to see the words 'Hewlett Packard' on the jerseys of a struggling North London team in the late nineties.

'I was on vacation,' says Charles, taking up the story. 'I flew into Rome, I flew back home out of London and everything in between was up to me. I saw a match in Holland when I was travelling around and that got me excited about soccer. Then I was in the soccer shop and there was my name on the shirt, and I was like: OK, this is my team now!' Given the chance reasoning for becoming a Spur, it feels like a fittingly 'Vegas' way to choose your team.

'Unfortunately, I haven't been back since '97,' Charles continues. 'It would have been nice to have got back to the old stadium but, sadly, it didn't happen. Oddly enough, I was talking about this to my brother over Thanksgiving. Apparently, my father brought back a Tottenham jersey when he was in London in the eighties. It was a pure white jersey with the logo, so obviously it was meant to be. I think it was more of a souvenir for my father but, for me, as the coverage and availability of soccer in the States has increased, it's really opened doors to people here to watch quality football compared to the MLS. It's a fun league but it's not the best players in the world.'

With football a minor sport in the States at that time, Charles shared his passion with a few friends who'd opted for glory over shirt sponsor namesakes, meaning they've usually claimed the bragging rights. His loyalty has been rewarded as the tide began to turn in recent seasons, however.

'I have a friend who is a Manchester United fan who egged me on to watch more soccer,' he says. 'He wondered how I'd plucked Tottenham out of the air, but we've had the better of them over the last few years! I love watching the squad now; what they've been able to do over the last few years is solidify something that is for the long-term. They're not just throwing £200m at it like some teams and seeing what happens, they're creating a team that is growing together. But I'd like to see one good signing in January to make the difference for us if we lose a few players to injuries.'

The urge to find like-minded Spurs fans led to Charles finding a new venue to watch games. That momentum would lead to the launch of Las Vegas Spurs in 2018.

He continues: 'There was a big group of us that would meet at the Crown and Anchor; a true English pub in town. They show all the matches so it's a great football environment, but we always felt like second class citizens when we went there because of the big number of Manchester United and Chelsea fans in the area that would dominate the pub. So finally, (co-founder and President) Sean and I, who I'd met at a number of games over the years, just decided to do this. We needed to find our own home that we could take over, hear the sound and see our match on the large screen. That's when we found G.O.A.T bar.'

Standing for 'Greatest of all time', a common American sports acronym, it's been a good home for the newfound collective. Despite being V.P though, Charles hasn't visited too many times. He's currently in the middle of a self-imposed ban based on the superstition that, when he turns up, Tottenham lose. Much like his chance reasoning for choosing Spurs nearly a quarter of a century earlier, it certainly fits the Vegas mould.

'I actually watched yesterday's match on my computer. Everton, I watched on TV. I was on vacation at my girlfriend's parents' place in Indiana. I'm still banned from going to the pub though while they're winning,' he confirms.

'I'm not allowed in, I'm telling you,' he laughs, when I query how serious he's being. 'Until the team loses with me not being there; then I'll be allowed back in. So, if they rip off nineteen straight wins, I'll be more than happy to celebrate outside by myself. It's funny but I feel sad that I can't go. I'd rather have the team winning than me being at the pub with everybody.'

It's a healthy mix of locals, ex-pats and tourists who have joined together in the few months since their inception. Charles continues: 'I would say half the supporters who come in are locals and support us on a regular basis and half are visitors that have gone on Facebook and done their research and found us. There are Barca and Real fans here in Vegas as well. We have a large Hispanic population. But for the most part it's the EPL and probably Manchester United with the biggest group. We're holding our own though now we have our own chapter and people know where to find us. This is our spot, we're going to have the sound on, there isn't any competition.'

Superstitions aside, the advent of the internet and growth in popularity of the game across the Atlantic makes following Spurs much easier than it was when Charles first headed home in a shirt with his surname emblazoned across the midriff more than two decades ago. By his own admission, it initially made keeping up with results difficult.

'It wasn't very easy at all,' he continues. 'They used to charge people to go in and watch the games as they had to pay for satellite. To say I was a true diehard Spurs fan during that time?

It was difficult to be honest. It's like saying you were a huge fan of American Football when you could only read highlights in the paper. I love it though. My devotion to the team is up there with any other sport I watch. I walk around and I'm proud to wear my scarf. I'll wear a Harry Kane jersey around town and people will start honking. I'll get someone shouting, 'Come on you Spurs!' It's rare that you think that would happen but there are loyal fans that are out there now.'

Charles has even converted his girlfriend to Spurs – and from the 'dark side' at that. 'She never really told me she was a Chelsea fan until after we got together,' he laughs. 'She had played soccer, liked their jersey and wore their colours. But now she comes and watches the game with me. They kick off at 4.30am here sometimes so she'll watch if they're not too early. It's great not having that issue at home though, having to pretend I'm sorry her team lost before turning around to snigger.'

With half the season played out already and the dawn of a new year upon us, Charles is supremely optimistic about what 2019 has in store.

'The team has more points than it's ever had at this stage of a season. If you look historically, they would usually be top of the table at this point if it wasn't for Liverpool playing so well. I think Spurs have played excellent football and yes, we've lost some matches, but we've won fifteen matches which is unheard of. I still think we could have a shot to win the league. I think Dortmund is a good draw for the Champions League because I don't think they're as good as they've been. We beat them easily last year so that's a good draw in my opinion.

'As long as Sonny comes back healthy and doesn't disappear for too long. Dele is coming back. I'm more worried about the backline than anything else as it appears to be injury prone. Do they need 100 points this year? I don't think so, but I think they need mid-90s which they're on pace for. The Liverpool and City match there were small turning points that cost us points. There's not a lot in it right now.'

Most pleasing for Charles, though, is the durability

Pochettino's Tottenham is beginning to show. He continues: 'I think the biggest thing for me is that in years past, people would have written off Spurs after the Arsenal defeat. Now they come back and rip win after win, rising from fifth to second in just three weeks. That's amazing and that's the difference between the team this year and teams in the past, in my opinion. It's great to see the consistency from the Spurs. They're probably the most consistent squad over the last five years in the Premier League.'

With interest in the Premier League booming and plenty of British fans making the trip out to Vegas for a weekend of golf, Charles's affiliation leads to some welcome repartee with those looking to tee-off at Desert Pines.

'I love asking visitors from the UK who they support,' he tells me. 'I can sometimes place the accent. It's fine when it's an Arsenal or a Chelsea fan because I can have a bit of banter. I just say: 'I'm sorry, your tee time is no longer available' or 'we're now closed for the day'. It's great because football bonds people and it's all good fun.'

My final question, after being left in little doubt of Charles's deep love for Spurs considering he shunts Gooners down the tee-times, is this: with Packard Bell being another prominent kit sponsor of the nineties, is there a possible alternate reality where Charles might have instead stumbled upon the white jerseys of Leeds United first?

'I guess so,' he laughs, 'but I think blue and white are two of my favourite combinations. I've never thought about it like that but, no, I don't think it would have ever happened. I love everything about Spurs. They work hard every day. They have a bit of flash, but they work hard as a team. The squad has been together for a while and it's great to see them get better. It shows what happens if you work hard, have a plan and put it together; it's exciting to watch and other teams and even supporters of other clubs acknowledge Spurs are exciting to watch and not a side they want to face because of the style of football. I love it, I really love it. I get pumped up and so excited. I think we're gonna win and I think we'll go deep into the Champions

League as well.'

My chat with Charles proves to be more enjoyable than the Wolves game that follows. Avoiding the last-minute urge to make the dash to London, I take heed of my post-Christmas bank balance and decide to walk the dog through the misty Derbyshire fields with BBC 5Live on my brand-new wireless headphones.

Despite numerous stats checks reminding us that Spurs are unbeaten in 39 games against newly promoted sides, including one from the club's official channel itself – a step too far for me in tempting fate, let alone superstitious fans like Charles - a humbling 3-1 defeat brings Spurs back down to earth and halts talk of a title tilt before it's even really begun. Only Arsenal's 5-1 defeat at Anfield, that effectively means Spurs increase their advantage over their North London rivals on goal difference, even in defeat, provides the smallest of consolations on a disappointing afternoon.

'I fell on my arse,' I tell my wife, wincing as I kick off the muddy walking boots that momentarily failed me climbing over a stone stile on an otherwise refreshing winter stroll. The only person going down heavier than me that afternoon was Hugo Lloris at Wembley, as he looked sluggish for all three of Wanderers' goals. I quickly banish thoughts that Charles might have inadvertently also cursed both the book and my hiking hobby.

It's just the third time Tottenham have lost at home by two or more goals under Pochettino, and the first defeat at home in a game they'd taken the lead in for two and a half years. Wolves had landed just four shots on target, demonstrating the 'smash and grab' nature of the victory, resulting in a very encouraging 2018 ending with a reality check. For all the progress, would 2019 be the year for silverware, a new home and renewed commitment from the key men taking Tottenham Hotspur forward?

The butterfly effect of the result does mean one thing though, in a bar more than five thousand miles away; Charles Packard, Vice-President of Las Vegas Spurs, is finally allowed back in his own venue.

JANUARY

9
NKOUDOU TO THE RESCUE
MALAYSIA SPURS

The New Year's Eve hangover is soon washed away, along with the memory of defeat to Wolves, by an efficient demolition of Cardiff City. A little back pain is reignited from my tumble off the stile; I'd already bruised my coccyx last summer after falling off a child's swing. It was a cruel injury blow so close to a World Cup that had ruled me out of Gareth Southgate's plans once and for all.

Neil Warnock, fresh from beating Claude Puel's Leicester City over the festive period, had spouted his mouth off about Spurs several times in the run-up to the game, suggesting his team do not "breathe" near top players in the box for fear of them going down – something he has some experience in – while encouraging his counterpart in the opposing dugout not to be "blinded by loyalty" when it came to the admiring glances of Manchester United. For a man once coaxed away from Huddersfield Town to Plymouth Argyle, it was sage advice indeed.

Following the 3-0 defeat, thanks to early goals from Kane, Eriksen and Son inside the opening 26 minutes, Warnock rounded up his analysis by suggesting Spurs should be forced to play at Wembley for the remainder of the season so that no other side gained "an advantage". Anagram fans everywhere are reminded of his affectionate nickname 'Colin', in reference to the letters 'W', 'N', 'A', 'K', 'E' and 'R' leftover for a surname. Have some fun at home and see if you can work it out for yourself.

It was becoming difficult to ignore the speculation. Mauricio himself had carefully sidestepped questions in one press conference before stating his desire to remain at the helm for 20 years; he then cryptically added that this would be something he'd need to discuss with Arsene Wenger.

Poch's class was further demonstrated in the 7-0 demolition of Tranmere Rovers in the opening game of FA Cup Third Round weekend. After a slightly laboured first half, punctuated by the first goal of an unlikely Serge Aurier brace, Spurs cruised through the gears to set up a visit to Selhurst Park with a Llorente hat-trick, a solo effort from Son that began in his own half and that surprise second goal from the Ivorian fullback. Serge would even attempt a shot at completing an unlikely hat-trick soon after; it sailed high into the stands. Normality restored.

At 6-0 up, with quarter of an hour to play, I'll admit to my heart being in my mouth at the sight of Harry Kane waiting to enter the field of play. Pochettino himself explained the reasons for risking the nation's captain for fifteen minutes in a long-won cup tie at League Two opposition: 'Respect the people, respect the opponent. They're not going to have many chances to see Harry Kane play here in a competition like the FA Cup. For different reasons I decided to make a change and put Kane on the pitch but one of them is that it's important to show respect to the people here so they could see Harry Kane, who is an icon in English football. It is difficult in that division to see it. It was important to see him in action.'

Whether fans of Tranmere Rovers agreed entirely was hard to judge, especially when the World Cup Golden Boot winner inevitably slotted home the seventh to secure the biggest away win in Tottenham's history. 'Surely you beat this score Harry, no?' queries the gaffer modestly as he shows deference to Mr Redknapp during the post-match interview on the touchline. 'We got nine against Wigan, Mauricio,' retorts Harry before returning the compliment that his side are "a pleasure to watch." It's a meeting of Spurs' recent past with the present that's enough to make even the most hardened fan go a little gooey.

'So proud of this lad,' tweets another legend of bygone days, Cliff Jones, the newly joint-fourth top scorer in Spurs history after the late seventh drew Kane level with the Welshman. 'We won't share 4th place for long and I wish him plenty more goals over the coming years.'

'Thanks Cliff,' replies Kane. 'A pleasure to share 4th spot with you but hopefully only until Tuesday!'

Sure enough, Kane is quickly presented with the opportunity to go clear third after winning a penalty following some VAR-based controversy in the League Cup semi-final first leg against Chelsea. A tight offside call followed by a rugby tackle from the onrushing Arrizabalaga draws unlikely claims that the Spaniard had seen his teammates claiming offside and had attempted to rearrange his limbs all the same. It's an argument as fragile as the lead Spurs will take to Stamford Bridge next month after Kane coolly slots home the winner.

When the visit of Manchester United arrives, the questions around the Old Trafford job appear to be firmly out of bounds but there are other concerns circling, not least the remaining 18 months left on Christian Eriksen's contract that could make him a likely departure in the summer if a new deal isn't agreed.

'Maybe he will sign next week or in six months, or the club and him are having different challenges and dreams,' Pochettino tells the pre-match press conference. 'He's a very special person. You need to give freedom, like on the pitch, you can't put him in the box. Like my dog, when you go in the park, you have to give freedom and trust.'

Given the analogy, clearly meant with affection, it can only be assumed that he's - wait for it...I'm building up to it. I'm almost ready...A GREAT DANE! Please don't leave now, you've come this far.

Instead of taking my usual seat at Wembley, I'll be watching at The Pit in Harrogate today with my dad. Watching Spurs play Manchester United in a pub in January immediately throws up several memories of yesteryear. The most vivid was following the first Christmas spent with the woman who would become my wife as we returned to our university city of Derby to watch Tottenham face the daunting prospect of Fergie's United in our favourite pub. The bar was packed with a rough 50/50 split cheering for either side for one reason or another, but we were all united in confusion upon seeing the Red Devils counterattacking in the final moments to almost snatch a late win. While the noise was too loud to confirm it, we had just exploded with elation at Pedro Mendes's speculative attempt from the halfway line that had surely been spilled by Roy Carroll. I'm still less 'over it' now than the actual ball had been over the line then. Younger readers might want to pause for a moment to relive it via YouTube and experience the injustice we all felt in the early days of 2005 at being robbed of a rare Old Trafford victory.

Another January clash came on a snowy evening in 2013 in a bar in Munich. Convinced the three-day stag do I'd ventured on would be delayed for a further 24 hours thanks to a light dusting at Manchester Airport, the search for a TV to force down another stein of local beer was rewarded with Clint Dempsey's late equaliser. The mate whose stag it was remains happily married with two beautiful kids now. Happy memories with a light flavouring of Spurs; my favourite kind of holiday.

This afternoon's game probably won't be filed under the same folder marked 'nostalgia'. A tight game is turned on its head when Marcus Rashford's pace helps the visitors capitalise on a wayward ball from Kieran Trippier. His powerful shot across Hugo Lloris somehow appears both devastatingly accurate and eminently saveable at the same time. The captain will eventually live up to his reputation in the second half with several top class stops, before David De Gea outdoes him by saving no less than eleven shots on target.

To compound the injustice of failing to gain a deserved point at the very least, a late tackle by Phil Jones on Harry Kane leaves him hobbling off the field shaking his head – it doesn't look good, and so it proves. A two-month layoff is confirmed the following day over a period that could include two trips to Stamford Bridge, both Dortmund legs, a potential League Cup final and the visit of Arsenal. Moussa Sissoko also limps off with a muscle injury. To cap off the evening, I get a parking ticket outside The Pit after failing to spot that the bay my car is in becomes a taxi rank after 6pm. Another successful Sunday, then.

There's plenty to reflect on then when I manage to schedule my call with Syahizan Amir Abd Wahab, or Amir to his friends, the 41-year-old President of Malaysia Spurs, ahead of an increasingly important trip to Craven Cottage. The Manchester United defeat, however, remains fresh in our minds.

'I'm surprised that they managed to outplay us using counterattack,' is his initial response to the match against Ole Gunnar Solskjaer's revitalised visitors – the Norwegian's pre-Christmas appointment having put an end to the Pochettino speculation for a little while at least.

'I wish it had been a Jose Mourinho team!' Amir continues. 'De Gea was great but the only thing that worries me is Sissoko and Harry Kane. I think someone should give Phil Jones a slap,' he jokes. 'Pogba's challenge on Dele Alli should have been a straight red and the game could have changed.'

Officially formed in 2009, a collective of Malaysian fans have been meeting since 2003 to watch Spurs games. Amir is their third President, having been involved in some capacity since those early days, and has played his part in their rise to 520 members with around 200 of these opting into an annual renewal. The winning combination of his warm personality and infectious laugh is evident from the first few moments of our chat as I begin to explore how he came to develop such a love for the Lilywhites.

'Prior to the World Cup in 1990, I was focusing on local football,' he begins. 'I was supporting Kuala Lumpur who won the Malaysian League three times in a row. I was a bit of a glory supporter! When the World Cup came along, I was thirteen years old and everybody talked about football. I watched England's games and I saw they had talented people. Thankfully I fell in love with Gary Lineker and Gazza and not David Platt or I might have been a Gunner,' he reflects with a shudder.

'After the World Cup, I started to follow Tottenham and saw them win the FA Cup in 1991. It wasn't easy to watch football back then because it was only shown once a week and we often only had one TV at home, so you had to watch with your family members. Without Gazza and Lineker and the World Cup, I would probably not have known about Tottenham.'

Tottenham's talismanic duo saw their stock rise further on England's unexpected run to the semi-finals; comparable to 2018, perhaps, with Harry Kane et al indirectly boosting the Spurs global brand. It wasn't the first time two players who'd announced themselves at a World Cup would leave Amir's family smitten with N17 from afar, as Amir would discover many years later.

'When I got older, I discovered that my late father had also supported Tottenham. I'd invited some of my friends over who were Tottenham fans and he recognised the jersey. He had supported them during the days of Villa and Ardiles. I was shocked – had it not been for this friend visiting, he wouldn't have revealed this. I believe Tottenham is in my blood.'

Like so many of his equivalents across the globe, getting to a game in person is more than a little tricky. After two decades dedicated to Spurs, however, it would be Amir's wife, Azni, who would convince her husband to make the leap. To add to the trip of a lifetime, they would also bump into a Spurs cult hero in the making.

'You think about visiting Tottenham but it's so expensive,' he explains. 'You have to spend one thousand quid just to stay for a few days – it's a lot here! One month's salary or so, so you seldom think about it. When I got married, we only usually visit Indonesia, Thailand and maybe Australia. We had never thought of visiting the UK. Then Azni said: "When we go to Jakarta, we spend one thousand quid. Just buy a damn ticket!"'

'We went to the Spurs Shop and while we were shopping, I realised it was van der Vaart by my side, buying his kids Spurs stuff. I don't think he'd played for us at that time, he'd only just signed. We approached him and he was very nice and took photos with us. I remembered I'd brought with me the Malaysian flag, so I asked him to pose with it. I think he was the first World Cup or Premier League player to pose with the Malaysian flag. I tell my friends that's why he performed for us - because he touched this flag!'

There would be more rubbing shoulders with his heroes after that first match. 'After the game, the players would go out the back to the car park. We met Gareth Bale, William Gallas and Younes Kaboul. Azni managed to meet her crush, Niko Kranjcar. He's so handsome!' laughs Amir. 'My wife has been supporting me since college, she is my college sweetheart. My first jersey was the 1996 Pony/Hewlett Packard shirt. I bought two – one home, one away – and she would always wear the home one. We're like a Spurs couple. She's been very supportive – I've been President for four years and she's been my First Lady. She will be there at every event helping out and had she never pushed me to go, I might still be hanging around Indonesia on holiday!'

There's little wonder Amir's friends have associated Spurs as part of his identity given his dedication to a team not traditionally as popular as some of the other heavyweights of the game who targeted Asia as a growth area for international fans long before the likes of Tottenham. It's largely down to the fact that anyone meeting his acquaintance for the first time between the mid-90s and present day could be left in little doubt about his allegiances.

He continues: 'Supporting Spurs then was like supporting Newcastle now because nobody wants to be a fake Spurs fan! There's no point! You must be a big fan to want to wear the jersey.'

Despite this, he assures me they have a great relationship with Toon Army Malaysia, a Newcastle United supporters' club who formed when the Geordies were a little more popular during the Shearer era.

'A lot of my friends refer to me as Mr Spurs because not many people supported Spurs here,' he continues. 'The top two teams are probably Manchester United and Liverpool. Arsenal managed to get more fans when they won the league and Chelsea also for the same reason. Most fans here choose a team because they won something – us, despite not winning something, we have Dele Alli and Harry Kane. Some of the fans we have support us because they like the way we play.'

Alongside his admirable passion, Amir's dedication to Spurs is also usually visible – and, in some cases, not so visible.

'Most of the time I have Spurs underwear on! Mugs, flask, pin badges - everything is Tottenham. I have six ties. You show your passion and show your club. When I attend meetings, people comment on it. Most of the time they won't be Spurs fans, but you earn some respect from them. Now I'm wearing Tottenham jogger pants and I've bought another two pairs! We must give good, positive vibes to the team. As a Muslim, and those who believe, we can pray; that's what we can give. If God is a Spurs fan, we can ask for them to win,' he continues.

If He is, he's got a dark sense of humour.

'It's better than sending out negative vibes. OK, they won't hear it, but God will hear it!' he reassures me.

Amir's presidency has seen the continuation of high-profile events to attract more fans from across Malaysia. As Tottenham's popularity grows, so do the audiences attending Amir's events – largely thanks to a healthy relationship with the local TV station.

'We have a very good relationship with the local TV station here and when they get an ex-player over, they get in touch with us. We've had events with Clive Allen, Gary Mabbutt, Jermaine Jenas, Paul Robinson and Darren Anderton. Mabbutt was the first and he was so humble. They are human beings and they share with us their experience. The first time I met these stars, it was huge, but now I am the president, I have to control myself! I was a bit excited meeting Jenas though because he is an awesome person and he scored against Arsenal all the time, so I was privileged having lunch with him. Gary Stevens is one of our members as well,' he adds, of the former

Tottenham defender who now earns his crust as a pundit for Malaysian TV. 'He's a very good friend and lives in Bangkok.'

Such regular face time with the good and the great of Spurs past gives him a different outlook on the current crop of players, not least one popular face in Mousa Dembele who left Spurs Lodge for the final time this week.

'When you consider Dembele is leaving for China, I understand. He is 31-years-old. He gets more money and two or three years more. It's a good thing and I wish him all the best. We need to respect the players and understand that even though they love the club, they are working! It's their job. If someone offered me double my salary now and my wife told me to go, I'd go!'

It's a sentiment shared by many as Dembele left almost uniquely with the universal love and support of an entire fanbase. A reflective video looking back on his time with the club was released by Spurs TV, complete with an appearance from a teenage Jan Vertonghen, alongside his friend of almost two decades, as they'd come up through the ranks of the Belgian national side.

After more than a decade of supporting Tottenham from afar, Amir first discovered there was a collective of other Spurs fans in his home country in 2003 through a newspaper advertisement.

'I read in the newspaper a column about the EPL and there was an advertisement about the location of fan clubs. There was Liverpool, Manchester United, and also Tottenham. I emailed Jack Wong, our first president, and he invited us along and we became part of an email group. Before I went along, I didn't know what certain things meant – what is COYS for example – because you've been watching alone. And then you learn it's [an acronym for] 'Come On You Spurs' and you learn songs. I learned a lot of things when I joined this fellowship of Spurs fans.'

The gratitude of Amir and his fellow supporters led to the launch of the Jack Wong Cup – a by-product of Malaysia's friendship with Singapore Spurs, who they play a match against on an annual basis.

'We won the first year in KL (Kuala Lumpur) by five goals to two. In the second year we won 7-1 in Singapore. We have a pool of players and have friendly games throughout the year. This time, given the big victory last year, I advised Ibrahim Rabbani, my Director of Football, to select more senior players because they had more senior players last time. But this time, they brought younger players,' he laughs. Amir's team were defeated in a tense penalty shootout that's still available on YouTube at the time of writing.

'We nearly won the game,' he adds mournfully, 'but it doesn't matter. Nobody loses in this tournament. It started just as a friendly tournament but now we buy a cup and have sponsors coming in. They spend a lot to come here and the main thing is that they enjoy the game. Now we have requests from Indonesia and Thailand wanting to join but it's very costly for them to come over.'

Battling inconvenient time zones is nothing new for Spurs fans in other continents but Asian fans have it particularly tough. While supporters in the Americas are often required to set their alarms and start the weekend early, most of the games in Asia start late and encroach on the traditional working week. Some games, however, just aren't worth staying awake for.

'During late games, it's not shown anywhere,' Amir continues. 'The places where we watch will be closed. We will watch the game in the middle of the night and then go straight to work; this is the passion. If the result is good, it's good! When we lost 4-3 to Inter Milan, I switched the TV off at half-time. I think I went to sleep crying! I am a lawyer and I have to attend court tomorrow. I woke up hearing about Bale's hat-trick so it was wonderful. The other players in that game deserve credit. We kept Inter Milan at bay. Jermaine Jenas was fantastic in that game,' he adds. The former England midfield is clearly one of Amir's favourites having previously shared lunch.

'My Vice President Mahmood Razak went to Japan and met

with Vakky Takuya of Osaka Spurs,' he continues, picking the thread of the dedicated Asian fan back up. 'They had to watch it in a karaoke bar because nowhere else is open at that time. The game started at 2am and finished at 4am. They had to stay there because there is no bus or train and a cab will be expensive, so they sleep there until 6am. Those are the kinds of sacrifices people have to make just to watch a game.' There are worse places to be stranded with fellow Spurs fans for the night than a Japanese karaoke bar, I imagine. It must be one Chas and Dave song after another.

As our conversation draws to a close, I'm genuinely sad to be leaving Amir's company. As we chat and laugh like old friends despite only making acquaintance an hour or so earlier, the bond that Spurs provokes leaves him assuring me that he can secure discounts on a 5-star hotel where Spurs have stayed before should I ever make the trip across the globe. 'Breakfast is 50p here,' he continues with the hard sell. As I gaze out into the freezing fog of my back garden, it certainly sounds appealing.

'Most of my best friends now are people I discovered through Tottenham. One of my best friends now, Rofizan "Peeps" Rahman, I met him at the toilet at my office,' he begins. It's an unconventional way to make friends, for sure. 'I'd see him all the time but then he wore a Spurs jersey, so I stopped him! I asked if he was a Spurs fan and gave him my card. He gave me his email. I emailed him right away about our supporters' club and he replied after one week. I asked him: 'why did you reply late? I gave you the email and told you to get in touch.' He said to me: 'I know but you were very creepy!' After that, they called me the toilet stalker!' While it's very funny in his telling of the story, Amir's recruitment drive in and around public bathrooms paid dividends, as Rofizan helped design the graphic for Malaysia Spurs.

'Some of the guys I wouldn't think I'd be friends with, but because he's a Tottenham fan, he's a good friend of mine. I don't think he'd want to be my friend either. But because of Spurs, it binds all of us.' It's a lovely sentiment to end our chat on.

I suppose the opposite of Amir's effortless bonding with Spurs strangers is working to find common ground with Arsenal-loving friends. It's something I've had plenty of practise in over the years, having known a fair few in my time.

During my school years in the late 90s, as Arsene Wenger turned Highbury back into something resembling a fortress, I was one of only two Spurs fans in my school in Chesterfield. Perhaps surprisingly, not one glory fan had abandoned Manchester United or Liverpool at that stage to support the Gooners that I can remember. Small mercies.

Then, at university, I arrived at my halls of residence to meet the lads I'd be sharing a flat with. Two Arsenal fans and a Chelsea fan – at the time, battling it out between themselves in the latter stages of the Champions League just as David Pleat was parachuted back in to save Spurs from the drop. We found an uneasy truce for a year or two. Perhaps tellingly, I'm no longer in touch with any of them.

In my early professional career, I went for lunch with a new line manager who became distracted by Sky Sports News in the corner of the café we were eating in. Spotting an opportunity for common ground, I enquired about who he supported. He responded by lifting a trouser leg to reveal Arsenal socks. Another blossoming professional relationship ruined.

A few years on, in a bizarre parallel to my own early career, I took a colleague who I'd just recruited out for lunch on his first day. The look on his face when he discovered that he'd agreed to work for a Spurs fan who'd already clocked his Aaron Ramsay screensaver was a sight to behold. Thankfully, our working relationship was much better, if a little frayed around the edges in the days surrounding a North London Derby. My general advice in our regular 1-2-1 catch-ups would be: if you're going to dress the desk of your boss in Arsenal regalia after a narrow victory, don't be surprised to find a Pascal Chimbonda shirt draped over your chair when you lose one.

The Arsenal fan I've co-existed most fruitfully with by far is my mate Chris. We met around five years ago when he began dating my old schoolfriend Claire. They are a wonderful couple with a beautiful dog that my Jack Tzu, Indiana Jones, tries to hump every time she visits. Neither she nor we have the heart to tell him that, following a painful procedure he's now clearly forgotten all about, each attempt is the equivalent of fishing without a rod. He's emptier than a Europa League match at the Emirates Stadium. Our dog is firing more blanks than Roberto Soldado.

Chris and Claire visited us regularly during their courtship before their engagement led them to ask me to perform a reading at their wedding. The subject was up to me and, naturally, I was intent on ensuring I delivered something special and memorable for them both. In the end, I settled for a self-penned poem which I can only assure you went down much better than it might sound. An excerpt from towards the end is below:

My only complaint in my friend's choice of man:
Did she really have to marry an Arsenal fan?
But other than, he's one hell of a bloke
Who'd probably crumble on cold Tuesdays in Stoke.

Eric Matey would be proud.

Chris and I participate in gentle banter when our two sides meet. It was especially gentle in the defeat at the Emirates earlier in the season when he shared a video of him silently celebrating with their beautiful newborn daughter asleep on his chest. And now, with a few months having passed since she was born, the time has finally arrived for us to meet her in person.

For anyone who has had a baby - or kids of any age, to be honest - you'll probably know how difficult it can be to keep an appointment. So, on Sunday 20th January, I made it perfectly clear to the new family that no time needed to be set. Turn up when you want; we'll be around. At the back of my mind, I had remembered that Spurs were at Fulham on the TV, but no matter. All would be fine.

We do have previous here when it comes to organising get-togethers at otherwise inconvenient timeslots relating to football. Such are our busy schedules, combining careers and children with stand-up comedy, gestating a baby and actively not gestating a litter of puppies, the choice of dates is often limited to get something solid in the diary. For this reason, I take full responsibility for agreeing with Claire to go for a curry during what turned out to be Spain and Portugal's 3-3 draw during the 2018 World Cup. As our poppadoms were served, it became increasingly clear to the football-loving half of the table that we were missing a stonewall classic. I know he blamed me, deep down. I blamed myself. A gurgling anger at my diary faux pas had continued to bubble within me all evening; although that might have been the Madras.

When they did arrive late that Sunday afternoon, the game at Craven Cottage had kicked off ten minutes earlier. I paused the match and we caught up as old friends do, especially when there's a newborn baby to be cuddled.

'Aren't you watching the match?' Chris enquired, leadingly. Not one to conceal a poker face, I knew in this moment that a) he wanted to watch the match, even though it was Spurs, and regardless of the combined blowback we might receive as the baby was passed around with the kind of precision Harry Winks was already imposing on the game and b) any likelihood of avoiding the score until later in the evening would now be impossible. This would be confirmed a few minutes later when he looked at his phone, burst out laughing, apologised and then explained that he was only chuckling because the circumstances were so extraordinary.

It's difficult to describe how I knew exactly what had happened from this reaction alone. Maybe I have an untapped psychic ability that remains undeveloped but intact. Maybe this life we all lead is nothing more than a re-run of endless outcomes in the same way that déjà vu is the echo memories of our alternate realities permeating our current consciousness. Or, maybe, and certainly most likely, Tottenham Hotspur Football Club have simply run out of ways to surprise me by being momentarily, utterly and hilariously incompetent.

All I can tell you is that, in that very moment, based only on the instinctive and understandable laughter it drew from my very best Arsenal-supporting friend, I knew that Fernando Llorente had scored an own goal.

The career of the big Spaniard since he joined from Swansea City had been a frustrating one. So often dragged off the bench in the dying embers of games to either attempt to salvage something or simply waste a bit of time, his only real opportunities had been in cup competitions where he'd twice registered hat-tricks against lower league opposition. While this might have garnered him the reputation of a flat-track bully, it was almost as sad as it was a time-honoured tradition to see a World Cup winning striker toiling away in a Spurs shirt.

Now, with a sustained period in the first team given the injury to Kane and absence of Son, the trip to Craven Cottage would be his first opportunity to prove he could step up to the plate with the January transfer window still wide open and, just a week ago, seemingly beckoning his name. His early response to this unexpected stint in the first team had been to instinctively deflect a whipped corner off his right leg and into the bottom corner of his own net. Oh, Fernando.

It would take until the early part of the second half for Dele Alli to draw Spurs level before limping off to further add to our attacking woes. And then, after various refills of tea and a discussion around the returning red-headed Ryan Babel - a player we agreed you might very easily forget existed until you heard his name again on an instalment of *Premier League Years* - the final minute of injury time arrived, and the following sequence of events took place between 92:00 and 92:53:

'Remarkably, this is going to be our first league draw of the season,' I tell Chris, unable to hide my disappointment at dropping such crucial points at one of the division's most toothless teams.

'Hold on a minute,' says Chris as Spurs make their way up the left flank, sensing what he perceived to be an inevitable equaliser from a Gooner's point of view in much the same way I fear Arsenal's ability to snatch a winner when they're struggling in injury time.

'I think there'll be a lot of pessimism in the Tottenham ranks if they don't win this,' says former Arsenal striker Alan Smith in co-commentary as the ball reaches Alli's replacement, the almost forgotten Georges-Kevin Nkoudou. 'Those questions about Harry Kane and Son not being there come to fruition...OH!'

That exclamation at the end of a somewhat prematurely damning assessment of Tottenham's afternoon would come at the realisation that the Frenchman had found the perfect cross to meet the head of Harry Winks, who nodded home to win the game with seconds remaining on the clock. No newborns were dropped or tea spilt in the celebrations that ensued.

As we wave our friends off with their new arrival shortly after the full-time whistle, the relative restraint Jacob and I showed around a sleeping baby and her Arsenal-supporting father when Winksy sealed the win is unleashed in the living room as we replay the goal again and again. What a cross. What a header. What a result.

'Helloooo u remember me?' tweets Nkoudou later that evening. Only just, Kevin, but we promise to never forget you.

The Fulham result would turn out to be a rare highlight in a disappointing January. Faraway from N17, the yearning for Heung Min Son's return only increased as the Asian Games gained new viewers with an ulterior motive. Unlike earlier in the season, where a South Korean victory was cheered across North London, Spurs fans were now actively supporting their opponents in a bid to get the star home a little earlier. While my £1 minimum stake on a weekday afternoon to enable me to view South Korea vs Bahrain via a tiny betting screen might usually point to a wider issue, it was seemingly the only way to keep track of his likely return. A 2-1 win after extra time for the Koreans, on the same afternoon Dele Alli was ruled out until March, meant another impending weekend of limited attacking options. Time to stick needles in my South Korea voodoo doll set, especially given newspaper reports would later suggest a move for Andy Carroll to plug the gap. It possibly works - they're knocked out by Qatar in the quarter finals.

Spurs have a crunch period of knockout football to contend with themselves with the second leg of the Carabao Cup semi-final at Stamford Bridge followed by a visit to Selhurst Park in the FA Cup without Kane, Alli or Son. With Moura benched and Llorente and Lamela upfront at Chelsea, I'll excruciatingly be attempting to avoid the score again due to an important gig at The Frog and Bucket, a famous Manchester venue that I've been waiting to return to for some seven months. It's been a while since Thursday nights have posed a scheduling issue for Spurs fans, which is handy given it's a busy night for stand-up comedy. Tonight, I would have to listen to the first quarter of the game on the radio before heading into the venue. I turned off just before N'Golo Kanté opened the scoring.

As demonstrated during Chris and Claire's visit, avoiding the score is a risky business, but I was confident of my chances. I wasn't gigging with anyone I knew to like football this evening - tick. Secondly, it was unlikely any of them even knew I was a Spurs fan, making an uninvited casual score update much less likely. Double tick. I turned my phone off and concentrated on the task at hand.

If you've ever been to a stand-up comedy night and commented on the general quality of the line-up, know this: we're doing the same about you as an audience. It was a notably quiet crowd in the first section for the opening act, but I was content with getting them going in the middle section to the point that I left the stage confident of further work. It's a bit like putting a decent shift in on your international debut, I suppose, before awaiting an announcement on the squad for the next round of competitive matches.

Content with my evening's shift, I had almost forgotten about the gentle Spurs-shaped bubble of excitement in my stomach completely – but only just. I was beginning to run through what time I'd arrive home, whether I'd got a beer in the fridge and which podcast I was going to play on the hour and a half trip home to be certain of not catching the arse end of a sports bulletin around the hour.

There was a fleeting consideration of heading straight to bed before rising super early to watch the match with my son before the school run, but this idea didn't last long. I'm more of a night owl than an early bird, and anyway, wasn't staying up into the early hours ahead of a busy working day exactly what my Asian counterparts would have been doing? As I pondered this, the headline act Chris McCausland arrived in the green room with his friend and assistant.

If you've seen Chris's Live at the Apollo set, you will know two things about him: the first is that he is one of the funniest acts on the UK circuit. The second is that he is blind. At this stage, if I'm honest, I thought I was on the home run. After the usual green room banter, which included several of us sharing where we'd be performing on the weekend's upcoming Burn's Night and Chris brilliantly quipping that 'that's what blind people call pancake day,' I shook hands with my comedy comrades and made for the door with a skip in my step.

As I left the green room, I only heard eight words as I made my way down the stairs towards the exit, just a few steps away from all direct human contact for the rest of the evening. They came from the familiar Scouse accent of Chris and were as follows: 'Oh wow. Chelsea won 4-2 on penalties.'

At that moment I felt a range of emotions, almost all of them being different shades of utter disappointment. Disappointment that we'd lost yet another semi-final, first and foremost. Disappointment at losing on penalties. Disappointment at not staying in touch with it all night given I'd found the result out anyway. Disappointment that my evening's plans, albeit ultimately destined to end in the ultimate dismal disappointment, had just been torpedoed. I had time to dwell on each and every one of these emotions as I sulked my way back to the car.

You might wonder if there was at least a small part of me

relieved that I had at least avoided the gut-wrenching experience of watching it 'as live' but, genuinely, there wasn't. If I can't experience a game in the flesh or live on TV, it's important to relive it in as realistic a recreation of the real thing as I can, otherwise what's the point? Win, lose or draw – hit me with it as if I'd been there. It happened with my dad once. I'd avoided the score all day and was about to settle down to watch the match when he called.

'Don't tell me the score!' were my opening words.

'You didn't watch it? Shall I tell you?' he'd enquired in a concerned tone, completely ignoring the one and only sentence I'd managed to blurt out so far.

'No thanks, Dad.'

'Are you sure?'

'Yes, I want to watch it 'as live', come what may, with all the disappointment and elation that brings,' I clarified as concisely as I could.

'OK then,' he replied. 'I won't tell you the score in that case,' he said sympathetically, before leaving a beat. 'But I wouldn't bother watching it if I were you,' he added, utterly unaware of how transparent his advice had been.

I did end up only watching the extended highlights in the end. By the time I reached home and turned on the TV, with impeccable timing, it was Sky Sports that greeted me as the Chelsea players wheeled away to celebrate their victory at the end of the scheduled re-run. It was almost as if I was destined to know the result before I could have ever sat down to witness it.

'I like two legs,' said my son the next morning as he excitedly sat down to watch the highlights with me, unaware of what was in store. 'Because if you lose the first game,' he continued, 'you get another go.' Spoken like a true Spurs fan, especially when we beat them 1-0 the first time around. Kanté's opener was blasted from the edge of the box and somehow went through the legs of three individual Spurs players including the otherwise impressive Gazzaniga to draw Chelsea level on aggregate. Eden Hazard, a player who always seemed to raise his game for Spurs, put them clear ahead of half-time before Fernando Llorente answered his critics with a kind of falling diving header that came off his shoulder soon after.

That goal would ordinarily have been enough to give Spurs the edge given the double value of an away goal. Not this season though, with both this rule and extra time scrapped - another typical sub-clause that would cruelly favour Chelsea over Tottenham. To penalties then, and a moment I feared given the raw tears of emotion my son had shed the last time his team had lost a semi-final. Between England and Spurs, it hasn't been much fun over the years.

Eric Dier blazed over the bar. Moura saw his effort saved. There were no Pickford-esque heroics from Gazzaniga as Chelsea's penalties were good. Tottenham's best hope of ending the trophy drought, and with it the one stick with which the media continued to beat Pochettino, had vanished. There were no tears this time. Just a downbeat 10-year-old heading to school without bragging rights.

Just a few days later, the FA Cup visit to Selhurst Park would at least offer an opportunity to bury the memory of Thursday. What followed was one of the most abject performances under Pochettino's reign and in recent memory. If anything, it was a reminder of what we had once endured week in, week out; month in, month out; even season in, season out. Perhaps it merely reflected how far we'd come that what was once anticipated was now so disappointing. With just a fading title bid and the Champions League left to play for, however, it felt like the moment that hopes of silverware for the season had ended once again.

The media had a field day at Pochettino's suggestion that finishing in the top four was more important than domestic trophy success. At Old Trafford, Ole Gunnar Solskjaer continued his impressive 100% record before pointedly reminding the media that he had to win trophies. It was impressive PR by the Norwegian, now odds-on favourite to take the role full-time, as Poch confirmed his intentions again to stay at Spurs for the project in hand once more. With fears of his departure allayed, there would hopefully still be plenty of time for the eagerly anticipated trophy haul to come one day.

Until the glory days truly returned, at least, and the boost in membership it might bring, Amir's unusual recruitment drive would simply have to continue unabated - haunting the public bathrooms of Malaysia on the lookout for cockerel pin badges.

Amir bumps into a Dutch superstar and soon-to-be Spurs cult hero.

FEBRUARY

10
FROM BORUSSIA WITH LOVE
GERMANY SPURS

When the busy fixture calendar eventually returns to league action at Wembley for only the second time in 2019, you'd be forgiven for thinking it might be welcomed. Instead, a midweek kick-off on a bitterly cold late January evening against Watford, combined with the depressing run of form and little relaxation on ticket prices, sees fewer than 30,000 in attendance. The desire to return home becomes ever more palpable, as does the longing to add fresh blood to an injury-ravaged squad.

For long periods of that freezing Wembley evening, Spurs look set to toil to another humbling defeat that would begin to raise those serious questions again about strength in depth and their ability to compete without key players. Craig Cathcart's simple header deflected off Davinson Sanchez to put Watford into a 37th minute lead and leave the travelling Hornets dreaming of an unlikely double over Spurs. The goal comes from a Hugo Lloris error after a corner tempts the Frenchman unconvincingly off his line. It would be their only shot on target of the night.

As a miserable looking Poch walked down the tunnel at the break and past half-time guest Pat Jennings, he might have been tempted to ask for tips. 'Jennings never punched them,' my dad would always tell me with nostalgia for a bygone age. 'He could catch them with one hand.'

As the depression began to descend over Wembley, even the energy provided by the returning Son wasn't enough to lift the crowd; that was until the positive run of Llorente to attempt to take on three defenders in his own box saw the ball cannon off his shin and straight into the path of the South Korean. With trademark killer instinct, he took it in his stride to smash the ball beyond Ben Foster, a goalkeeper once beaten by a Paul Robinson freekick on a visit to White Hart Lane.

Earlier in the game, Llorente had missed a header from six yards out that had end-of-season blooper reel written all over it, so his assist, however accidental, was welcome in the continued rebuilding of his confidence. Seven minutes later it would be supercharged as he showed strength and composure to nod the winner, almost in slow motion, across Foster's goal and into the back of the net. The Spaniard's emotion is raw as every player congratulates him after he races directly to Pochettino to celebrate. It's yet another victory grabbed from the jaws of that elusive first Premier League draw of the season as there'll be no last-minute sucker punch for Spurs. Instead, the final moments are punctuated by a booking for Isaac Success wrestling a winking ball boy in injury time, with shades of the infamous Eden Hazard incident in his tussle with the taunting teenager.

The most remarkable result of the night came on the south coast where Chelsea were demolished 4-0 by Bournemouth which, coupled with Manchester United, Manchester City and Liverpool all also dropping points in games they were overwhelming favourites to win, meant that only Spurs and Arsenal gained ground on the teams around them in an extraordinary round of fixtures. It's a welcome boost to the appearance of the league table to sweeten yet another transfer-free month. Only Spurs would impose a two-window transfer ban on themselves.

As the tiresome debate around who and what Pochettino needed to truly mount a title challenge in the second half of the season began again, one thing appeared certain: in much the same way Moussa Sissoko had redeemed himself, and despite the misses, the mishits and even the own goal, Spurs fans had found an endearing new hero in the determined displays of Fernando Llorente.

February begins with encouraging - if not always entirely

convincing - victories over Newcastle and Leicester at Wembley. Both games require late goals from Son to put a seal on the three points as the talisman once again steps into the gaping breach left by Harry Kane's absence. Despite still looking some way off their scintillating best, it means Spurs go into their Champions League knockout tie against Borussia Dortmund just five points from the Premier League's summit with a cushion of ten points to fifth and sixth-placed Arsenal and Chelsea and nine ahead of a resurgent Manchester United. Whatever lingering frustrations remain in the stands around the stadium delay and transfer policy, it's certainly a healthy position to be in with twelve games to go.

Ahead of the appetising looking first leg at Wembley against the Bundesliga leaders, I'll be chatting to Franz Stockebrandt, honorary Chairman of Germany Spurs – he relinquishes the official title to his son Patrick. Franz is 66 and lives in Oberhausen in the North Rhine Westphalia district. It's less than an hour's car journey to Dortmund in one direction and the Dutch border in the other. It also means he remains close to his hometown of Gelsenkirchen, home of FC Schalke 04, and a city best remembered on this side of the channel as being the scene of England's 2006 World Cup quarter final defeat to Portugal. He moved for love and now he and his wife Elisabeth, alongside adult sons Patrick and Dennis, are all Tottenham diehards.

Franz's presence is most notable on Facebook, where he is extremely active in the Germany Spurs Supporters group he administrates. It's how I first contacted Franz having noticed a striking profile picture of his entire family wearing retro Spurs kits in the doorway of their home. Franz sees it as his duty to share content with his fellow German fans across the country and, as such, delivers news relating to all things Tottenham. He even provides blow-by-blow updates during games for anyone unable to watch it live in both German and English.

'We also have a WhatsApp group for Germany Spurs members,' he tells me. 'The Facebook page is open to non-members. I live here in Germany in an area where there are more Schalke fans. Dortmund and Schalke are the same as Tottenham and Arsenal; Dortmund hate Schalke fans and Schalke fans hate Dortmund. It's very, very crazy!'

Franz has made time to speak to me after waking up from the night shift. While he is officially retired, he still does a little work on the side to supplement his income as an on-call security guard. The rest of his time appears to be entirely devoted to Spurs and his duties within the supporters' club.

'I'm a little bit tired. I have lived in America for five years, but my English is not the best,' Franz confesses modestly. Realising he's struggling with the pace of my questioning mixed with a regional accent, I take it down a notch while trying not to sound like Steve McClaren interviewing for a Bundesliga 3 team. Naturally, as an Englishman interviewing a German after a recent penalty shootout defeat, there's only one place to start.

'When it goes to penalties, people are nervous,' Franz begins, on the Chelsea loss that remains painful. 'I think they needed to clear their minds. There was too much going on in their heads. Relax and clear your mind and visualise the ball in the net. And then you must have some luck.' It all sounds so simple when a German explains it.

Franz has supported Spurs since 1979 when, as a 26-year-old, he visited London with his wife on holiday. 'I played football from a young age and admired the English style,' he says, taking up the story, 'so I looked in the paper and Tottenham were playing Southampton, I think. I asked my wife if she wanted to go to the game and when we got to the stadium, people asked where we came from and people were very nice to us. It was super! From that day, we loved this club and became members.'

I'm reminded of a similar story of my own parents being put up for the night and not buying a drink when the pub they visited after the 1984 UEFA Cup Final discovered they'd travelled down from Barnsley. Such is the warm welcome extended to visitors to White Hart Lane, I suppose. That famous night against Anderlecht was a game Franz also attended - 'it was very, very fantastic!' he recalls, enthusiastically.

That first, chance experience on holiday and the connection it planted with Spurs would spark a lifetime of devotion for both Franz and Elisabeth that would be passed on to their two sons.

'In the nineties we would set off at one in the morning to see Spurs and we'd go to one home game every month,' he tells me. 'My money was good, I was self-employed. We'd drive Friday night to Calais, get the ferry to Dover and go to London from there. We'd spend some time in London, go to the game and then come back! By Sunday morning we'd be at home. Now I have a little retirement and not so much money, but I think we'll come back to the new White Hart Lane soon.'

It was quite the pilgrimage for the Stockebrandts with two young sòns – not least because the results weren't always quite so consistent back then. 'You had many games where you were a little bit nervous,' laughs Franz. 'My son Dennis once came over for Spurs against Manchester United. At half-time we were winning 3-0 and by the end we had lost 5-3!' It's a game etched in the memory of every Spurs fan who lived through it and can at least be remembered positively for the blistering first half performance that would include the goalscoring debut of the late Dean Richards, who tragically passed away far too early aged just 36.

'For my son, it was a terrible game. I was on holiday with my wife and watched the game in an Irish pub in Ibiza. I was the only Spurs fan in a pub full of Manchester United fans. At half-time I could stand tall but by the end, I slowly went home!' laughs Franz.

There were plenty of fruitful trips across to N17, however, even during what could generously be described as one of Tottenham's most inconsistent decades. Franz's favourite Spurs game during that period was the trip across to see Spurs win the League Cup in 1999 against Leicester City at the old Wembley stadium.

'It was an incredible game,' he continues. 'Justin Edinburgh saw red and we were really nervous. But then Steffen Iversen crossing for Allan Nielsen in the final minutes for a fantastic atmosphere.' It wasn't Franz's only Final; he was at the replay against Manchester City in 1981 when Ricky Villa danced through the defence, as well as 1987 – the only FA Cup Final Spurs have ever lost. 'We also came over around that time for a Junior Spurs camp and met Gary Stevens and Paul Allen. We met many people and have many great memories of this time. I love the English people.'

The nineties were also a period where two German Spurs players achieved cult status at the club before another German, Christian Ziege, would go on to become a fan favourite.

'It was nice seeing Klinsmann go to Tottenham,' recalls Franz. 'What's not so good was him leaving after one year. He came from Stuttgart and it's always said here that he keeps an eye on the money! And Steffen Freund, he was cult hero. A nice guy.'

Franz has only ever seen Spurs play on his own home soil during several recent meetings with Dortmund, and he also crossed the Swiss/German border to attend the infamous Champions League qualifier against Young Boys of Berne in 2010. It was an 800-mile road trip to see Spurs that at least saved the hardy Stockebrandts a ferry fare. The home side raced into a 3-0 lead after a characteristically horrendous start from Spurs before Seb Bassong and Roman Pavlyuchenko pulled a couple back to thankfully set up the comfortable overturning of the tie back at the Lane.

'Ultimately, we love soccer. Well, football,' he corrects himself, scalding his own perceived faux pas. 'Sorry for "soccer"; I lived in the United States for five years and we say soccer and not football! We love football though and when the team plays well and loses the game, that's OK. You cannot win all the games.' This is undoubtedly an outlook he would have had confirmed irrevocably having followed Tottenham so closely in the nineties.

Franz only very recently returned to his homeland following his wife's homesickness after living in Kansas City. I'm delighted to discover he was linked in with the local supporters' club during his time there and drove 500 miles to see Tottenham on tour, where he also spent an evening with Steffen Freund and the Chicago Spurs. Eventually, though, the pull of home was too much. 'Our kids and family are here so we came back,' he confides.

Like most countries, the Premier League is now available on subscription TV in Germany in much the same way Bundesliga action can be found on BT Sport here. It makes keeping up with Spurs relatively easy from afar – even if, in his younger days, Franz would more often be found in the stands of White Hart Lane.

Members of Franz's collective are all over Germany as you might expect, making it difficult for all fans to come together regularly. 'We have people who do meet for the game,' he says. 'Not all members can come to the game - when it's the Champions League, people have to work. But at weekends we can have a clubhouse here in Gelsenkirchen where a group of us can watch the game together.'

I enquire about how some other members of the club might have landed on an allegiance to Spurs and whether they combine their support with a Bundesliga team, but it doesn't quite translate. 'I have a friend from England and she is from Durby...not Durby, Derby,' he says before letting out a big laugh at his own expense. 'Derby County is her big team. She is a very good friend to me. She hates Nottingham Forest!' It's a charming diversion as Franz's English really begins to warm up. As ever, my shame at barely having mastered my own mother tongue is tugging on my conscience as I attempt to simplify my questions and he returns to the thread.

'Me? Oh no, I'm 100% a Spurs fan. I love to watch football on TV or in the stadium here in Germany, but I am not a fan of any other team.' It goes without saying, I suppose, as I again look at Franz's profile photo with his family. Behind them in the kitchen, a wide range of memorabilia is clearly visible on their kitchen wall. 'We are a crazy family!' laughs Franz.

And the self-confessed Spurs-crazy Stockebrandts still have high hopes for the remainder of the season. 'I think we have a good team. We have no new players, but I hope we can win the league. Manchester City is very, very good and Liverpool is playing very well. It is hard to win the league in England. I think we can stay in third until the very end and in the Champions League it is all to play for – and with Mauricio Pochettino we are always in with a chance. He is a very good manager.'

Before we end our chat, Franz unnecessarily apologises for his English again before joining the growing list of international friends I intend to meet up with for a beer at a game one day.

'I am planning on coming over to the final game,' he says. 'My sons speak much better English than me! It was very hard learning English when we moved to the United States. When you're young, you can do it every time but when you are old, it's very hard!' he laughs.

With the promise of Tottenham's new stadium being the only place in London to watch Champions League football – a possible PR gaffe in waiting that had poked fun at Arsenal and Chelsea's Europa League involvement but was still to be realised – the arrival of Borussia Dortmund to Wembley began with a slightly underwhelming feel to it. The game was not quite a sell-out – something of a surprise given the prestige of the match – as perhaps the Wembley factor combined with the familiarity of an opponent we vanquished 3-1 in the previous season's group stages were two potential factors for the lull in atmosphere as the famous music played out over the national stadium's tinny speakers.

The first half was a cagey affair with Dortmund looking in control for large periods and the impressive Jadon Sancho a constant threat. The best chance of the half had fallen to Lucas Moura, however, who controlled a ball into the box with his thigh before sending a volley just wide of the post. It would have been the sort of goal played on repeat for years to come had it sneaked in.

After the break, Pochettino's men found a new gear. It took just two minutes of second half football – a point lamented by my 10-year-old back at home who had endured the first half before reluctantly being sent to bed at half-time with the promise of the second half available for viewing with breakfast before school the next day – for Spurs to win the ball through a high press from goalkeeper Bürki's short pass out to his full-back. The ball was played to marauding deputy left fullback Jan Vertonghen, who delivered the perfect cross to find the peeling run of Son to open the scoring with a superb guided volley.

The Belgian assist maker would later find himself on the scoresheet in the 83rd minute, bursting into the box to meet Serge Aurier's cross from the right with a first time shot that left Bürki with no chance and drew the trademark Superman celebration. By the time Fernando Llorente outmuscled his defender to nod home Eriksen's corner in the 86th minute, less than three minutes after replacing Moura to score his first ever goal from the bench, a small, delirious riot had been sparked as he joined the crowd to celebrate.

Despite the continued absence of Harry Kane and Dele Alli, Tottenham Hotspur had delivered a European performance almost unsurpassed in recent years to secure the only three-goal first leg lead in the eight Champions League and sixteen Europa League ties taking place. To add a rosy red cherry to the top of the cake, Arsenal would go on to lose 1-0 in Belarus less than 24 hours later against BATE Borisov, leading to a million declarations that Arsenal can't even 'master BATE' on Valentine's Day. The prospect of so many Gooners cancelling tables for two at the local Italian to settle down for a night in front of Arsenal TV while Spurs fans were so besotted by the boys in lilywhite only added to the unconfined joy of what had taken place at Wembley.

The love-in continued in the post-match interviews as the incredibly likeable Son apologised to Man of the Match Vertonghen for running in the opposite direction to the provider of that perfect cross during the celebrations that followed. 'I didn't run to Serge for mine!' quipped Jan.

There was extra cause for celebration down the road from Dortmund in Oberhausen too, where Franz Stockebrandt found reason to recruit a few more potential members for Germany Spurs. 'We have more German people here who like Schalke.

There was a big party when Dortmund lost the game!'

The home game against Dortmund had been the first in a challenging upcoming schedule that again looked to be potentially season-defining. The home game against Arsenal, perhaps the most anticipated game on the calendar of every new season, was sandwiched between trips to Stamford Bridge, Turf Moor and the Westfalenstadion for the second leg where Spurs would look to complete the job for a place in the quarter finals.

While there was a welcome break created by the unfortunate FA Cup elimination at the hands of Crystal Palace, it was the knock-on impact of our South London neighbours' continued run that added yet more uncertainty around the official move-in date for the new stadium. With March widely mooted as being a realistic target date, the home game against Arsenal had been ruled out by Metropolitan Police as being already too high a risk fixture to incorporate the occasion of a new stadium opening into their risk planning.

Next up was Crystal Palace, originally scheduled for 16th March, moved back to a midday kick-off the following afternoon for TV broadcast but now at risk of being postponed should Palace progress beyond Doncaster Rovers. After that, it would be the visit of Brighton on April 6th - also FA Cup Sixth Round weekend, and a competition Brighton were still involved in as well, risking further unavoidable postponements. Huddersfield on 13th April would be the next fixture that offered any certainty before West Ham the following week – presumably not an option for the same reason as Arsenal.

With the number of remaining home fixtures running out, one potential extension route for a few more games in the new digs had at least now been presented by the Champions League following such an unexpectedly brilliant performance that would live long in the memories of the 70,000 that witnessed it.

The return of FA Cup action not involving Spurs would at least present what appeared to be ten days of welcome respite and vital recovery time for a tired squad suffering with injuries. With a tricky looking visit to a resurgent Burnley in the early kick-off eventually marking a return to action in late February, the caution among Spurs fans still felt justified off the back of Dortmund; so often a flat performance has followed a world beating one in recent seasons. Surely the window of rest would mitigate against the predictable blowback?

Well, no, not really.

With confidence boosted by the return of Harry Kane to training, once again several weeks earlier than anticipated from a medium-term injury, the World Cup Golden Boot winner is named in the starting line-up for the first time since suffering an ankle ligament damage against Manchester United in January. 'He's an animal,' Pochettino would say of the England captain.

After a couple of sighters, he's on the scoresheet in the 65th minute, showing great strength to hold off the trailing defender and poke the ball beyond Tom Heaton following a trademark driving run. Unfortunately, his goal comes between Chris Wood's opener and a lucky break of the ball for Ashley Barnes to tap in a winner seven minutes from time. It's a damaging defeat at the beginning of a crucial week and "the day that Tottenham's title challenge died" according to the Sky Sports bluster. Pochettino angrily and uncharacteristically confronts Mike Dean and his assistants at the final whistle over Burnley wrongly being awarded the corner that led to the opener. He apologises later, but it's a telling public display of rage at the end of a deeply disappointing afternoon.

No matter, though. Where better to put things right than at Stamford Bridge against a freshly vanquished Chelsea. Their defeat on penalties in the League Cup final the previous Sunday had seemingly sparked internal turmoil following a very public managerial bust-up over Kepa Arrizabalaga refusing to be substituted that had dominated the tabloid sports columns ever since. Coupled with an additional 30 hours of recovery for Tottenham and the absence of half an hour of extra time in their legs following Chelsea's fruitless extended period against Manchester City on Wembley's big pitch, things looked promising.

About that...

With both sides striking the woodwork in the first half – Hazard for Chelsea and Harry Winks coming within inches of emulating Eriksen's stunning goal to put Spurs on their way to the memorable 3-1 win the previous season – Chelsea found a breakthrough when Pedro escaped the attentions of Alderweireld before poking the ball through the legs of Lloris at his near post. As Tottenham toiled to find an equaliser, the captain was involved for all the wrong reasons again, rushing out to receive a back-pass from Trippier. Under minimal pressure, the England fullback played the ball in the direction of his goalkeeper without looking, rolling the ball agonisingly and embarrassingly beyond Hugo. Holding his head in his hands as the ball reached the empty net, Trippier's despair was matched by millions of Spurs fans around the world.

Remarkably, Pedro's opener is the only shot on target of the entire game. While indicative of how cagey an affair it was, the failure to test the eminently dodgy Willy Caballero feels like a missed chance. Wins for the other four teams in the top six means yet more ground is made on the comfortable cushion Spurs had built over the course of the season and lost on those above. It's not squeaky bum time just yet, but the once comfortable marooning in third place and hard-earned cushion from the chasing pack is now looking at serious risk of being overturned by the teams below; meanwhile, the chasm to the blistering pacesetters at the summit grows further.

Football results are put into context after the game, however, as BT Sport broadcast an interview between Robbie Savage and Glenn Hoddle. Speaking publicly for the first time about the day he suffered a cardiac arrest just minutes after going off-air, it's powerful viewing as he acknowledges the speed in which first aiders reached him and administered CPR and a defibrillator to save his life. It's a sobering watch as the Spurs great reflects on his own mortality. Some things are much more important than football.

The Stockebrandts outside their memorabilia-filled front door.

MARCH

11
HUGO'S GLOVE
OZSPURS

There are a number of key ingredients that go into organising a successful supporters' club weekender. First, you need a vast and sprawling country where fans spread across a great distance can come together to reacquaint or meet for the first time to enjoy a Tottenham match together in something resembling a convenient time slot for their time zone. Next, you need a variety of entertainment to make the occasion worth travelling in for – perhaps a golf day or, better still, an ex-player dropping by.

A dedicated pub with a Tottenham-only policy is vital, as is pre-empting any potential switch in the schedule that could count against you. After all, with plans being put in place months in advance, the risk of a switch to Monday Night Football is a very real one. Once all these elements are arranged, there's just one factor remaining that cannot be controlled: a Tottenham win.

When UK-born Mark Lawson, President of OzSpurs, plumped for Burnley away for the annual Oz National in his adopted nation of Australia, he could have been forgiven for feeling moderately confident in his choice. Mark, however, knew better.

'We're very much in the curse category,' Mark laughs. 'Our first National was in 2004 when we beat Liverpool 1-0, so we were off to a flyer. We've had a National every year since…our second win came in 2017! The run was ridiculous.

'Half the people blame me because I tend to pick the weekends. I started off with the big games. I did away at Old Trafford where we were 2-0 up at half-time and lost 5-2. I picked an Arsenal game and we lost. Then I started going for the easier games: Bolton, Burnley, Wolves, West Brom – everyone who I thought we could take on. We've snatched draws from the teeth of victory time after time. When we finally had a win two years ago, the great curse of the National was gone. Since then, we didn't have a game in 2018 and then lost to Burnley last week. It's a good job we don't rely on Spurs to keep us happy.'

By the time I speak to him on Thursday morning, the physical and emotional toils of the previous weekend have left him visibly under the weather. It's where my video call to Brisbane begins.

'I'm alright,' says Mark with a firm twang of Australian in his British accent. 'Little bit croakier than usual! It's not entirely self-inflicted. I went through half the week wondering if this was a horrible hangover or illness – I must admit I didn't stop drinking to find out! It was only when I got home on Monday and went into the recovery position that I discovered I'd just been sick all weekend.'

With the disappointment of defeat or elation of a win heightened by the occasion of sharing the experience with your fellow compatriots, what happens on weekenders when we don't win?

'It certainly slows the night down for a while,' he continues. 'I'm going to remember that game for the rest of my life because of a very surreal experience. I spent the entire match stood at the bar chatting with Darren Anderton which isn't something I ever expected to be doing in my life. I just stood there, drinking beers with him while people came up in the pub and had photos while a real life professional told me how badly Tottenham were playing and how horrible Burnley were!

'It was annoying losing to Burnley but it's not the worst one we've had. We've had Nationals where the game has been switched away from the weekend and we've had no game! At least we got to watch a game and cheer Harry Kane score a goal. The rest of it was just horrendously familiar for anyone who has supported Spurs for longer than five years.'

Fresh off the back of the disappointment at Turf Moor, we're chatting the day after – for me at least - Tottenham's 2-0 defeat at Stamford Bridge, that means the double figures points lead over the pack chasing down the top four of just a few weeks ago is now a much less comfortable five points. Only Spurs can make the seemingly unassailable look quite so assailable.

Of the Chelsea result, Mark continues: 'I saw the game. It was a 6am kick-off where I live and there is nothing good about that. We have had some of our most enjoyable games I've seen at 6am in the morning. What do you with yourself at 6am when you've won at the San Siro? You want to jump and dance, you want to go down the pub and instead you have to get in the car and join the commute. You've got this slightly happy but misplaced buzz about you all day. On the other side of the scale, I've been awake for fourteen and a half hours of a day where Spurs played shit. It doesn't just ruin your morning, it ruins your whole bloody day. The best time to watch football really is three in the afternoon.'

There is little doubt that there are better ways to head into a North London derby than the worrying run of form combined with uninspiring performances in the league. Mark has something of a theory around when that seems to happen.

'There's a bit of a pattern if you go back to Dortmund. Every season Spurs play an unbelievable game that nobody expects when you could almost forgive them for being tired and injured and you don't expect anything - and they put on a world class performance. I remember it a few seasons ago against Man City when the challenge looked on and then they underwhelmed for the next four games. They did that against Dortmund and then arrive at Burnley thinking there's a win for turning up. Then they go to a fired-up Stamford Bridge and didn't deserve to get anything out of that.'

It's a fair observation and one that is inevitably linked with the idea of being 'Spursy' that has dogged the club for years – capable of world class displays on their day but often found lacking when the going gets tough.

'We're slowly getting past this stage but we're not there yet,' continues Mark. 'I think the only thing that can get us through it is Pochettino because he clearly doesn't accept this; you can see that in the man. You can't work out the logic of the team because they know they are getting murdered when they go back in.

'We have wonderful players but not many leaders. There isn't a Dave Mackay of old or a Roy Keane. Dier is the closest we've got to that and if he can be reinforced to be that person in the team, he can have that impact as well. As for Arsenal, if Pochettino gives them hell, who knows? We go into it with trepidation but with more hope than we used to in the old days!'

Mark knows all about the old days from a family connection to Tottenham stretching back to the dawn of the 20th century. His great grandfather was at the 1901 Cup Final while his own father and grandfather spent many hours on the terraces at White Hart Lane. His earliest memory came as a five-year-old trying to spot his own dad in the crowd at the 1981 FA Cup Final. A pre-booked family holiday to Majorca two days later meant forsaking a ticket to the replay; they watched Ricky Villa's unforgettable winner via a grainy reception on a small Spanish television. 'I'm not sure he ever got over it,' Mark adds.

His own first match came in a 1-0 win against Charlton Athletic in April 1987, with the winning goal being one of a record-breaking 49 that Clive Allen would bag that season. Mark would go on to name his cat after the Spurs hero. There can be no greater honour.

These days, watching Spurs is largely a night-time activity each Saturday, with kick-off times dictating just how much of the weekend Tottenham will inhabit. It's usually accompanied by a curry, a few beers and a colourful selection of friends.

'I will have a normal full day with the family, and then after the kids are in bed I'll head off to town,' Mark explains. 'We'll normally get to the pub a few hours prior to kick-off. Flags are pinned up and the songs and chants normally kick in half an hour or so before the game. One consequence of the midnight games is that a few hardy souls may have been drinking in the pub for a bit longer than is advisable. I've seen a few over the years that haven't made it to half time, and for some of the more boring games, you might find the odd person having a short power nap between beers.

'We'll usually get a hundred or so for the bigger games in Brisbane and I try to talk to as many people as I can, but in my close group of mates there's Phil - he got the Brisbane group going right at the start and we've been friends for a very long time. There's Duncan, a New Zealander who declares in most games that he's watching the worst referee he's ever seen. There's Ian - an Aussie who was originally a friend of Duncan's but came along to some OzSpurs events and enjoyed them so much that he started supporting the team and is now as passionate as they come.

'There's Daniel, the group hell raiser who normally fits Spurs games in around Death Metal concert attendance. He's now a father and recently had his trademark dreadlocks shorn off - it still looks weird. My old friend Mark Allwood, the father of two boys he is constantly trying to get out of their Barca and Real kits and into Spurs shirts. Mike, who spends his money on Spurs kits and seems to own every home, away and third kit since the days of Admiral in the 70's. Seeing him walk into the pub in an early 1990's shell suit top is a wonderful thing. And finally, there's Nathan - he doesn't make it out every time, but when he does, he is a presence. He's the lead singer of songs, chants and all things volume related and it's more fun when he's there.'

It's as formidable a 'crew' as any regular match going group back in the UK and the comradeship is no different, even if the commitment of travelling hundreds of miles is more commonly replaced by giving up on precious hours of sleep ahead of the working week instead.

'The lunchtime games are hated in England but they're the best for us,' Mark continues. 'Where I live in Brisbane, it's a 10.30pm kick-off which is when we get a pub full of people. You'll get a good number at that time for any game, but Arsenal will be very busy. The geography of where we live means there are a lot of people living an hour north or south, but they'll come in for this game – it's a major commitment for these people, so there'll be a number of people who I haven't seen for a while.'

It's a phenomenon that is unique to the international

supporters' club, and something that Darren Anderton himself commented on to Mark over a beer during their chinwag. Anyone *this* passionate about Spurs in England would be in the stadium. 'You'll never replicate actually being at the game,' adds Mark, 'but as far as being in Australia is concerned, it's as good as it gets.'

Mark moved to Australia 16 and a half years ago for love. 'I'll tell the non-soppy story,' he laughs, before recounting a short work trip to Sydney in 2002 that ended with meeting the woman who would become his wife just a couple of years later. 'I met her on the Friday and by the time I had to go home on Tuesday, it was a really difficult thing to get on the plane. You never plan on these things and I think my mum wishes I was still living down the road, but I was young and impetuous enough at the time and it worked out pretty well.

'I've not been back for two and a half years but I'm hoping to have a big Christmas at home this year, so I'll be looking at the fixtures with interest. I'm reconciled with being here and I'm happy but there have been two times when I've sat here miserable thinking "I should be there". The last game at the Lane was one obviously; that was so hard to watch from here because I could have been there, but only brutal common sense and money told me I couldn't."

The second game that pained Mark to miss might be more of a surprise – and, having witnessed it first-hand during the 2016/17 season, I can assure him that he did miss very little, even though the occasion was perhaps a notable one.

'It was that first Champions League game at Wembley against Monaco,' he continues. 'That was the first time in years a domestic team had called Wembley home, the first time in the new Wembley, 90,000 fans in there and I couldn't be there. I haven't been to a Champions League game yet as Spurs didn't qualify when I was there and that's something that's on my list. I don't care if it's a group game against Basle or a semi-final against Real Madrid, I just want to be there and hear that music and buy some stupid merchandise.'

While leaving his family and friends in England behind to start a new life down under was clearly a huge wrench, giving up a Spurs season ticket to live on the other side of the world was arguably an even bigger one. The experience of watching Tottenham while in Australia for the first time remains one that Mark vividly associates with first feeling at home in his adopted nation.

'When I got here, there was a minor TV channel that showed one Premier League game a week that might be Spurs but usually wasn't. I think I typed into the internet 'Spurs Australia' wondering if there were other fans here. The website had only been going a year and was one of those old-style chatrooms, so I bookmarked it. I'm not a shy person but not the most outgoing either, so I watched it for a little while and then registered to take part in the conversation, engaged in a few online chats and after a few months of doing that, I went along for a game.

'They never missed a match at that time because there might not be another one for three months! This thing was absolutely in its infancy at the time in a place called Shark Bar. There was a great big fish tank with a shark in there, the poor thing. There were no big screens, just a couple above the bar; one had the football on, zero sound, and you couldn't hear the guy next to you. I walked in with a Spurs shirt on so I wasn't completely anonymous and there are ten people there and you walk over like a bit of a loser and introduce yourself but that's what everyone has to do. Even to this day, every chapter has an organiser whose most important job is just to be friendly and integrate new people into the group.'

It's a nice touch to ensure new fans are welcomed and brought into the fold. And, as Mark reflects, it's not a difficult job either.

'The great thing about Spurs fans is you don't need to get to know them! You already do,' he smiles. 'There's no awkward small talk, you just talk Tottenham. It's your specialist subject, you don't feel ill at ease about it. Shutting up is the problem! I remember that very first night and those ten people; two of them are still really good friends. One of them I room shared with last week in Perth. That's how it started, and I went a few times before seeing us win, but there was a group of readymade mates. It's hard moving to a new country – you realise you meet most of your friends at school and university with perhaps the odd workmate. It's tough making new friends and I didn't want my friendship group just to be my wife's friends. I left so much behind in England, not because I wanted to, but that was the choice I made, so coming here with Tottenham was huge for me.'

The newly launched OzSpurs had started in Sydney and Perth around the same time in 2002. The same began to happen in Melbourne and Adelaide in small numbers to begin with. Mark recalls being the 75th user on the website – although it's unlikely he could have guessed the impact his registration would have on his life in the years ahead.

'OzSpurs went from being an informal group to official in Perth initially and that was spread to the rest of Australia. That was in place from 2003 and those people are still legends and thanked for what they did. The guy who was Treasurer did as much as he could but had a busy life. In 2006, I heard they needed a Treasurer and I'm an Accountant by trade, so I put my hand up for it. There was no electoral vote, I think they just grabbed me from there! It's a group of friends working together with an altruistic goal. We love the Club and want to help - we just want to have good nights out and want Spurs fans in Australia to know we're here and if they want to reach out then we will grow.

'I was Treasurer for nine years doing a lot of the day-to-day running with another guy running the website and then in 2015 someone stepped down as President and I thought it was time to give it a go. During that period, Spurs announced their first tour in 32 years. That's when being involved in the committee goes from being a fun four hours a week to a full-time second job. You want to make the most of the opportunities; you don't want to wish you'd done it differently because it might not happen again for another 32 years.'

With plans for Tottenham's visit to the southern hemisphere providing quite the baptism of fire for the newly appointed president, he began to get to grips with his role liaising with the club. One coup quickly sealed was the visit of Ossie Ardiles for an evening spent with the fanbase down under.

'We had people from all over Australia travelling to Sydney, so we wanted as much stuff for them to do as possible,' Mark continues. 'There was a golf game. We also asked every Spurs fan on the day to go to the Opera House at lunchtime on the day of the game for an OzSpurs photo – holy hell, did that work out well!' he laughs, in reference to the image that went viral among Spurs fans around the globe as hundreds of supporters displayed their colours in front of the world famous backdrop.

'We are a committee via chatroom which can be interesting as it's not as easy as sitting in a room and getting things done,' he continues. 'But for a lot of people in Australia, for whatever reason, they are genuine, true Spurs fans. I'm an ex-season ticket holder, I know what genuine Spurs fans look like. Some of them have never seen Spurs play in the flesh but you can't devalue their passion, it's the same! You see them when we lose, it's awful. My opinion on friendlies has never changed; they're not worth seeing. But my opinion on seeing Spurs in the flesh on a beautiful pitch in Sydney – it was different to any friendly I'd ever seen. You could see Spurs fans wiping away a tear because it meant so much to them, for whatever reason. It was an incredible experience.

'I can't kick a football to save my life, but it still took me until about the age of 32 to realise I'd never make the team. I always wondered what the most I could do with Tottenham was and always thought once I'd got a job and sorted myself out, maybe I'd get involved and get a job with the club or something like that. When I moved here and saw OzSpurs, I did think the most I could ever do was become the President of Australia Spurs. And let's not overblow it, it's a very grand title, but there have been a few times when something has happened with Spurs in England and a journalist wants to get an Australian view, the first person they go to is me. And I'm like, wow, I'm that guy! And people do say they don't know how I do it, and it's true that it's a lot of work, but how lucky am I to have this role? It is an honour and privilege and I do it because I've got a strong belief of why it's here. It's a community that brings people together, both online and in person, to express their passion and give an outlet to their frustration.'

Mark has even helped advise on a new venture that Spurs are planning in Australia, with the opening of a new academy at the University of Wollongong. It's the first real investment in Australia aside from the pre-season tours and will be a five-year partnership with coaches based there permanently. 'I asked if they're going to teach them what we, the fan and customer want?' Mark continues. 'I'm going down there next month to be part of the launch to talk to these trainees about what it means to the fans. I want you to be sad when we lose, not see a picture of your flash car when we've been beaten by our rivals. I want to feel like you're almost as sad as I am. I don't know if that's what coaches would say to them anyway, but because I'm President, I get to have those conversations.'

Despite Mark sounding as content as you might expect to be given the access and privilege his commitment to Spurs has been rewarded with, he has something of a bombshell for me as we come towards the end of our chat. 'It might sound odd after everything I've said,' he begins earnestly, 'but I actually announced on Sunday that I'm going to step down at the end of the season. There are a few reasons: it takes a huge, huge amount of time and I have three young children. And secondly, I could keep going on forever, I really could, but there's nothing that could happen that I haven't already done. Spurs have been here twice. On a weekend when we flew in Darren Anderton and I stood in the pub with him, we've grown into this group that's doing things that every Australian Spurs fan would know about as well as launching our own merchandise range and lots of chapters.

'Which brings me to the third reason – being OzSpurs Chairman is bloody great and why should I be the only one to experience this? There's more than me who deserves to do this so someone else should get a go as well.'

While Mark's commitment will surely be missed by his adopted compatriots in the years to come, there's at least one light at the end of the tunnel for his members: he'll be conceding his duty of choosing the fixture for next season's Oz National.

'I will love turning up next year and wondering what we are doing rather than having the agenda burned into my brain and dragging everyone out of one pub to the other,' he laughs. 'But it's been so much fun, and I cherish every moment of it; I also look forward to getting a bit of free time because sometimes I get in from work and do a few hours of OzSpurs every night so I'd also quite like to watch Netflix sometimes as well.'

And so, to Arsenal. If we win, all will be rosy. A defeat, and things look decidedly tight in the top four race with a quarter of the season still to play. Whether the current run of form is a blip or something to be more concerned about remains to be seen, but it will surely be tested against our greatest rivals and current leaders of the chasing pack.

'I think we've got everything to lose and not much to gain,' says Mark. 'If we win, there's everything to enjoy about beating Arsenal but the view among the fanbase throughout the season, which has been far too complacent, is that we're looking at first or second with third seen as a gimme – and it isn't. Third is probably where we should be, and charitable commentators might say we've done well having not had a ground again all season. But if we drop out of the top four having seen ourselves as title contenders and then not qualifying for the Champions League, I think we'd be in a lot of trouble.

'I desperately hope the Burnley and Chelsea results will act like the Newcastle 5-1 defeat from a few years ago and terrify the players into getting us through. If we have the season we've just had and don't start the new season in the new stadium, playing in the Champions League, I can't believe we won't go through a summer not losing people. Nothing is all over if we lose but if we miss out on the qualification, I think you start looking at some of the players leaving. I've spent a lot of years watching Spurs in the 80s and 90s so I'm a bit of a pessimist. I'd love to say we'll go in and kill the buggers, but my experience has been that we don't!'

With my own dad coincidentally on a bucket list trip to Australia where he'll be checking in with the Adelaide chapter, I provide him the details he needs for his own late night OzSpurs foray. I'll be heading down to Wembley with my mate Hadders, who last joined me for the Manchester City defeat in October. Usually opting for the car, it will be the first time I've caught the train to Wembley from his hometown of Peterborough after our own pre-match beer and curry routine the previous evening. We arrive at King's Cross three and a half hours before kick-off, with plenty of time to grab a hangover soaking breakfast before heading for the Novotel to join the special event that Punjabi Spurs have laid on.

There's a special guest teased as attending that Paul Pavlou of Yorkshire Spurs suggests is a UEFA Cup winner but won't divulge further information on. My hunch is Micky Hazard or Graham Roberts and it's duly added to our morning's agenda after the all-important sausage and egg sandwich.

The Metropolitan line offers a direct route from Kings Cross St Pancras underground station through to Wembley Park. You can't get it wrong; not unless you're me and Hadders, that is, who have been late for every occasion and appointment we've been invited to since I was born prematurely in 1985. We were once so late to a game at Craven Cottage that the match was kicking off by the time we reached Putney Bridge Station and had begun jogging almost a mile through Bishop's Park to the ground. It's kind of 'our thing'.

Our first issue comes when we realise we've headed through the wrong barrier on the Tube and a lack of signal cuts out access to Google Maps. Some might say the steady stream of Spurs replica shirts we'd seen walking in the opposite direction to us was a clue, but it wasn't one we'd picked up on. Instead of heading back out and retracing our steps like normal people, we plump for the train to Euston with the intention of getting ourselves quite literally back on the right track from there. When we arrive, Google suggests it's a two-minute walk to a neighbouring station to join the right platform for the Metropolitan line. All well and good until we find ourselves walking vaguely back in the direction of St Pancras, further compounding our navigational issues, growing frustration and lingering hangover.

We make our way back through the correct gates at St Pancras some 45 minutes later, back where we'd started. Shaken by our ordeal, that had involved an impromptu stroll around the sights of King's Cross, but now at least surrounded by a sea of lilywhite, I decide to doublecheck with the platform guard that the next train *definitely* goes to Wembley.

'Nowhere near,' he replies dryly. 'It's the one after you need to get.' Suitably chastened for the stupidity of my question and desperately wishing I'd brought the car, I thank him for his assistance, and we continue to wait patiently.

'THE NEXT TRAIN DOES NOT STOP AT WEMBLEY,' he announces into a handheld device that booms the announcement across the platform. 'PLEASE WAIT FOR THE SECOND TRAIN FOR WEMBLEY STADIUM. DO NOT BOARD THE ONCOMING TRAIN.' Feeling increasingly stupid with each repetition, he broadcasts this warning to the entire platform five more times in the three minutes that follow. 'He might as well just say 'Carl' on the end of that,' quips Hadders, helpfully.

Ten minutes later, our train passes back through Euston Station and beyond, ending the most frustrating circuit since Johnny 5 released a sequel. Call me sensitive, but even the automated voice announcing our arrival at Wembley Park sounds sarcastic as we eventually alight.

With an hour and a quarter to kick-off, there's still time to grab a pre-match beer but no time to meet the legend promised to be attending. It was Keith Burkinshaw, manager and architect of several great teams between 1976 and 1984, who had dropped in to mingle with fans. Now in his eighties, he understandably limits the number of appointments he makes, meaning my opportunity to have a quick chat about signing Ardiles and Villa, lifting the UEFA Cup in his final match in charge and even being the only man to manage Spurs for a season outside the top flight since 1950 was gone. The disappointment at my own ineptitude is palpable.

On reaching the stands, our usual vantage point hosted a few new faces, suggesting a surprising number of season ticket holders had traded their seats in. The unfamiliar chap beside me had a small boy with him no older than around six-years-old. While he would only be a spectator to the varied rollercoaster of pain, ecstasy and anxiety experienced by the adults around him in the afternoon ahead, it made me wonder what age the tribal turmoil of such a fixture becomes some form of neglect. If it can be categorised as such, I surely know I've been guilty of it in the past.

True to form, trouble kicks off in the Executive Box behind us just two minutes into the game. As with Leicester City the previous season, a group of mouthy Gooners do their best to incite the masses of Spurs fans in front of them after Alexandre Lacazette misses a gilt-edged chance - and they achieve it. A panic-stricken solitary steward, who'd presumably been grateful for such an uneventful posting a few minutes earlier, urgently requests support as several burly blokes fly up the stairs past him and towards their tormentors. There's the usual pushing, shoving and 'hold me back' palaver before plastic pint cups are launched and then things begin to calm down. A further flare-up follows as two fellow Spurs fans remonstrate with each other as the hot heads who ascended the stairs three at a time to express their rage are eventually returned to their seats. 'There's kids up here!' one of them screams down while the vaguely purple bloke in the row behind us breathes deeply from his rage-fuelled exertions.

Before sharing the next revelation of this fracas, I feel I need to state that I operate a strict equal opportunities policy to hooliganism. If you're a hooligan, that's your choice; while I don't support it, I do support your right to it regardless of age, gender, race or disability. Everyone needs a hobby. I'd go as far as saying

I'm practically one of you after once settling down to a testosterone-driven afternoon's double bill of Green Street and The Football Factory during my university days, where things certainly got a little bit 'tasty' in between mouthfuls of popcorn. However, it was around this point that me, Hadders and everyone else around us clocked that the bloke at the epicentre of all the trouble only had one arm.

I've never been involved in a fight at the football. I've certainly never come close to instigating one. While it's difficult to place myself in the mindset of someone who wants to knock seven shades of shit out of someone else for supporting another team and then actively act upon that instinct, I am fairly certain one thing I'd appreciate on my checklist before windmilling in would be a functioning right arm.

Arsenal certainly look a little handier (I'm so sorry) on the pitch in the early stages. Coming off the back of a 5-1 win against Bournemouth, they're in confident mood and look dangerous on the break. A back three of Toby, Jan and Sanchez seem happy to play a relatively high line as Spurs take the game to the visitors, but it's punished just after the quarter hour mark after a long hoof upfield isn't dealt with by Davinson. His mistake leaves Aaron Ramsey through to take the ball around Lloris under pressure and put the visitors into the lead. The instigators of the trouble behind us pipe up again, leading to another flashpoint, before mercifully disappearing into their box for the remainder of the match.

Both 'keepers are called into action just before the break, with Lloris denying Iwobi before a superb double save from Leno denies Eriksen from close range and a surprisingly good volley from Sissoko on the rebound is pushed over.

Talk returns to the excessively sleeved tearaway behind us during the break. 'I imagine he lost it at West Ham away,' I suggest to the chap in front of us at half-time once he's safely out of earshot and, indeed, at arm's length. 'I think he came with it but then threw it at the Arsenal fans,' he responds. 'How else has he lost it?'

Tottenham's reprieve comes with quarter of an hour to play when Mustafi shoves into the back of Harry Kane as he attempts to attack an Eriksen set piece. Harry converts the spot kick – it's a North London derby after all – and I embrace anyone in grabbing distance in the pile-on that ensues. The little boy beside me with his dad looks momentarily petrified, unsure where the guttural roar from me, his own father and everyone around him has come from. I compose myself for a second, remembering to crack a smile and rub his head. He beams a grin back that suggests he's just become Tottenham for life, even if he doesn't quite know it yet. The poor little mite.

The goal gives Spurs fresh impetus to push for a winner in the final stages. Instead, impending disaster looms quite literally at the hands of Sanchez, whose physical approach to an off balance Aubameyang in the final minute leaves the referee with little choice but to point to the spot again.

Behind the goal, Hadders and I hold our heads in our hands as the action plays out below us. It seems to take an age for the Gabonese striker to place the ball on the spot but it's less than a minute in reality. It is enough time to imagine every Arsenal fan I know rubbing the result in as they complete the double over us. It's enough time to visualise the cushion protecting Tottenham's top four place evaporating almost completely by the time the weekend is over. It's enough time to urge him to miss with every single fibre of my being.

As the clock ticks over to 90 minutes, he steps forward and hits a low penalty to the right of Lloris who gets down superbly to push the ball to one side. There are mere seconds to absorb the elation of the stop and realise the ball is still live as Iwobi plays the ball into the middle and a miracle block from Jan Vertonghen sends the ball over the bar. Surely the only thing worse than losing to a last-minute penalty against your greatest rivals would have been to prematurely celebrate the point earned by a goalkeeper's save before watching the rebound be converted.

Replays suggest Jan's intervention perhaps isn't quite as miraculous as it first appeared – he wasn't far off being level with the penalty taker as the ball was struck – but the sense of injustice it leaves the Gooners on our return train home with is worth the entrance fee alone. 'They're shit,' repeats one Dreamcast-clad knuckle dragger to his mates repeatedly on the correct train back to St Pancras. 'We should have beaten them easy,' he continues. You didn't though, pal, and I reckon you've managed to spell 'Mum' wrong on those three middle fingers.

'How was it? Tense and horrible?' inquires Mark as dawn breaks in Australia. 'Sounds pretty similar to here,' he adds when I describe the slightly muted and nauseous atmosphere right up to the final moments, complete with the anecdote about the one-armed hooligan.

'I was worried I'd be the chapter that everyone skipped past!' he jokes. Thanks to Hugo, I'm hoping you're still here.

That famous shot in front of the Sydney Opera House.

APRIL

12
FINALLY HOME
HONG KONG SPURS

'Hello! My friend! Are you looking for somewhere to park?'

'Yes,' I reply, a little bewildered.

'I know somewhere. Because you are my friend, I will let you park there,' says the septuagenarian stranger who has just appeared outside my car window. The car park I'd been relying upon has closed its gates. With the High Road shut to vehicles, I'm running out of options.

'OK...' I reply, taking a deep breath, uncertain if I'm about to fall victim to the most embarrassing car-jacking of all time. 'Where is it?'

'It will be easier if I get in and direct you that way,' he replies, opening my passenger door unchallenged and clearing a path through the empty Red Bull cans and Haribo wrappers that have fuelled my impromptu journey. It is 7.13pm on Wednesday 3rd April 2019. Tottenham Hotspur are just over half an hour away from kicking off the first match in their incredible new stadium that is visible from my driver's seat and I've just let a pensionable Londoner into the Kia. Allow me to explain how we got here.

After the point grasped from the jaws of defeat against Arsenal the previous month, things had moved along quite nicely in the stadium department. Crystal Palace had been confirmed as opponents for the opening game and tickets had predictably sold out in record time. As a Hotspur Plus member with a longheld place on the season ticket waiting list slowly getting closer to zero and several hundred loyalty points, I'd sat with three separate browsers open on release day, refreshing pages, waiting patiently for the timer of doom and swearing incessantly at my phone. None of the above had worked. Devastatingly, I had come to the realisation that I would not be present for the first competitive match at the Tottenham Hotspur Stadium.

I did have some small consolation. With two test events required to ensure the Palace game wouldn't revert to Wembley, I had at least secured a pair of tickets for the Legends game against Inter Forever to take my Dad along to. We sit amongst the Yorkshire Spurs and cheer on Gazza, Keane, Berbatov, Klinsmann and Ginola as well as Chimbonda, Stalteri and Tainio for anyone present who favoured the looser definition of the word 'legend'; you know the type - the sort of people who say it to pizza delivery drivers or to the mate who brings back an unexpected pint when it isn't their round. 'What a legend!', they'll say. We've all met one.

'This is truly stunning,' was the abridged reaction of me and my dad on reaching our seats in the lower North stand and basking in the beauty of our new surroundings. Taking time to absorb the view on the walk to the ground, we'd already been blown away by the scale and ambition of its exterior. Even seeing videos and images daily for almost two years hadn't prepared either of us for seeing it in the flesh. Our new home; and it was incredible.

From inside, there was an ambience of White Hart Lane. It sounds ridiculous until you begin to realise that was always part of the plan. With the very soul of the club at stake, this wasn't swapping Highbury for the Emirates or Upton Park for the London Stadium. This was swapping White Hart Lane for a bigger, better and more beautiful version than anyone could imagine – but it was *still* White Hart Lane. It was hard not to feel a little emotional looking up at the spectacular golden cockerel sitting atop the biggest single tier stand in the country.

Home. Home again.

One Legend who hadn't dug out the shin pads was Ledley King. The previous week, he'd been guest of honour at the Yorkshire Spurs Q&A alongside Graham Roberts before making a dash across the globe to join OzSpurs for a flying visit. He was a notable omission from a star-studded line-up.

'I've been in that stadium this week,' said 1984 UEFA Cup winning captain Roberts before bringing out Ledley. 'It is incredible. And I'll tell you something,' he continued, momentarily channelling Kevin Keegan's famous rant. 'We'll beat Crystal Palace there in a few weeks' time and then we'll beat Man City in the Champions League,' he rallied, to the cheers of a few hundred Yorkshire Spurs members in attendance.

Ledley was great value for the ticket price, chatting warmly about his time with the club and passing comment on the likelihood of his old mate Gareth Bale making a return. The night had got off to a melodic start with Ro Huntriss, co-founder of Yorkshire Spurs, belting out a medley of tunes on the old Joanna that would have made Chas and Dave proud, before our former captain held a meet and greet before setting off for the airport.

Having missed J'Neil Bennett's superb opener for the youth team against Southampton the following day – a moment the 17-year-old is unlikely to forget, wherever his career eventually takes him - I left the Legends game a little melancholy but at least content that I had been there to witness the 5-4 defeat to Juan Sebastián Verón and co. first hand.

I would instead be flying out to Keflavik the following morning for a short break and to also join Iceland Spurs for what would prove to be a fruitless trip to Anfield. 'I am at my girlfriend's sister's naming ceremony so I will miss the match,' messaged Birgir when I told him of my impending visit. It was probably for the best. Had Moussa Sissoko shown the same composure in front of goal that his all-round game had developed in the previous six months when clean through at 1-1, it could have been very different. Instead, I and many more Icelandic Spurs fans around me in the dedicated Spurs bar in snowy Reykjavik witnessed a worrying fourth league defeat in five following losses at Burnley, Chelsea and Southampton.

Despite finishing the job professionally in Dortmund, only the gloves of Hugo Lloris against Arsenal at Wembley had stopped a Premier League rot that had long ruled Tottenham out of the running for the title and had instead dragged them back into a bitter battle to even retain a top four position. Spurs were now behind Arsenal and a whisker above Chelsea and Ole Gunnar Solskjaer's resurgent Manchester United. Whisper it, but on the eve of a move to their billion-pound new home, Pochettino's Champions League quarter finalists were in the midst of their worst run in years and effectively on relegation form.

With another short break punctuated by a disappointing Spurs result, I attempted to enjoy the remainder of our childfree Icelandic trip in the small campervan we'd hired to tour the south coast in. With the grip of winter still firmly taking hold, we'd park up at various campsites on our three day visit to spend the night before waking up to explore the breathtaking scenery. Having returned to the van from the latest waterfall we'd just wandered beneath on the morning of Tuesday the 2nd - 36 hours before we were due to meet Crystal Palace – I logged onto the Spurs ticketing system out of habit to forlornly look at the sea of 62,062 sold out seats one more time. It was around then that something strange happened.

I don't really know what had made me do it apart from optimistically and almost unconsciously logging in several times a day of late before logging back out. Except this morning, it was different. There, along the very top row of block 508, were eight seats, together. I immediately let out an animalistic shriek in response to the unexpected view before me. By the time I'd reserved one into my basket, the others were disappearing. A frantic call home to my Dad confirmed he couldn't make it at such short notice and so I had a decision: could I make it back in time? Ticket purchased. £55. I would be at the first competitive match at the Tottenham Hotspur Stadium. Fingers crossed.

The light and airy feeling I had for the rest of the trip was largely down to procrastinating over the logistics of making it home in time. Our scheduled 9.00am flight back to Manchester meant we should reach Chesterfield by 3pm. After landing just before 1pm, we made the dash back across the Pennines so I could drop our bags, have a shower and head south down the M1. I was making good progress until a junction closure around

Luton meant a 45-minute detour that included hundreds of vehicles in both directions heading through the smallest village in the world. By the time BBC Radio 5 Live had begun their pre-match broadcast at 7pm, I was still more than 10 miles away in heavy traffic and fearing the worst.

Trusty old Google Maps kicked in to earn her keep at this stage. Bobbing and weaving down side alleys and backstreets, I freed myself of the congestion and, cutting it extremely fine but at least now within walking distance, I arrived at the industrial yard I'd left my car at just 96 hours earlier for the Legends game to see them shutting the gates at 7.12pm.

'Sorry mate, we're full,' said the foreman as I pleaded with them to find me a corner to squeeze into. Panic began to set in. There was nowhere else to leave the car. Yellow-jacketed stewards guarding fenced off residential areas watched on unmoved. Sleep deprivation was making it hard to think straight, but the reality seemed cruelly simple: I was 500 yards from the stadium with half an hour to kick-off and I was going to either miss the match or have my car towed.

I began to think about the infuriating Ford trails that ran before Premier League games on Sky where happy groups of friends dumped their forty grand motors directly outside a stadium on match nights and happily wandered towards the turnstiles in their hideously generic hats and scarves. In the real world, that new car would have been on the back of a truck before they'd even started digesting their first prawn sandwich.

'Hello! My friend! Are you looking for somewhere to park?'

By the time I'd let the old boy into the car, he was waving a parking permit at me. 'You can park on my drive,' he said, pointing me towards the street stewards who had now sprung into action and were looking puzzled as to whether they needed to report a man his thirties falling victim to some weird sort of hybrid car-jacking combined with a reverse abduction.

'He is my friend,' shouted my captor across from the passenger seat. 'He's parking on my drive. Let us through!' he demanded. 'Is that true mate?' said the parking steward, ignoring his parking permit and looking at me eye to eye as he assessed the situation and tried to work out if I was trying not to cry.

'That's right,' I said, weakly, as Stockholm Syndrome kicked in and I wondered if I'd ever see my kids again. The steward suspiciously moved the gate aside as he made a mental note of the details he'd need to recount at my murder trial, and I drove onto the empty street.

'Can you park it there?' enquired my new friend as he pointed at a gap that was just about wide enough to fit a scooter in. 'Not really,' I said, politely. 'Can you move that one across a bit?' I enquired, pointing at the wonkily placed vehicle already dominating his driveway.

'No, that belongs to my friend; he's upstairs asleep,' he replied as he made to exit my car. As I began to picture a half-and-half scarf poking out of a bath full of acid at the other side of his first-floor window, it seemed like the best time to part company for all concerned. 'Sorry,' he said as he climbed out and went back to prowl for his next victim, leaving me behind the hi-vis guarded perimeter fence without a permit but with acres of tarmac to leave my car in. I spot another steward looking bored on the end of a different road in the rabbit warren I've inadvertently become trapped within.

''Scuse me, mate. I was supposed to be parking on the drive of a friend,' I begin, continuing the ridiculous lie. 'Am I alright just leaving it here instead without a permit?'

He shakes his head and confirms the tow trucks are in the area. My heart sinks. Surely now my chances of seeing kick-off have gone. As I dive down Pretoria Road away from the stadium, a glance up towards the Haringey Irish Centre and an emergency stop offers hope where there was none – one yellow jacket waving me towards a space in return for £20. As I perform a borderline handbrake turn into the space, I hand over the cash – it's the kind of transaction I would baulk at the cost of usually but currently it feels like the bargain of the century - before grabbing my coat and sprinting towards the stadium, through the turnstiles, up to the fifth floor and right to the very back of the stand. As I reach my seat and sit down, the lights drop, the spotlight lands on the pitch, Paul Coyte takes the microphone and the opening ceremony begins. I've made it. And, let's face it, being fashionably late but equally somehow just in time is sort of in keeping with the entire redevelopment.

A stirring short film, a community choir formed in the aftermath of the 2011 London riots that began just down the road and a marching band playing 'Glory, Glory' to the team's arrival onto the pitch are just the beginning. With rumours that Tottenham-born Adele was pencilled in for the original opening ceremony last summer, a slight downgrade on ambition had been required for this evening. Out of the tunnel emerges Wynne Evans, the opera singing Spurs fan and star of the Go Compare adverts. Any correlation in the booking of a bloke from a comparison site for the inauguration of a bigger and better stadium than the one down the road was entirely coincidental, I'm sure.

What followed was a ridiculous, rousing, beautiful and hilarious few minutes as Wynne wandered around the pitch in duet with the sensational Lanya Matthews to send the crowd into delirium before a spectacular firework display exploded from the stadium roof. Meanwhile, the Crystal Palace team stood and at least attempted to look unmoved, throwing in the occasional calf stretch or jog on the spot to represent their unerring focus.

When the match itself kicked off – initially feeling like a side show to what had gone before it - the slow realisation that Tottenham Hotspur were playing football in their new stadium in front of us began to kick in. Emotion and excitement aside, the potential indignity of failing to beat Palace on such a huge evening in both Tottenham's history and season was tangible. Forget the pomp and ceremony - this was a side in real danger of dropping out of the Champions League positions that had seemed so secure just a few weeks earlier.

Chatting to the lads around me, we all had a similar tale to tell on how we'd acquired tickets the previous morning. Whether it had been a late release of a tiny batch or a cancelled minibus on the ticket exchange that had returned their allocation, we didn't really care. We'd all given up hope and yet now we were there and that was all that mattered.

After a dominant first half ended goalless, Spurs found the breakthrough via Heung Min-Son's deflected shot to open the scoring. It was by no means a classic but the relief it generated reverberated around the atmospheric new digs in a way I can't recall experiencing at a football match before. Christian Eriksen's poke home from close range for the second in the 80th minute got Spurs back to winning ways and reinstated a cushion to the chasing pack beneath them.

In the run-up to the opening match, I'd chatted with Stewart Banister, President of Hong Kong Spurs. Our call takes place on a slightly groggy Sunday morning for me after a fun gig in Stoke-on-Trent. While he's enjoying the early Sunday evening in Hong Kong, I neck my first pint of tea of the day. Notably, Stewart has retained a stronger Greater London twang than some of my previous ex-pat interviewees, despite spending a significant proportion of his life in Hong Kong.

'I'm in the street at the moment – I'm actually in a bar with the wife. It's a bit noisy here but you can't really avoid that in Hong Kong,' he begins.

Stewart is in the restaurant trade where he owns his own business. It's what first took him from the UK to Hong Kong and it's what brought him back to live there after years of following Spurs home and away.

'When I was in the UK years ago, I was a chef,' he begins. 'I came to Hong Kong at a fairly young age, left the business and went into telecoms for a number of years. But in 2007 I went back into the bar and restaurant business – back to my roots, as they say. Years ago, my dad worked out here in telecoms but in a different sector. He worked all over the world and he came out to Hong Kong under a contract many years ago and I came out to visit on holiday and fell in love with the place. Although I've been back to the UK a few times for lengthy periods, I've pretty much been based here for many years.'

Given work commitments and the distance to travel, visiting home isn't easy or particularly frequent these days. With the new stadium move finally complete, however, there's fresh impetus to board a plane home.

'I get back much less than before,' Stewart continues. 'Several years ago, it used to be fairly regular. These days, it's maybe once every two years. Now we're back to the new stadium though, that's on everyone's list! There'll be a queue of Hong Kong-based fans trying to get to the first few games. We're also fortunate here because the sponsor is a Hong Kong company. We have a good relationship with AIA and can get tickets for away games in the Champions League – it's a bit of perk! One of the directors of AIA is also a Spurs fan who has relocated to Singapore and I know another director who keeps good relationships with the supporters' club there.'

An online forum was the birth of the Hong Kong supporters' club in a country where live coverage of Premier League games has been plentiful over the years. Watching together with like-minded fans, however, was more of a challenge.

'It wasn't too bad keeping up with Spurs. The difficulty was finding a pub which would show our games as a priority,' he continues. It's a familiar tale, especially for fans going back further than a decade when Tottenham's international standing as one of the 'big' English clubs had begun to slip after a couple of decades of severe mediocrity.

'In terms watching live games, it wasn't too much of a problem as we get fairly good coverage of English Premier League matches in this part of the world, especially in Hong Kong. It was more to do with getting the fanbase together so we can go into a pub and negotiate a deal whereby you show all our games no matter if Liverpool are playing Man United and you think you can get a bigger audience; you're still gonna show the Spurs v Wigan game because we've adopted this as our pub, we hang our memorabilia on the walls and get a discount off the drinks.

'It was important to get a base so we could say this was our pub no matter who else was on TV. The pub that we're in now is owned by a Spurs supporter who is also on the supporters' club committee and he approached us. We need a fairly sizeable place because sometimes we get attendances of well over a hundred for the big games, so we're packed in there like sardines. It's a great atmosphere and a good laugh.'

While football is considered the number one sport in Hong Kong, the levels of commitment shown by Stewart's band of Spurs fans is still considered unique. Never is this more apparent than during the testing time differences thrown up by evening games – and it's not just the high-profile ones either.

He continues: 'When it comes to the Champions League, these games are quite regular in terms of the late, late kick-off. We're normally seven or eight hours ahead of London time and any nighttime kick off in Europe is gonna be early hours in Hong Kong. As you get into the latter stages, such as the quarter finals now, those games become much bigger or more important and people want to come out and watch the games with the other supporters. A lot of people don't have those TV channels at home anyway because the current provider for those games is a premium network.

'Last season when we played Juventus, that second game we had about sixty people in the pub for a four in the morning kick off. A lot of people who are walking past are thinking we're maniacs – 'what are they doing out so late? Oh, they're Tottenham fans! That's understandable then.' You wouldn't see that with many other clubs – Liverpool maybe – but Arsenal or Chelsea? Never. They wouldn't be out in the early hours.'

When it comes to the late games, everyone has their own method on how to fit their working lives around Tottenham. Stewart acknowledges that it's certainly easier for some than others – himself included.

He continues: 'On the Spurs live games we have a Facebook page and a WhatsApp chat for the members. Any announcements we do through that, putting up the venue and additional activities. We try and get as many fans down for the game as possible. Recently it's been a bit difficult because so many games have been on very late. Hong Kong itself is quite a compact place, but a lot of people like the ex-patriates and the ones that have kids, move further out to the outlying areas, so it's not too easy to get out at the weekend.

'If we're playing at 4am, there are still bars that are open but the guys that can make those games are the ones that start work really early. They get up much earlier than usual to go to the game and then go to work. Or they are people who have their own businesses. One of the guys on our Committee, Mike Gerraghty, he's an insurance broker. He doesn't do a lot of work, except on the golf course,' he teases. 'After the game he can go home, go to bed and do some work in the afternoon, I guess. The guys who can make the really late games have got flexible working hours. If you're a nine to fiver and live further out making transport more difficult in the early hours, those guys normally can't make it – and they're the majority. It's not a problem for the early afternoon games though where we have a 9.30pm kick-off. Even I'm allowed out for those!'

Living in one of the most international countries in the world means one of the most diverse fanbases, too. It's an aspect of the supporters' club that Stewart is rightly proud of.

'The fanbase is very diverse, not just in terms of local Chinese and ex-pats, it's also a diverse age group,' he says. 'You've got the older guys like me and the younger guys who obviously have a bit more energy these days! Let's say they are at the earlier stages of their working career, so they take a few more chances around getting three- or four-hours' kip before they go to work. I've slowed down a bit because people's marriages can suffer from this sort of thing but a lot of us are still fairly hardcore, we still make the effort.'

As well as the late nights and early mornings, there are plenty who will make the trip across the globe to watch Spurs in the flesh as well. Regretfully, it's not something Stewart is able to do quite so often these days.

'We've got a lot of supporters based in Hong Kong who make fairly regular pilgrimages over to London to watch games. The hardcore element is still there but for people like me, you've got to take it a bit easier. We're trying to expand the business at the moment and I'm really busy with a new project, so I need to make sure that I'm not too hungover most mornings!' he laughs. 'The older you get – you can still do the drinking, you just can't handle the hangovers! I recently acquired a Thai restaurant in one of the main districts in Hong Kong with a business partner. We're trying to acquire another restaurant in a neighbouring district too. That keeps me pretty busy.'

Stewart tells me about a recent planned initiative he's received details of where supporters' club members will register directly with Spurs. It makes a lot of sense and has struck me throughout this project that the football club don't appear to have a direct line into this huge international network. It appears to be a loophole they are understandably keen to close and capitalise on, especially in the lucrative Asian market that Stewart takes pride in being a key component of.

'Our guys in Hong Kong were instrumental in building the network of supporters, not just with Tottenham, but with each other,' he tells me. 'As social media grew, it was easier for us to connect with other clubs in the Asian Pacific region. Hong Kong being a main transport, business and tourism hub, we're viewed upon as the main supporters' hub in the region. They recognise the growth of the fanbase in China and we assist them in communications with the clubs here as well. We also have strong links with Singapore, Australia, Thailand and Indonesia. A lot of that was initiated by us to build those contacts. We're all good mates and any time their fans are in Hong Kong, they know a lot of us personally and we meet up for a beer and come to the pub to watch the game with us. It extends beyond Asia though – we get a lot of Americans, lots of fans from the UK. All over the world, really.'

While Stewart's Tottenham connection is lifelong, the continued growth of fans joining them for games is an intriguing one. With Manchester United and Chelsea being particularly well-established in that corner of the world and English football's popularity continuing to grow, why Tottenham for the hardcore locals that join every week over perhaps more prestigious names?

'Liverpool have got three supporters' clubs here,' he begins. 'Two of them are quite sizeable but they're mostly local lads. The third one is a mix of locals and ex-pats. They are well supported. There's a lot of Manchester United fans but only one supporters' club that seems to keep changing its organisation. Chelsea are smaller than us, Arsenal pretty much non-existent but they used to have a supporters' club. Of course, you know a lot of Arsenal fans, but they don't seem to be organised too well.' A bit like their back four then.

'There are Celtic and Rangers clubs out here as well which are medium-sized but smaller than us. I'd say we're second only to Liverpool. There are a few miscellaneous clubs like Southampton, Newcastle, Sunderland - even Norwich City have got one. I know a lot of West Ham fans. They used to have an organised club, but they don't seem to be very active anymore. They have a lot of fans here but don't seem to be gathering at any location.

'Although we've won bugger all since 2008, a lot of the local Chinese fans just love football and they love the players,' Stewart explains. 'They also love a lot of the passion they see from the ex-pat fans and how much we love the club even though we haven't won a lot recently. It's the style of football and the attitude of the team's British fans - how hardcore and devoted they are. If you compare that to your Arsenal and Man City fans or whatever, you'll find a lot of the local and some of the ex-pat fans of those clubs that when they're having a bad day at the office or not playing too well, a lot of them don't come out or show their passion and won't go and see them until they start winning again. Spurs fans go and watch the games through thick and thin, even if we're playing badly or have a dodgy manager – before Pochettino or whatever – Spurs fans still come out and support the badge more than success.

'Some of that rubs off on those local supporters and that's what really inspires them. That, plus the stylish players of recent times like Harry Kane, Dele Alli – that sort of combo really motivates the local fans to be a little bit more hardcore as well. We give it back and we appreciate their loyalty. We look after each other. It's a really good mix.'

According to Stewart, that loyal mixing of fans of all nationalities and ages is quite rare compared to their rivals, as he explains: 'All the other supporters' clubs out here tend to see the locals and the ex-pats drift away from each other due to a slightly different culture and the way they follow. We're one of the few larger clubs where our fanbase is still unified. We do things together, there's no segregation. We sit together and watch the games. If you look at the Chelsea supporters club here, the ex-pats watch the game separately from the locals because they don't like the way locals sit down in front of the TV – they view themselves supporting their clubs in different ways. Our local Chinese are singing and know all the songs. They sing as much as the westerners. We're the unique supporters club in Hong Kong that is truly integrated.'

Who'd have thought the Chelsea fans weren't up for integration? I'm oddly proud that this hierarchical system hasn't extended to Spurs, where the British fans don't appear to consider themselves above the locals. It feels true, somehow, to the team on the field and its culture and philosophy.

'Tottenham's fanbase in the UK is pretty diverse and that's reflected in Hong Kong and other countries,' Stewart continues. 'It's the same in Singapore, Malaysia, Thailand – that's what makes us special.'

And Stewart has a clear message for Spurs fans visiting Hong Kong in the near future: 'If you come to Hong Kong, get in touch with us on Facebook, tell us you're coming over and myself or some of the other guys will greet you down the pub and introduce you to the rest of the supporters. We do this already and people just know how to find you on social media. We welcome fans all the time and sometimes we have multiple groups – a few weeks ago we had a couple from Norway Spurs and another couple from South Africa Spurs. We ended up introducing them all to each other, people exchange business cards and sometimes we even hook them up to do business with each other. If someone needs a local accountant or something like that – there's a market for business exchange.'

For anyone who has ever endured a business breakfast networking club, the idea of such a thing existing but with beer and other Spurs fans is infinitely more appealing. And now Spurs are back to their roots, is there any likelihood Stewart might ever return as well?

'If I moved back to the UK – and I have no idea what my movements are likely to be over the next few years – I'd be back to going to every home and away game for sure.' For now, at least, Stewart remains happy and comfortable launching the next business venture in his adopted country. For Tottenham Hotspur Football Club, though, the temporary move is already but a memory.

Spurs are home.

Stewart (far right) with members of Hong Kong Spurs.

13

VAR, MY LORD
NORWAY SPURS

The midweek that followed Tottenham's opening night victory had seen the visit of Manchester City in the Champions League quarter finals. On the face of things, it was the worst possible draw against the quadruple-chasing favourites in a last eight that had seen Tottenham drift to an outside shot to lift the trophy ahead of only Porto. The Portuguese champions, meanwhile, provided a plum-looking opponent for Liverpool.

If the spectacle of Palace in the Premier League had been exciting, the sound of the Champions League theme reverberating around the Tottenham Hotspur Stadium lifted its surrounds to new heights. There was no more fitting a venue to host Europe's top club competition across the entire continent.

With the words of Graham Roberts still fresh in my mind, there was a strange sense of optimism ahead of facing Pep Guardiola's collective of superstars. Yes, the odds were against us, the form guide was frightening and the win against Palace had been far from convincing, but it felt like the long-awaited moving day had given everyone the bounce required at a time when the team had so desperately needed it. There was no pressure and no expectation after the draw had been made. Had the match been at Wembley, we might have viably feared a drubbing; instead, there was hope.

In true Tottenham style, a fair chunk of that newly-discovered buoyancy was extinguished early on as Raheem Sterling's mazy run from the left wing into the box resulted in a shot that appeared to innocuously deflect off Danny Rose for a corner. That was until a VAR review adjudged that the England fullback had used his arm to divert the ball away from goal and a controversial penalty was awarded. The look of Danny's bemusement had only been matched by his cursory glance at the Go Compare bloke a week earlier.

Captain Hugo was the hero again, diving to his right to push Sergio Aguero's spot kick away and keep the scores level. While Tottenham had their moments, City looked in patient control for long spells as they soaked up pressure without really threatening. Their most potent moment towards denting Tottenham's chances came when a full-blooded challenge between Delph and Kane saw Harry's ankle come off worst. The sight of our top scorer hobbling back towards the dressing room again, with his season surely now over, was not the housewarming present anyone had ordered. He'd have to wait until 2019/20 to grab that elusive first goal in the new stadium after only managing a combined couple of hours of football under its floodlights.

Speaking of first goals, the talisman's injury would again bring the best out of Heung-Min Son, who stepped into the matchwinner's shoes again to give Spurs a narrow lead ahead of the second leg. Through sheer determination following a heavy first touch inside the box that almost took the ball out of play, the South Korean worked his way back from the byline to create an angle and strike a powerful shot under Ederson. It was game on ahead of the visit to the Etihad.

A Lucas Moura hat-trick to seal a comfortable 4-0 dismantling of basement side Huddersfield Town between the two quarter final legs continued the winning home run with seven goals scored and none conceded in the opening three games. With one eye on the Etihad, it had felt like a training game for long periods as Pochettino made changes to rest key men. Adding a late brace to his first half strike, Moura's contribution had made the game look comfortable and put him in the running for a starting berth in the return leg. As fans lingered in the stadium after the full-time whistle, the Brazilian brought his baby daughter onto the pitch to kick a ball around and delight anyone with a heart not made of stone. With a tricky run-in to come, the spirit of those final days at White Hart Lane was already being rekindled between players and fans in a way that the vastness of Wembley had never allowed.

Ahead of the match, I'm speaking to Vidar Edell, a gentleman I met before the Arsenal game in March and who was Chairman of Norway Spurs until earlier this season when he decided to step down. He was certainly someone who had appreciated the opportunity to meet Keith Burkinshaw more than me, having experienced the great man's era in charge first hand. Better still, the first person he'd set eyes on when arriving at the Novotel that morning was Keith himself. He'd managed to get a picture which he proudly shared after I'd arrived late, again. To soften my disappointment, he'd generously brought a copy of the book he'd commissioned a few years earlier, telling the story of his historic supporters' club.

'It is in Norwegian, of course, but it is a good way to learn our language,' he'd told me, somewhat optimistically given that I got a GCSE grade B at French and can still only just about order a beer, pizza and communicate that I enjoy playing ping-pong. Time to polish up on a new language.

'Chesterfield?' he queries, as our chat recommences over the phone and he starts by finding out where I'm from instead of other way round. 'I've never been there. Are they still in the professional league or what?' I explain the recent woes of my hometown team and Vidar listens with interest, his knowledge of the English game clearly extending beyond the Premier League. But back to Norway Spurs and the bits I haven't quite managed to absorb from the beautifully produced hardback tome he gifted me.

'In 1982 the supporters' club was formed by a bunch of very young kids,' he begins. 'I think they were 12 – high up in the north of Norway. They kept that going for four or five years but it almost folded in '87 before being revived by another group.' Perhaps that FA Cup Final defeat to Coventry City had been the final straw.

'And then in 2006, after only being a member for a few years, a guy I knew on the Board asked if I'd be the Chairman. I was working in a bank at the time. I accepted and expected to last for a few years, but it turned out to be twelve years! We've doubled the membership during that time, which includes lots of qualified people including writers. We publish our own award-winning supporters' club magazines and have done so throughout our existence. In 2017, we made the book to mark 25 years,' he adds, proudly.

Vidar tells me the once youthful group of founding fathers are all now fully-grown adults, one of whom is now a newspaper editor in the west of Norway. 'I haven't met them, but I have heard they are superb people,' Vidar continues.

'We have around 5,000 members now, but the potential is bigger – much bigger. We should aim for 10,000 or 15,000 but of course we first need to do things on the pitch. Manchester United and Liverpool are both around 40,000 and I know quite a few of these guys. There is a Liverpool fan who is running a company and he tells me he's hiring people all the time. He checks their qualifications, all looks OK – then he asks, by the way, do you love football? And do you have a team? He tells me that if they are a big Liverpool supporter, he hires them. But if they are a Manchester United supporter he says, I'm sorry I can't hire you then! This thing is running through society here. One of the guys I meet in the pub all the time is a Minister for Transportation in Norway and he has a Spurs flag in the office. The coverage of English football is huge, and Spurs Norway has a huge chance to grow.'

I'm intrigued by how the teenage Vidar came to see Spurs for the first time. 'My first match was in 1977 at White Hart Lane when I was only 16 years old. I came across only to watch Spurs with my best mate at the time. He's still very close to me but is the editor of a Manchester United supporters' club magazine now and they have 40,000 members. We went to our parents and asked if we could go to the UK and they told us absolutely not! My friend's father was a businessman and he arranged us a meeting. My friend and I took the ferry from Gothenburg to the UK alone which, looking back, was crazy. How we managed, I can't remember. And then we stayed one night in the UK before my friend's father and older brother came to see us. We went to Spurs v Manchester United in February 1977. Spurs lost 3-1 but by then I was beyond salvage at the time. It started there.'

Vidar's Chairmanship has overseen big growth in the club, especially since Spurs visited Norway a few years ago and Vidar was asked to present the team with a traditional gift before their game against Inter Milan at Oslo's Ullevaal Stadion in 2016.

'This match was arranged in August by a private company,' Vidar explains. 'We didn't get involved too early, but my deputy was very involved in the process. In the end, we had a stand outside the stadium, but the crowd wasn't big because it was still in the summertime. Inside, many of the people were Spurs Norway members. The day before the match we had a Q&A session in the pub with Ledley King. He presented himself excellently, he was a superb guy. The day of the match we had a lunch event as well. Some of us were invited to the hotel that Spurs were staying in and met all the players and Pochettino. Everything was superb. Then I presented them with the welcome gift of the Viking ship on the pitch.'

From a 16-year-old getting on a ferry to watch his first Spurs game to the President of Norway Spurs presenting a traditional gift to the team in Oslo decades later. It's a great story.

'There's a huge interest for English football in general here,' he continues, 'because in the '60s, '70s and '80s we had live matches broadcast to Norway, at first in black and white. It was part of the pools which was run by a national company and regulated by the state. They'd show different matches so you could bet on them. The first few years it was only midlands teams for some reason, but Spurs would play also. It started there for me as a very young boy against Villa in 1971 and around that time I became so obsessed with Spurs. A few years later, The Glory Game came out and I got that book for Christmas from my parents. From that moment on, there was no way back. I was so in love with Spurs.'

Hunter Davies' book remains a primary source of affection for

Spurs fans who remember the teams of the early '70s and remains a fantastic read to step into a different world of football in a bygone age.

'Norway is a very stretched country and there are pockets of Spurs fan everywhere,' Vidar continues. 'I think the biggest collection is here at Bohemen Sportspub in Oslo. It's a Spurs bar that shows all Spurs matches and because we have such a big number and level of beer drinking, I think it gives us a lot of leeway – even though the landlord is an Arsenal supporter!' I bet that's fun on North London derby weekend.

The pub is run with Vålerenga - a side best remembered in England for running Chelsea close in the European Cup Winners Cup quarter finals in 1999 back when Thursday night football really was on Channel 5 and accompanied by Jonathan Pearce screaming like a banshee.

'They play in the Norwegian Premier League. We usually have the pub to ourselves but people from other clubs go there as well. Sometimes they'll have five or six games going on at the same time and it's very segregated.'

A recent health scare coincided with Vidar stepping down from his role as Chair of Norway Spurs. While he's no longer directly involved, he's happy to just be enjoying the football as a member these days.

'Last year I was diagnosed with kidney failure, so my eldest son donated a kidney to me in August,' he explains. 'It's been a lengthy thing, so I only got out of hospital early in November. I haven't been much as a result this season but some of my friends were going to Barcelona away, so I went with them. I came over to see Chelsea away and Arsenal at Wembley also. I always come over for the final game of the season as well, I've done that for a few years, including the last game at the Lane. And when it came to the first game in the new stadium, I'd have done anything. I was so desperate to see that game that I would have dug out my other kidney to get over!'

I'm pleased to report Vidar is fully on the mend and made it to the first game without the need for major surgery. 'My boy is a healthy kid because his kidney is working like hell. I have lots of energy and appetite for life. Kidney problems are bad. It's not painful, just really depressing, and my body was shutting down. A new kidney has reshaped me.'

Much like Vidar's friends at Sweden Spurs, a 24-hour trip is not uncommon. 'It's quite easy. We can get a very early Ryanair flight to Stansted and you're in Liverpool Lime Street at 9am in the morning. If it's an early kick-off you can have a breakfast, a few beers, watch the match, have a few more beers and return home. It's very convenient. Compared with the old days, airline tickets were the most expensive and then maybe a hotel and the matchday ticket cost basically nothing. Now, it's the complete opposite. The airline is not expensive at all, the hotel, well, we are not very snobbish,' he laughs. 'It's the match ticket that is very expensive.'

Even for overseas fans, the delayed return to the new stadium has had an impact. And, while health issues might have dictated otherwise, the extended stay at Wembley scuppered Vidar's plans to travel over more frequently this season.

'I was hoping to spend most of my life at the new stadium this season. It's so important that we are there now, it's vital for everybody, especially the players. It is also important because of the money machine we will become now as well.'

On the eve of one of Tottenham's biggest European games in recent history, Vidar's memory stretches back to when Spurs going deep into continental competition was a regular occurrence. In his younger days, he'd often make the journey south to join in.

'I remember going to Anderlecht away in '84,' he says, referring to the UEFA Cup Final first leg that would form the foundations for one of White Hart Lane's most famous nights a fortnight later. 'It was quite special because at the time I was in the Navy and I was young and strong and brave and a real idiot with the drinking. I had no fear at all. We took the ferry from Dover to Oostende and were greeted by buses and an armed police escort. Something really went wrong and there was a rampage of Spurs fans through Brussels. What had coloured that day was that the day before, a Spurs supporter was murdered in the Red Light District, so the mood was quite aggressive at the time.'

It's a story I'd never heard before but reports at the time confirm that an 18-year-old Irish born Spurs fan from North London was shot dead by a Belgian barman. At the time, the reputation of the English football fan abroad was heading towards rock bottom. Belgian riot police, gendarmes and soldiers were primed to deal with the situation, with more than 50 moved into stables converted into makeshift prisons near the stadium. Having travelled abroad watching Spurs myself, albeit in an era of carefully managed fan zones and private transport laid on by clubs to minimise the risk of trouble, I've seen almost zero aggravation that could provoke such problems among fans at least. It's hard to imagine what following the team to Europe could have been like in those dark days.

Vidar pulls no punches as he continues: 'At that time I had no fear and I didn't take care of myself. Because of this, it was a good time for me to go, but now I think people would be very frightened in that situation. This was just a few years before the Heysel disaster with Liverpool in the same city but, in some ways, this wasn't surprising as the policing was absolutely shit. That is how I'd describe it.'

On a brighter note, we get to comparisons between Pochettino and where he might rank compared to managerial greats such as Bill Nicholson and Keith Burkinshaw. Vidar is in little doubt that the Argentinian is well on his way to being mentioned in the same breath as those two Tottenham titans.

'We are in a new era really,' he begins, thoughtfully. 'Bill Nich and Keith Burkinshaw was an era where honesty and loyalty was part of the game. In this age, there is not as much anymore but I feel Pochettino could be an exception. He states that he wants to stay and make Spurs great again and I think things look very well. I don't think it is easy to compare him with those two, but I can see similarities; he is a strong character. He wants to reach his goals, but he will not betray his loyalty and truthfulness, I feel.

'At the Spurs Norway AGM in September we had Ryan Mason come to give a speech. When we asked him who the most important figure was at Spurs, most people would expect him to say Harry Kane, but he said Pochettino. He said that if we can keep him onboard, the future is very bright. And I agree with him. I think we are on the verge of becoming one of the world's greatest clubs. We are already number 10 in the economic league and I think the new stadium will kick us up that as well. We will be a force to be reckoned with and we have everything in place, including the beginnings of a superb team.'

Vidar is similarly positive about the season that is ending, despite the worrying form the team find themselves in. He continues: 'I think Spurs had done superbly this year until the recent blip. We've played at Wembley much longer than anticipated which I feel has had a draining effect. We've had serious injuries to vital players, especially Harry Kane. He is so instrumental for us and when he is away there is nobody natural to come in and take his place. To be philosophical, how can you back-up Harry Kane? It's hard because if you have quality then what player is going to sit on the bench always? We tried it with Janssen, it didn't quite work out, Llorente the same thing, I think. That's a big issue.' It's the transfer dilemma that has dogged Pochettino ever since the England striker burst onto the scene that is likely to continue for a few more seasons to come.

Like the friendship between clubs in Asia or across America, Norway Spurs are no different with their Scandinavian cousins – with regular get togethers often turning into one big party.

'Sweden is the club we know the most,' he explains, returning the compliment that Sverker had paid them. 'They are nice people. They like to drink a few and so do we! When we were in Copenhagen three years ago with my girlfriend, we went to visit Denmark Spurs as they have their own pub and we went to see a match. We lost to West Brom I think, it was a shambles and a terrible match – but nice beer!'

Tottenham's connection to Norway on the field is also a significant one. While the huge stars of Norway's golden '90s generation might be better remembered for wearing the jerseys of other Premier League sides, with Solskjaer and Flo boosting the popularity of Manchester United and Chelsea respectively, there were also a few big names to wear lilywhite during that period as well.

'There have been a few Norwegian Spurs players like Erik 'the Viking' Thorstvedt - I've been in TV studios with him and met the guy,' Vidar tells me, proudly. 'He told us about his time at Spurs and episodes with Gazza – lots of fun and lots of madness! He's a pundit now. Then there's Øyvind Leonhardsen who never really liked the limelight anyway. I think he's a youth trainer outside Oslo. Steffen Iversen, I've heard he's a friendly guy. His father was a top scorer in the Norwegian league for many years. Then the other 'keeper, Espen Baardsen, he's in London now. I think he was born in the U.S. and emigrated – he is more of an international guy, I don't think he speaks much Norwegian. Oh, and the 'keeper Frode Grodås who came from Chelsea on a free. I don't think he played any matches. So, there were six of them.'

And is there a new golden generation coming through Norwegian football that Spurs should be on the lookout for? 'They have changed the manager and he's doing better than the last few. I wouldn't call it a golden generation, but they have someone who is shining – a young central midfielder called Berge who plays for Genk in Belgium. He is the son-in-law of a good friend of mine. I think Spurs should probably go for him. He's not the finished article but he shows good promise. And he wouldn't be too expensive!' I can feel Daniel Levy's ears twitching.

Before we finish our chat, Vidar tells me about an interesting collection he's developed over the years – and a related project he's been working on. 'I am a big collector of Spurs memorabilia. Things like the official handbooks – I believe I might be the person outside of the UK with the most handbooks on the planet. They are very hard to get. I had a connection with Andy

Porter who was Tottenham's official historian. He died sadly, but he taught me a lot and I came to learn about this guy called John Ripsher who was our first manager from 1885 to 1895. All these things are sketchy because they were so long ago, and nothing was documented. But he ended up in Dover, they were poor, he had some health issues and when he died, he was buried in an unmarked grave.'

It's a fascinating story that I wasn't previously aware of. Vidar has researched it extensively. He continues: 'Thankfully, the Club learnt about this back in around 2007 and they took the trouble to erect a proper gravesite for him with the Spurs logo on. I believe Mabbutt and other officials from the Club were there. I'd like to go out there to take a picture of the gravesite and write an article for our supporter magazine – it should be quite an interesting story. It's vital for us to look forward to the glory days that are hopefully coming now, but also to look back. These were the men who were there at the beginning.'

It's a warming sentiment and a reminder of the giants that went before us whose shoulders we stand upon as we head into the Champions League last eight. Ahead of Man City, however, Vidar would prefer to keep his predictions in the longer term. 'I believe Spurs will enter a period of huge success and become a really big club,' he says with confidence. You can't say fairer than that.

Despite Vidar's confidence, I have sobering advice for my 10-year-old son as we get comfortable on the sofa ahead of Manchester City. I had intended to remind him all day that, despite the aggregate lead, we remained the underdog. Every bookie in the country was backing Manchester City to turn us over comfortably and we needed to enjoy the match as best we could. Managing a child's emotions as hormones kick in can be something of an ongoing challenge; factor in a love for Tottenham Hotspur and you've really got a recipe for disaster. It was important to have this conversation early.

Amidst the rush into the house following under-10s football training to see the sides lining up ahead of kick-off, and the excitement of the Champions League theme tune, I forgot to deliver my pre-prepared monologue until a few minutes after the game commenced.

'Jacob,' I began, as Manchester City poured forward. 'Don't forget, we're still expected to go out tonight,' I continued, just as Raheem Sterling was granted the freedom of Manchester by Kieran Trippier to receive the ball on the left. 'I hope we go through,' I added, as the England forward set himself on the edge of the box. 'But,' I hesitated, as he bent the ball into the far corner beyond the despairing reach of Hugo Lloris inside four minutes. I stopped mid-sentence, flabbergasted by Tottenham's ability to illuminate my words before I'd even been able to utter them. We gave each other the kind of knowing look that suggested he had already begun to steel himself to the life sentence I'd bestowed upon him. I need say no more. That's my boy.

Back Spurs came, though, with Moura's driving run feeding Dele, whose ambitious through ball for Eriksen was redirected by the defender and into the path of Son. The South Korean finished with unerring composure to put Spurs back in front overall and secure the all-important away goal that would mean Manchester City now needed to win by two clear goals on the night. We'd barely had time to register this fact when Eriksen fed Son on the edge of the box to fire another superb strike beyond Ederson for his third goal of the tie and give Spurs a firm foothold in the game. The scenes in our living room matched the delirium in the stands, and among Spurs fans across the world, as a three-goal cushion had effectively been secured inside the opening ten minutes.

It would be a cushion that would last for 99 seconds, as the Spurs backline failed to reset and were dragged hopelessly out of position to leave Bernardo Silva with far too much time to slot in the equaliser on the night. The lacklustre deflection off Danny Rose that led to the ball trickling beyond the dive of Lloris made the goal even more farcical. For anyone other than the watching City and Spurs fans who were mid-palpitation, this was already becoming a classic.

When Sterling converted a 21st minute Kevin De Bruyne cross to give the hosts the lead on the night, the game broke the record for the quickest five goals in a Champions League match. It was little consolation to fans of a Tottenham persuasion, who could feel the inevitable playing out before them, even if watching it through the lens of what resembled an end-to-end 5-a-side match rather than a Champions League quarter final was a quirky new subplot at least. The Belgian playmaker was the architect again in the 58th minute, with a driving run feeding Aguero to finish powerfully at the near post and make up for his penalty miss in the first leg. Having thwarted the opportunity to give City the early advantage in North London, he made no mistake to put them ahead for the first time with just half an hour of the tie left to play.

Spurs regained the overall advantage through first half substitute Fernando Llorente. Preferred over Oliver Skipp to replace the injured Moussa Sissoko late in the first half, the big Spaniard can be a divisive figure as his physical presence often appears outweighed by his lack of mobility in an otherwise pacey, athletic, counter-attacking forward line. His conviction to divert a corner off his thigh – a moment that is replayed countless times in a lengthy VAR review to ascertain whether it hit his arm first – means Spurs are again on course for the semi-finals with an agonising seventeen minutes remaining.

The maturity of Pochettino's team is evident in the final stages as they manage the game to restrict Guardiola's side to little more than a half chance blasted high over by Gundogan with five minutes remaining. And then, with two and half minutes of added time elapsed of the five indicated, most of which came from the Llorente goal review, Spurs spot the opportunity to break from their own box and release the mounting pressure. Son's ball out to Eriksen sees the Dane immediately closed down and, as he inexplicably turns to play the ball backwards, his pass is intercepted by Bernardo Silva and into the path of Aguero.

It is an instinctive touch from the Portuguese playmaker that would create one of the most controversial moments in

Champions League history.

As play continues, Aguero cuts the ball inside for Raheem Sterling who fakes to shoot, moves the ball onto his left foot and powers it past Lloris to seemingly complete his hat-trick. The live pictures are complete with the kind of shuddering camerawork that only comes from a goal of this magnitude or FA Cup First Round weekend as the Etihad shakes to its foundations and I swear repeatedly at the television in front of my son. It's a devastating blow, as painful as it is expected. Even after all these years, Spurs find new ways to cause us suffering.

Except, this time, it was different.

As the screens around the stadium signalled a VAR review to the groans of the crowd, television replays immediately showed Aguero to be offside. By receiving Eriksen's errant pass via Bernardo, the Argentinian's left foot hadn't quite made the trip back into an onside position after a tired and slow trot back. Spotting Sergio's dangling shoelace before the decision was confirmed, the crestfallen Jones family were already screaming with delight at the TV a few seconds before the decision came through – the score remained 4-3 and Tottenham were still on their way to the semis. It's enough to make Pep remove his charity shop jumper/cardigan hybrid as the premature star jumps down the touchline turn out to be in vain.

It had been an evening of incredible drama right down to the final seconds that would be a defining moment in the season's Champions League to date and far surpass the emotion of Tottenham's sneak in through the back door of the group stages. For City, hopes of a quadruple had been extinguished as they were eliminated at the hands of English opposition for the fifth time. For Spurs, it was new ground under Pochettino once more as his threadbare squad advanced to the European Cup semi-finals for the first time since 1962.

'I still can't believe it, Dad!' are the final words from my son as he drifts off to sleep in his Spurs shirt. I lay with him a little longer than is necessary as his gentle snores suggest he's beginning to dream of Madrid. It will be the youthful fellow underdogs of Ajax Amsterdam who stand in our way.

Vidar (right) on one of his many trips across to see Spurs in action.

14
ONE HELL OF A HANGOVER
SPURS CANADA

If you've ever been to a teenage party where the house got trashed and the host's parents came back halfway through, you might be familiar with the slightly awkward return trip to help tidy up the following morning. Indeed, if your mate Kev who threw the party gets so drunk on four cans of Carling that you have to call his parents because he's being sick everywhere and you don't know what to do because you're only sixteen and feeling pretty woozy on half a shandy yourself, it's also a very solemn face you have to pull as you wave him off in the back of his dad's car to A&E.

While these rites of passage are just part of the average British teenager's assimilation into the adult world, it is quite the unexpected treat to feel that same mix of slight embarrassment, mixed with the relief that it didn't happen to you, in the company of 55,000 people. And yet, that is exactly what happened to Tottenham Hotspur Football Club and their merry band of still ever-so-slightly dreary eyed fans on the early afternoon of Saturday 20th April 2019.

A little over 60 hours after the last few fans had filtered out of the Etihad Stadium, the turnstiles would open again to 'welcome' Spurs back to the scene of one of their most memorable parties. The customary low-energy atmosphere of the weekend's early match, often caused by the broadcasting powers insisting on away fans being required to set off before the dawn chorus to arrive for kick-off, had the air of a wake – albeit with the addition of a small, possibly still tipsy collective of distant southern relatives, singing and dancing in the corner.

Phil Foden would score early to secure a 1-0 victory that would feel a bit like discovering someone else's vomit in the carpet that required removing from a Tottenham perspective, but no matter. The expectation of points had been remote for every team visiting East Manchester this season and Spurs were no different, especially on the back of such a spectacular midweek result. That the remainder of the weekend would see Manchester United lose by four at Everton, Arsenal be overturned on their own patch by Crystal Palace and Chelsea fail to capitalize on all the above by drawing 2-2 with Burnley on Monday Night Football, it had been a remarkable weekend's action to end an extraordinary week. Oh, and my mate Kev who hosted the party is still an absolute lightweight to this day.

On the back of a quite wondrous week of football, I've booked in a chat with Spurs Canada – not Canada Spurs, as he reminds me early on – and their former Chair John McClelland. It's fitting I should speak to John on the crest of one of Tottenham's all-time peaks given he became a Spurs fan by chance around one of their deepest nadirs. His first game in the flesh happened to fall around the end of Juande Ramos's reign in 2008 and the subsequent appointment of Henry James Redknapp.

'I had been to the UK after I graduated from University,' he begins as we get settled into our chat after reliving the thrilling few weeks we've had by way of an introduction. 'I did the backpacking thing around Europe and first stop was London. Then, years later, my wife wanted to go somewhere for our anniversary and England was top of the list. It was a case of looking at the schedule trying to figure out if I could see a match. It was certainly a bucket list thing for me to see a Premier League game.

'I found out all about how you actually order tickets as an international fan and it seemed to be quite the process! With the ticket in hand, I made my way on the Tube, then from Seven Sisters to the stadium on foot - should have taken the bus really, but hey, who knew it would be such a long walk!'

After his marathon journey, the least John might have

expected was a decent view of the pitch at least; not to be, as he explains: 'When I finally got to my seat it was directly behind one of the big standing poles. Other supporters were waiting to see my reaction, but I just laughed and so did they. It was a great game and a great experience even though we were bottom of the league. I remember Ledley, Lennon and Modric all playing well, and the overall match day experience had me hooked on Spurs.'

John's Tottenham origin story leaves me with one lingering question: given his ambition was to see a Premier League match in the flesh, was there a Sliding Doors-esque alternative reality where he might have become a fan of another London club? 'Thank God I didn't go to West Ham or Arsenal!' he laughs. 'The football Gods were clearly smiling on me that season.'

John and Harry's first game came just a few days before one of the most memorable games in Tottenham's recent history: a high-scoring draw at the Emirates where Spurs entered the final two minutes of ordinary time 4-2 down before Jermaine Jenas and then Aaron Lennon's jubilant equaliser was celebrated amidst a half-empty away end.

'I can't remember the 4-4 match,' John continues. 'All I know is that when I got home after vacation I started following the results of the Premier League and then I found out that there was actually a Spurs Canada,' he says, reminding me that it is was the unilateral decision of the supporters' club not to conform with Tottenham's preferred naming convention of Canada Spurs.

'I found the Spurs Canada website - it was a terrible website at that time – and I found out that I could become a member. I think we had about 90 members so it was pretty small. There was a Toronto chapter, a small chapter in Vancouver, the BC (British Colombia) Spurs. They probably had 10 or 15 members, mostly ex-pats that lived in Vancouver, and they would meet up for games.'

John can't quite place the first time he saw a fellow Spurs fan on Canadian soil. But his outgoing approach to introducing others to the cause would help fuel an exponential growth in his corner of the country.

'If I saw someone with the Spurs emblem in a parking lot, I would always say 'Hey Spurs fan!' or something like that and I'd always talk to people which I think is why we became successful in the new Ottawa chapter. Every time I saw someone, I would talk to them about Spurs Canada. I would go to the same football pub to watch every match – and that's one of the big differences in Canada. You can watch 95% of the matches on TV and then the other 5% you can stream.'

With five time zones across the country, John has it better than most for convenient kickoff times on the East Coast.

'It's generally 10am or 3pm here,' he continues. 'If you live in Vancouver, it would be three hours earlier. We have approximately 350 members across Canada with around 60 of those here in Ottawa. Vancouver would have a similar number and then Toronto has 150. There are another 75 members across Canada that just wanna be participants but don't have a chapter to go to. Over the last 10 years, there have been many chapters in many locations across Canada and they've all pretty much failed because if you don't have a leader that's going to be involved that wants to do the legwork, it's not going to work out. Even in a major city like Montreal, we've had a couple of tries there and it just didn't work because no one wanted to be that leader.'

John is well-positioned to advise on the subject. Alongside his several years of Chairmanship, he had also been the founding member in Ottawa.

He continues: 'When I became a member of Spurs Canada I was on their database and the president at that time happened to have family in the area and was coming up for a weekend visit. He contacted me as I was just about the only member in Ottawa, so we had to figure out where we were going to watch the match. We decided on a place called the Georgetown which was known as a good place to watch football. It was a great atmosphere and we decided to start a chapter in Ottawa right then. I would go up to people specifically who were clapping for Spurs and tell them what we were doing. Sometimes they would look at me like I was nuts.' It was this perseverance that would help see John's newly formed Ottawa chapter begin to flourish.

'I remember specifically there was a guy called 'Darts Mike',' he continues. 'I'm not sure what part of England he's from but he's got a really thick accent – I think it might be the Newcastle area. He would just show up and play darts, have a pint and then watch the game by himself and it was obvious he was a Spurs fan, so I went and chatted to him. He gave me a look like I had three heads! It took a few years to get him onboard but now he's a fully-fledged member.

'Once we formed, we stayed at the Georgetown pub and I approached the general manager about letting us put a Spurs Canada flag up there. His reaction was along the lines of: 'OK, but it's not my fault if it gets vandalized!' I actually brought a ladder and bolted this thing to their walls, and we had our first Spurs Canada Ottawa headquarter flag there.

'We stayed there for a few years, but the problem was they wouldn't do anything for us despite, from a business perspective, that we would bring people to their location when not a lot of people are there. In the morning they might have a few stragglers having breakfast but not a big sports event. The service levels dropped, and they went out of business in the off-season, so I went out to search for my own venue with my own criteria around how they must be central, must have parking, must have the TV channels and stuff like that, a proper beer selection, all on a checklist.'

John's thorough search for a new home in Ottawa, combined with impressive negotiating skills, helped him seal the deal on a new home for the growing congregation to gather.

'I went out and found a place called Hometown and it's a big sports bar with a nice outdoor patio. I talked to the owner and just laid out what we could do for them. Based on the previous year's numbers, I could be confident we would have 14 people on average per game and showed them the numbers on our Facebook page and website. We offered to use their logo and get them on the Spurs website. Eventually the owner said he would open for every match no matter what time – even the odd early match at 7:30am.'

John's new venue was charmed into offering special discounts, prize items for draw and money back offers to reward fans - so much so that they would hold unannounced member's days.

'We wouldn't tell the members or else people would show up just because they know it's free! We'd just announce when the match bills were coming around each time that the bill was on the house!'

As Spurs Canada continued to grow in Ottawa, an unexpected boost to Tottenham's popularity would follow the recent arrival of Jermain Defoe to North American shores that had already significantly helped to boost interest.

John continues: 'I got an email from Spurs membership with a heads-up saying they were coming on tour the day before it actually hit press, so that was kind of cool. When they came to Toronto, we made scarves and a banner that said 'thanks Jermain' because I'm pretty sure one of the reasons they picked Toronto was because Defoe had signed up. There was a big campaign that was on radio and TV. The headline in the paper was: A Bloody Big Deal!

'Defoe's arrival had made a difference to our membership for sure. We held a big event with the money we had in the bank and all the members had a great time. We even hired a double decker white bus that carried people from our pub in Toronto to the stadium so people could have that experience. We also donated $3000 to a local Toronto football youth charity.'

The tour fuelled a few significant additional benefits that would last for much longer than the ninety minutes in Toronto as well, as John explains.

'Tottenham made an agreement with an organization called Maple Leaf Sports Entertainment that own several franchised sports teams including Toronto FC. They cut a deal so that the Spurs Canada group would change pubs to their venue. They had this massive bar called Real Sports and at the time when it opened it was the largest sports screen in North America. We agreed that would be our main pub for at least the next year and Levy signed off with TFC that every supporters' club in Canada would get $1000 Canadian every week.

'So – and this is crazy - every match we would show up and they would have a section cordoned. Our match would be on the largest screen with our volume turned up. Our members would show up and it's a free breakfast or free lunch and here's your three-pint ticket. We were charging $25 to become a member of Spurs Canada. That year, we would say to people: what's 38 (matches) multiplied by three pints and a free meal? - and many wouldn't believe us. But we certainly got great benefits that year, so thank you Mr Levy!'

The Tottenham tour also helped John rub shoulders with some famous faces including Canadian football's prodigal son and a Spurs cult hero.

'Paul Stalteri was part of the event and I got to go on stage and do a speech,' he says of the meeting with the fullback best remembered for a last-minute winner at Upton Park that looked to have all but relegated West Ham at the time. 'I got to meet him, Ledley King and Brad Friedel which was pretty neat. Stalteri is our honorary chairperson. He is part of the national Canadian football team programme these days.'

One cultural note I've picked up during our chat is the Canadian tendency to refer to the beautiful game as 'football' rather than 'soccer'. 'If you are a big supporter, you just call it football,' John explains, 'and then you know if anyone looks at you confused, you just have to clarify that it's not NFL or the CFL!'

John did make a trip to the UK earlier this season with a view to watching a Spurs match while he was over. Instead, thanks to FA Cup-related postponements and the delay to the new stadium, he ended up in the slightly less salubrious surrounds of South London instead.

'My holiday was planned months in advance and part of the plan involves whether there is a Spurs match - because if there's not, you know I'm choosing a different time!' he laughs. 'We came to Britain for ten days but unfortunately the game was postponed so I went to Charlton Athletic instead! I froze my butt off, but I had great seats because only one third of the stadium was full.'

Before our chat ends, John tells me about another Spurs-related bucket list item he is desperate to tick off some time soon.

'I would love to see Spurs play away from home. I wouldn't care where, it's more about the experience. Just taking a bus or train ride with a bunch of supporters and getting to a town or city to take over a few pubs or a square and just having a good time and experiencing things as an away fan. It's something I've never done but it's something I would like to do.'

One small person craving the experience of seeing Tottenham play at home rather than away is my son, Jacob. With last summer's World Cup having a galvanising impact on his love of the game in much the same way Euro '96 had for me at his age, he had only visited the old White Hart Lane stadium once. With plenty of Wembley games under his belt and a painfully dull goalless draw up at the Stadium of Light to show for his efforts since, the Brighton fixture falling in the unusually late Easter school holidays means we're London-bound for his first visit to the new ground.

The usual mix of Haribo and chat is slightly off-kilter these days as he tends to counteract the long drive south with whichever handheld device he's laid his hands on as we head out of the door. I've got BBC 6 Music for company while he involuntarily yelps and shrieks at whatever game is dominating his Kindle screen, and punctuated by mouthfuls of e-numbers between Mansfield and Luton.

Learning from my car parking faux-pas against Palace, and with little room in the passenger seat for any pensionable 'samaritans' this evening, we park in the grounds of Haringey Borough FC a mile or so out from the ground to walk in. It's a friendly reception from a club I'd kept an eye out for since FA Cup First Round weekend and it's nice to think that the by-product of our £15 parking fee is diverting some much-need investment back into grassroots football.

'Why do we have to walk so far, Dad?' is the familiar moan from my pre-teen. Those Ford sponsorship commercials really do have a lot to answer for. Even on the third or fourth visit, the stadium's majesty is enough to transport grown adults into 10-year-olds as we get closer; imagine what it must look like to an actual 10-year-old. We've arrived with enough time to browse the superstore, take a few pictures and grab a pulled pork burger with a pint of reasonably priced Neck Oil – brewed by the brilliant Beavertown in the bowels of the huge stadium - before I can no longer delay the inevitable for him as we attempt to learn the meaning of deferred gratification.

'Can we go to our seat yet? I want to see it!' Jacob pleads. Our vantage point sits midway up the North Stand facing towards the wall of sound and the cockerel tonight. With the stadium still half empty, we climb the dozen or so steps towards the entrance to our block with the panorama that's about to hit him coming into focus with each stride.

'Smile!' I say as he takes in the view and turns to pose for the camera so his mum can share in his reaction. He's staring at me, slack-jawed at what he's witnessing. 'I can't,' he replies genuinely. 'It's just too amazing!' It's a photo I'll treasure forever.

The game itself is perhaps not quite as memorable. Chris Hughton, still a popular figure at Spurs having spent half of his sixty years either on the field or in the dugout at White Hart Lane, has set his side up to defend with their lives tonight as they seek precious points in their battle against the drop. As a result, the game has a similar training exercise feel that the Huddersfield match had – except, this time, the more organised Seagull's backline combined with Spurs appearing drained from the exertions of recent weeks makes this look an altogether trickier proposition.

Step forward Christian Eriksen. Rumoured to be seeking a new challenge in the summer in one of the worst kept secrets in football, the Dane had dropped below his usual high standards for considerable periods this season. While his detractors would point towards a disappointing propensity to fail to beat the first man on a corner – my own dad included – and with his eye seemingly straying towards new pastures, he had remained a talisman and matchwinner at key times against Burnley and Inter Milan and would do so again here when Spurs needed it most.

With two minutes to play, frustration in the stands growing and every Brighton man behind the ball, Eriksen received the ball 30 yards out, strode forward into space and arrowed the ball into the bottom corner beyond the despairing dive of Mat Ryan to take the roof off once more.

It's as crucial a goal as any so far this season, giving vital breathing space in the top four chase, with just three games left to play. It's taken 29 shots on goal with just five on target as Brighton threw everything on the line to grab a crucial point in vain. The 79% possession highlights how embarrassingly one-sided the whole affair had been but that moment of magic from the Dane would seal all three points and pile the pressure on Manchester United and Arsenal the following night. It would be a test both would fail against Manchester City and Wolverhampton Wanderers respectively.

Outside, a neon traffic sign urges fans to 'Please Walk Slowly' – a message that appeared to have been the gist of Hughton's halftime team talk. 'I'm on it for Ajax,' says my mate Dan, the ticket guru who is hitching a lift back to Nottingham with us, on the long walk back to Haringey. 'Amsterdam is my spiritual home.'

Spurs finally had one foot firmly in next season's Champions League. It was now time to focus on what had seemed unthinkable for so long – booking a place in the European Cup Final.

MAY

15
ONE MOURA GAME
PUNJABI SPURS

They say if you know your history, it's enough to make your heart go woah-oh, or something. While it's never been medically proven, it's hard to deny there isn't a little flicker when you delve back into the archives. So when historians relive the moment Spurs booked a place in the Champions League semi-finals half a century from now, and the book you're currently reading is considered an account of the dawn of the greatest period of dominance football has ever seen (fingers crossed, eh?), it will be worth reminding them what had transpired in the previous fifty years or so that had made it such a spectacular achievement.

Back in 1962, as Bill Nicholson's double winners tried to defend their second league title, there had been another European Cup semi-final against Eusebio's Benfica. A hugely unfortunate 3-1 defeat at The Stadium of Light left Spurs with a mountain to climb in the second leg – a situation exacerbated fifteen minutes in when they conceded again in front of more than 60,000 at White Hart Lane.

Spurs reduced the deficit through Bobby Smith and a Blanchflower penalty, but it would be a near miss that would haunt the club for decades. It would take Harry Redknapp, then just a 15-year-old West Ham trainee having signed with Spurs as a schoolboy, to eventually guide them back to European football's top table almost half a century later and within touching distance of matching that maiden campaign at the first time of asking. We'll draw a veil over the Adebayor-inspired stuffing at the hands of Real Madrid.

The defeat had steeled Tottenham towards a sprint finish in the league after a shaky spell during late winter – sound familiar?

– but, ultimately, a home defeat to eventual champions Ipswich Town, on their way to overturning Burnley at the summit of the First Division, proved decisive.

Those looking to the history books for guidance could perhaps find some parallels. The late winter wobble had extended well into Spring after the defeat of Brighton, as the invincibility of the Tottenham Hotspur Stadium was broken by West Ham. The ignominy of being so close to the away end as the gloating Hammers secured both the first away goal and away victory at the new ground - a badge of honour they also claimed at the Emirates over a decade earlier - had brought everyone back down to earth.

If the stakes for the visit of Ajax weren't already high enough, they carried a little more trepidation as a result; losing to West Ham can do that to you. It was well-warranted as the young Dutch side played fearlessly with a nod to the great attacking sides of the mid-90s and earlier still in the days of van Basten, and Cruyff before him. With the two favourites for the competition slogging it out in the other semi-final and Barcelona securing a convincing 3-0 lead to take back to Anfield, the meeting of the two rank outsiders would end in a 1-0 home defeat for Spurs in a game where they never really got going. Work to do in Amsterdam, then.

A trip to the south coast to face Bournemouth, a side Spurs had despatched with relative ease on six out of seven occasions since their promotion to the Premier League, would provide the opportunity to instil some much-needed confidence at least, and that much-needed sprint finish in the league. With victory offering the chance to secure a top three spot, it would also remove the growing worry of being caught by their rivals for the Champions League places. That was until an uncharacteristic display of anger saw Heung Min-Son dismissed just before the break before Juan Foyth, a half-time sub for Eric Dier who had been lucky to escape a second yellow himself, lunged in to see red just two minutes and 13 seconds after coming on.

If the display hadn't been 'Spursy' enough, an exasperated

Pochettino would see his nine men battle and compete doggedly for the remainder of the game before conceding a 91st minute Nathan Ake winner from a set piece. The identities of Tottenham old and new had never seemed so intertwined as the chance to secure Champions League football now looked certain to be decided on a nervy final day against Everton.

'I can't get tickets,' Dan texts after the match as a disappointing day is completed with the realisation that we won't be on our way to Amsterdam. 'I've tried everyone. Let's keep our powder dry in case we reach the Final.' It wasn't looking promising on either front.

Some respite would arrive the following day in the shape of Arsenal Football Club. So often our tormentors over the last few decades, the balance of power in North London that had been argued for the best part of fifteen years was now unequivocally back in Tottenham's favour having kept their near neighbours out of the Champions League for two consecutive seasons. Another year of supremacy had looked guaranteed for large parts of this season, too, until Tottenham's standing in lower midtable of the form guide had left the door open for a late twist in the tale.

Step forward Chris Hughton. Deploying tactics not dissimilar to the Seagull's visit to Spurs just a few weeks earlier, and with his club confirmed safe for another season thanks to the inadequacies of Neil Warnock's Cardiff City, the former Tottenham fullback saw his side hold on for a deserved point at the Emirates Stadium against an Arsenal team who became increasingly desperate in their search for a late winner. There were tears at the end as Aaron Ramsey cited his move to Juventus was about playing Champions League football again – a claim that was enjoyed by Spurs fans everywhere given it would now take a ten-goal turnaround on the final day to usurp Tottenham from their top four berth. Anyone who'd supported Spurs for longer than five minutes knew that wasn't the sort of mathematics that should be ignored. It would not be over until it was over.

The night before Ajax, Liverpool faced Barcelona in the other semi-final looking to overturn a 3-0 deficit. It could have been worse in the Nou Camp when Ousmane Dembele scuffed a tame shot into Alisson's hands in injury time when one-on-one. That moment would prove to be pivotal as Liverpool completed an astonishing comeback to book a spot in Madrid. To paraphrase one presumptuous Spurs fan on Twitter some 24 hours before our own return leg: I'd come to terms with the prospect of losing the Final to a bit of Messi brilliance but I'm not sure I can cope with it being a James Milner penalty.

While a small proportion of Liverpool supporters have an ingrained intensity that's enough to wind up even the most placid of fanbases, I'd never particularly minded them until the 2-2 draw at Anfield the previous season. They'd always been a more palatable alternative to Arsenal, Chelsea and Manchester United in the barren seasons when European football was something Spurs fans spectated rather than participated in, but the online vitriol aimed towards Harry Kane that would continue into the World Cup became especially tiresome.

I watched Liverpool's 2005 'Istanbul' final on my first ever holiday with my girlfriend, now wife, in Rhodes. We were in the hotel bar with a few dozen other tourists in that rubbish bit of a holiday waiting for the bus to take us to the airport and I found myself sat next to a slightly unhinged Liverpool fan I'd inadvertently befriended. The only time we'd seen him all week was when he was arguing with his girlfriend by the pool, at the restaurant or on their balcony.

They'd subsequently split up and she was on the way back to the airport in a taxi, so I was the next best thing and, perhaps subconsciously sensing everyone else was giving him a wide berth, he stuck to me like glue during the first half while knocking beer bottles over, swearing at the TV and generally being a bit of a nuisance to anyone in earshot.

3-0 down at half-time, he was inconsolable. Even though I'm not sure I believed it, I told him all wasn't lost: get one back early in the second half, grab another halfway through and pile on for a late equaliser. I remember him telling me he was feeling better about things. We all know how that went. By the time Alonso stepped up for the penalty at 3-2, he was stood directly behind my plastic patio chair and I'm convinced he'd have ripped my head clean off if Xabi hadn't missed it first.

The coach arrived to pick us up ten minutes into extra time and even I was gutted to be leaving behind what was clearly a Final for the ages; I can't imagine how he felt. As we passed every bar on the way to the airport, the few of us who cared about the match would strain our eyes to see what was happening on tiny distant screens; the commentary in Greek on the radio was a tricky listen for figuring out what was happening.

He, and all of us, found out the result over the coach tannoy when the driver said 'Liverpool. Win.' in a thick Greek accent and off he went again while Susan from Stockport was just nodding off. I'm pretty sure everyone on that bus wanted to kill him, with his now ex-girlfriend waiting at the airport with his passport at the front of the queue, but we'd made a bond. I felt like I'd been there for him in his time of need. I celebrated with him like it was Spurs because, on finding out his team had achieved the near impossible on a coach full of Mancunians who hated him, all he needed was a mate to share it with. When we got back to Manchester, he asked if we could swap numbers and said he'd text me for a meet-up, but it never happened.

I thought of him after that Barcelona comeback as I reached to the back of the cupboard in search of some long-forgotten ouzo. I wondered where he is now and how he's getting on. Did he settle down and sort himself out a bit? Was he there in the crowd at Anfield? Did him and his girlfriend ever kiss and make up?

I would have text him to find out, but it's been 14 years and Lynsey made me wrong-number him and delete his contact from my phone before we'd even made it back over the Peaks. He's probably in prison to be fair.

And so, it was on to the Netherlands, where the Amsterdam Spurs had laid on a treat for visitors to the Dutch capital. Clive

Allen, Graham Roberts and special guest Martin Jol, a man I would personally credit with laying the foundations on the pitch to get our great club back to where it is now, were all in attendance for a Q&A. He's still got no hair, but nobody cares.

With Champions League football as good as secured and a 1-0 deficit to chase down, there was certainly a cup final feeling among the travelling faithful as Spurs walked out into the Johan Cruyff Arena; not that Jacob and I could comment as we looked jealously on from our sofa in Derbyshire. There was no need for the same pep talk I'd attempted to give my son ahead of the Manchester City game. He knew the score this time – quite literally. So, when Dušan Tadić forced a corner in the fourth minute, we were already braced for a stressful evening. When Matthijs de Ligt, the 18-year-old Ajax captain who'd been linked with Tottenham the previous summer, broke free of Kieran Trippier's marking to head home the resulting cross and double the Dutch side's aggregate advantage, Jacob also learnt what déjà vu meant.

Had Heung Min-Son's run and shot not cannoned off the near post and away to safety almost immediately from the restart, there might have been cause to suggest we were watching a re-run from the Etihad. Instead, another mistake from Trippier to allow Tadic to feed Hakim Ziyech for a superb second left Tottenham needing to match the heroics of Liverpool the previous night to join them in Madrid.

'If we go another goal down, it's bedtime,' I told my son. 'School in the morning.' He put up a half-hearted protest but we'd both accepted the inevitable by this point. By the time Spurs emerged for the second half, they needed to score at least three goals without reply. With one eye already on the Final, the stadium PA system blasted Bob Marley and the Wailers out as the teams returned to the field – and seemingly with good cause. After Fernando Llorente's much-scrutinised tie-deciding goal at the Etihad three weeks earlier, Spurs had found the back of the net once in the eight hours of football since - Christian Eriksen's late winner at Brighton. They'd had more red cards than goals in the intervening period. Don't worry about a thing, indeed.

If nothing else, Liverpool had at least provided Tottenham with a blueprint to believe 24 hours earlier. Spurs duly pulled a goal back ten minutes into the second half. The trickery of Danny Rose and long ball infield was knocked on by Lucas Moura to Dele who drove at the heart of the Ajax defence. With De Ligt still upfield and the little Brazilian sprinting into the space left behind, Lucas takes control with two incredible touches to break into space and then slot the ball across the retreating Onana into the far corner and reduce the deficit.

'There are the first signs of concern here in the stadium,' says commentator Darren Fletcher three minutes later as Spurs attack again to the sounds of whistles from the stands. This time, Son releases the much-improved Trippier on the right flank who plays a pacey, low ball into the box that diverts towards goal by Llorente. The big Spaniard sees his shot from four yards out saved miraculously by the Cameroonian 'keeper who then attempts to dive on the ball and somehow lets it slip from his hands. With speed of thought matched only by his feet, Moura takes control of the situation to create an inch of space and fire the ball into the far corner to equalise on the night with half an hour to play. Suddenly, the young heads of Ajax have dropped and the world-beating Tottenham we're treated to so occasionally are here. My son and I roar gutturally in one another's faces in the way that only football can make you from time to time.

The game calms down for a while, but not before Ziyech hits the post for Ajax with just over ten minutes to play. 'Things are happening,' says Jermaine Jenas in co-commentary without ever clarifying what; but he doesn't need to. Vertonghen hits the bar with a header with less than five minutes to go before a lunging follow-up is cleared off the line. A huge save from Lloris two minutes into the added five is followed by Llorente heading over from a corner with just over a minute left on the clock. The sight of Lloris heading up for the corner before downheartedly returning to his post is usually a sign of the last knockings in any cup tie. The booking Onana receives for taking more than twenty seconds to retrieve the ball, as Jacob and I despair on the sofa, feels like little more than a side note as the first tears begin to fall from my son's eyes.

'Come over here for a cuddle,' his mum says. 'He's OK here for a minute,' I reply on his behalf. 'It's not over yet,' I add, without believing it for a second. The agonising Llorente header over the bar was surely the final action.

What happened next will likely remain unsurpassed in my footballing life and, quite possibly, my entire life generally.

With Spurs throwing everything at their opponents from Onana's long goal kick, a clearing header from De Ligt to meet Trippier's hoof forward falls to Sissoko and the Frenchman sends another long lump upfield that's knocked down by Llorente. Outmuscling the young Ajax captain, who has dropped too deep to defend his own poor clearance, the ball rebounds off Fernando in the sort of clumsy way to which we've become accustomed. There's a slip from the defender which allows space for Dele to play a delicate ball inside to the advancing Lucas Moura, who instinctively lashes the ball towards goal between two defenders, beyond Onana and into the bottom corner.

It's a match-winning hat-trick in a Champions League semi-final in the most dramatic of circumstances. All three goals are scored with his supposedly weaker left foot. For the first time in the tie, Spurs have the lead. There have been 95 minutes and one second played as the ball crosses the line.

The next few minutes are a blur. I know that I sprinted from one corner of my living room and back again to pound my fist against a wall. I know that my son's tears instinctively turned to howls of joy and that my wife and dog joined in. Up in the stands, Harry Kane and Davinson Sanchez make their way towards the field of play where Pochettino, Dier, Wanyama and more are celebrating on the pitch while several thousand fans lucky enough to have a ticket are a mass of jumping limbs embracing one another. The Spurs pile-on that ensues in the far corner is in sharp contrast to the Ajax team who lay face down on the field.

There's just enough time to restart, and for the home side to make their way worryingly into the opposition half for a moment, but by the time the full-time whistle is blown, Harry Kane is pitch side and testing out that ankle as he sprints to join the action – it's later revealed he gave a chunk of the half-time team talk - while Pochettino grabs anyone within hugging distance as he loses all control of his emotions. It's a magical moment that no Spurs fan could have dared to dream of; not least Josh Sandhu, founder of Punjabi Spurs and generally a bit of a blubbering mess himself, high up in the stands. He's in good company.

'We said before the quarter final draw that if we did get through that Ajax is a perfect European tie for us to go to,' he'd tell me a few days later once he'd returned to his home in Wolverhampton and composed himself a little. 'It's a historical European team, it's a great city anyway and it just ticked all the boxes, so we were gonna go no matter what. After what we did at City, which was just unbelievable, and then losing 1-0 at home, it was a case of win, lose or draw, we'd just get out there anyway and go and enjoy a historic game. We are still in the semi-final at the end of the day.'

Josh's approach to the semi-final was echoed by many. The consensus appeared to be around not getting too greedy. We'd used up our miracles in Manchester. Perhaps it comes from more than a decade waiting for a trophy beyond a League Cup – a collective decision not to get our hopes up too high for fear of them being dashed.

'I love their fans as well,' Josh continues. 'They've got a loyal fan base and they are fantastic. You just knew it was going to be a great spectacle and it did not fail to deliver, everything about it. I've got to say it's my most complete trip ever as a fan without a shadow of a doubt. Obviously, the result was the icing on the cake, but the fans in the square and the fans in the city the day before was brilliant. You can walk around and just chant anywhere. You'd see another Spurs fan walking around who would chant back to you. There was no trouble with the police, they didn't overpower us and really let us enjoy the city. We just had a really, really good time so even before the game I said win, lose or draw, it's no problem. We've had a great time, a great run and a great trip, they've done us proud.

'When we went 1-0 down, fans were obviously getting a bit on edge, but even then, we said we just needed two, so nothing has really changed and it just carried on. Then we conceded a second and everybody felt this sombre atmosphere. And then for that 2nd half to happen the way it did it was just unbelievable,' he says, the disbelief still audible in his voice. 'I've never experienced anything like it in my life. It was just unbelievable, absolutely unbelievable.'

The good-natured atmosphere extended beyond the game as well with Ajax fans accepting the cruel twist of fate with good grace. Josh continues: 'There were guys applauding us at the end of the game, that's always a nice touch. We were walking around the stadium singing and I had Ajax fans shaking my hand and vice-versa once we got to the central square. Everything about it was just complete. The Bob Marley song that was played at half-time stood out for me, don't worry about a thing, every little thing is going to be alright. That was the song we walked out of the stadium to and sang all the way into the city. Everything about it was just magical.'

Like so many who'd shared their experience after the game, both inside the stadium and across the globe, an unplanned and uncontrollable emotion had also overcome Josh. 'I've cried three times over Spurs. The first time was when we went 1-0 down in the cup final in 1991 but only because my cousins were picking on me when Pearce put that free kick in. I was only ten.

'The next time I cried, it was tears of joy and emotion, when we left White Hart Lane for that final game. I had some tears then only because everything I loved and admired and grew up with and experienced with the club was there. It was the end of an era. But I never ever thought a football match, an actual football match, would bring me to tears. I can't even count how many times I had tears or welled up, it was just mad, just the greatest thing ever. To know that my club has reached the pinnacle, has reached the ultimate stage for any club competition, for any club team in Europe, is such a proud moment, to be part of that history, it was just the best. I just got overwhelmed mate. I was like a baby a couple of times, I must have cried God knows how many times. A couple of lads asked if I was alright, but it's where we've come from to get here,' he gushes.

'It's the attachment we have with our club. I always said when I had nothing, I had Tottenham Hotspur Football Club. If I was down as a kid, I had football, whether it was playing it or watching our heroes like Gazza or Klinsmann or Ginola. And we've not been showered or spoilt with too many days of success and glory but when it comes, we really enjoy it. I'm just so proud of the boys throughout the season. Playing away from home again most of the season, we've qualified for the Champions League again and we're in the Final. We haven't signed a player yet, but we've delivered what was needed from us. Talking to everybody about it, nobody can get their head around it.'

Josh's summary of an extraordinary season is a fair one and, while he admits to possibly getting carried away, it leaves him confident enough to make a bold prediction about Madrid.

He continues: 'I'd even say winning the Final, I don't know if I could feel what I felt against Ajax. We'd have to be six down and come back! That might be rubbish, but it was just unbelievable. 3-0 down at half-time, a hat-trick, we hit the bar and they hit the post. The game itself was just an emotional rollercoaster. I didn't cry after the City game, I was just in shock. People asked if City was the best game I'd ever been to and it's up there, but the best was beating Arsenal 5-1. Ajax is knocking on the door of that now. We were there an hour and a half celebrating, the team came out twice to join us. It will live with me forever.'

Since the final whistle blew, rumours over ticket allocations and loyalty points were rife. With Liverpool getting a 24-hour head start on travel plans from the UK, flights had more than quadrupled in price, while hotels across Madrid were already cashing in on the increased interest. Despite this, Josh was already well on his way to organising the group trip of a lifetime.

'Everyone has different plans, driving in or flying in from everywhere. It's just crazy. I can't describe or express that feeling since the final whistle blew in Ajax.

'It's not like before where you play all season and hope for a cup final at the end of it. We play big games every other week, like Real Madrid last season, Dortmund, the big games in the Premier League. If you've won one of those games, you feel that euphoria anyway – how do you surpass that as a fan? In my eyes, they are already winners. They've made me so proud.'

Josh's Tottenham origin story goes back over 30 years. Brought up in Stoke-on-Trent surrounded by Manchester United fans, it was a quirk of fate that led him to discover Spurs as his footballing love.

'When I was a kid, I was just a football fan and obsessed with everything football,' he explains. 'If there was a sticker with a football on it, I'd want it. I collected my first sticker album in 1987 and the only team I completed was Tottenham – so that became my team. I didn't know where Tottenham was, I didn't realise it was in London. I lived a stone's throw from Stoke's old Victoria Ground, and I'd see loads of people going to football all the time. Port Vale weren't far, so I grew up thinking all football grounds were all close by because I lived so close to one!' he laughs.

'I used to follow the results on Ceefax and collect all the posters. I remember the euphoria of Gazza signing and then the 1990 World Cup cementing that feeling. I knew that Tottenham were my club. Then watching the 1991 semi on my own and running around the house going mad because my team was in the FA Cup Final. Everyone I'm related to is a Manchester United fan so when they beat Palace the previous year, it was a party atmosphere and I remembering wishing my team could do that – so to do it the following year was my proudest moment ever. My walls were splattered with posters of the 1991 win for about five years – I never took them down - so I was heartbroken when Gazza and Lineker left. Then Klinsmann arrived and my love for Tottenham just grew and grew.'

Not put off by the stars of 1990 departing and the mid-90s nadir setting in just as Manchester United grew to the peak of their powers, teenage Josh was more obsessed than ever before as he scraped enough together to watch his heroes in action. It would be a rare foray into Europe under the floodlights following the Worthington Cup win over Leicester that would provide his first Spurs match in the flesh.

He continues: 'I learned about the history of the club and the great players we had along the way. I was on £2.83 an hour in 1998 and saving up for a good year or so to get a ticket for a game; my first Spurs match turned out to be Tottenham versus Kaiserslautern in the UEFA Cup. I'd moved to Wolverhampton by then and I asked my brother who lived in London if he could take me. I got a train down and he took me there after work. Neither of us had been to White Hart Lane before and I remember missing kick-off by a couple of minutes.

'My seat was in the West Stand and all I could see were these glowing lights on the pitch. The first person I saw was David Ginola. I think my seats were in the front row and I can't remember much about it – Steffen Iversen scored the winner, a penalty – but I was just in awe, admiring the players, intoxicated by the stadium, the atmosphere – just the whole experience. These were my boys and I was there! I loved all football and I'd been to see Stoke and Wolves before, but I remember thinking this is my life, but this isn't my club. On that night in 1999, it was just falling in love and knowing this is it; this is my club.'

Just over a year later, Josh's long-distance relationship became more conventional when he moved to Wembley. At first, he struggled to get tickets until a friend of his brother's began offering a spare season ticket. 'I used to buy it for £22 and I did that for a good few years. They'd always get to the Arsenal, Chelsea, Liverpool and United games but not the Everton, Newcastle, Bolton, Villa...I'd go on my own and watch the game and I did that for a number of years.'

Fast forward a couple of decades and the Champions League Final will be Josh's 39th game of 2018/19. It's a far cry from just a few seasons ago when he gave up going so regularly due to affordability after getting married. 'I'd go to five or six games a season for about seven years but I'm back on it now,' he continues. 'People say you jump on the bandwagon, but I jumped off just as we were getting good! But I'm back now.'

I reflect on my own childhood, longing for the days when someone might accuse me of being a glory supporter for following Tottenham. Quarter of a century later, I'm still waiting, but it's getting closer at least. 'I wish somebody would call me a glory fan too, it'd be brilliant,' Josh concurs.

Spending more quality time with Tottenham also coincided with the launch of Punjabi Spurs, a project that's close to Josh's heart for reasons beyond football. 'I love the global growth Spurs are trying to achieve,' Josh continues. 'Spurs are probably the best when it comes to America and Australia but not when it comes to places like India. And then you've got a lot of people of Asian origin in the UK who are Spurs fans and the stigma of going to games, you should avoid this, people of colour have this or that problem. I wanted to beat that and not to do it in a way that created a divide, I wanted to do it in a way that celebrated the relationship between the culture of football and individual cultures.

'I remember being in Turkey and looking at these fans. Fans in Israel and Dortmund – aren't these fans amazing? But we have that as well, and I wanted to celebrate on a bigger scale and not be segregated because Spurs are a really diverse club. People say it's breaking down barriers, but I think it's building bridges. It should be about what we do with football because it gets a lot of stick and is linked with hooliganism and racism – I want to flip that around. That's individuals and that's the minority causing those kinds of problems. Football is the language of the world. That's what we do through the supporters' club. Spurs took that onboard and they welcomed it with open arms.'

Launched in 2017, they had a spectacular half-time introduction in October – a match I remember well given it was the first time in five attempts that Jacob had seen Spurs win a game!

Josh continues: 'In the first year, we did a cultural dance at half-time that's never been done in Premier League football – it's been done in basketball but not football. Bhangra dancing is part of the Punjabi community, so they said they wanted to dance to what they dance to – but we said this is about embracing cultures. We're at Tottenham so we're going to combine the two.

'The first songs were western songs mixed with Asian songs and then there was Chas and Dave. It was brilliant, it got such a good reception, and then we won our first game at Wembley! We scored two minutes after half-time!' he laughs. Josh is clearly claiming that three points as his own, and well he might, considering he was halfway back to his seat when the winning goal went in. The video was popular both here and in Punjab. 'I had family in India messaging me asking if I'd seen it,' Josh continues. 'I replied telling them that, if they looked closely, I was in the background!'

That was just the beginning for the newly formed supporters' club – something Josh credits the support of club representative Jonathan Waite with, who sadly passed away suddenly earlier this season - and they've been doing good deeds in between football matches ever since. Josh continues: 'After that, we took Ledley King to the temple to celebrate Diwali. We paid respects to the diverse cultures who lost their lives on Remembrance Day. The Punjabi culture is about selfless service, so we ran a soup kitchen in Tottenham with Ledley King. We're trying to do ground breaking stuff and we've got Jonathan to thank for the support he showed us in those early days,' Josh continues, before revealing that they'll be taking Spurs legend Ossie Ardiles to the Punjab for a tour to reach new fans in India over the summer.

As our chat comes to an end and we exchange giddy predictions for Madrid, it seems a fitting time to reflect on the season that Spurs have given us so far. Josh is in little doubt that the achievements of the previous ten months have far surpassed anything we could have reasonably expected given the stadium delay.

He says: 'My outlook was always that, no matter what, we were going to end up in the new ground. Whether it was straight away or a few months, it didn't matter to me. It wasn't nice going to Wembley, but I knew we were going home. I felt for the boys not getting the support. You'd look at our team thinking they don't deserve this – what more do you want from these guys? The players on the pitch have delivered for us as much as they could, and Wembley was good for me as a fan as it was easier to get to. I had no qualms about Wembley and was in no rush to go home, but when we did it was a rush that went back into the club.

'There's a unity and a glow about the club again. I drove to Bournemouth three and a half hours by myself and three and a half hours back. People ask me why I do it but it's like a drug, you just never know what is going to happen and you don't want to miss it. That's what being a football fan is about and if it wasn't for that, you wouldn't witness the Ajax game or the Arsenal 5-1. That's what football is about and victory against Liverpool now – I don't know what I'd do. But the boys have done brilliantly this season and I'm proud of them; I've never been prouder.'

With that sentiment in mind, there is only one way to finish a chapter about one of the most iconic games in our storied history. Providing a piece of commentary up there with 'And still Ricky Villa!', it comes courtesy of BT Sport's Darren Fletcher and is supplemented by the near orgasmic moans of Jermaine Jenas in co-commentary, a former Tottenham player who would be reduced to tears by the end of the night live on air. Take it away, boys:

'Here's Deli Alli. Here's Lucas Moura, OH THEY'VE DONE IT! I CANNOT BELIEVE IT! LUCAS MOURA WITH THE LAST KICK OF THE GAME! THE AJAX PLAYERS COLLAPSE TO THE GROUND! TOTTENHAM HOTSPUR ARE HEADING TO THE CHAMPIONS LEAGUE FINAL!'

Incredible. Still utterly unbelievable. Madrid? We're on our way.

JUNE

16
DON'T CONCEDE EARLY

'Well done, mate!'

'Congratulations! You must be thrilled!'

'When's the big day then? I bet you can't wait!'

In the 48 hours that followed Tottenham Hotspur's breathtaking win over Ajax, I and many more Spurs fans around the world had been greeted by everyone they came across like a new arrival was on the cards or an engagement to be married had been agreed. The genuine outpouring of incredulity and warmth from football fans of all teams (barring a few notably quiet London rivals, of course) was unlike anything I'd experienced before – I suppose that's what happens when you've only really got a Carling Cup win for comparison.

On the eve of what would now be the penultimate game of the season against Everton, and in anticipation of a higher than usual influx of fans from around the globe for the conclusion of the Premier League campaign, the football club organised their annual Supporters' Club celebration event at the stadium. Compered by regular half-time host Paul Coyte and with a guest appearance from Ledley King – a hero I was beginning to feel quite blasé around, such was our obvious connection following a brief chat in Leeds a few months earlier – this was an insider's event attended by fans from around the world to hand out player and supporter awards before rounding off the afternoon with a stadium tour. Given this access-all-areas offering wasn't yet open to the general public, there was a ripple of excitement in the room at this revelation in a variety of languages, including within the gaggle of Yorkshire Spurs attendees that included Paul, Ro and I. Yorkshire is practically its own language, after all.

There were two standing ovations given by the couple of

hundred fans in attendance; one for the arrival of the former captain and club legend who is better than John Terry and the other for Stacy Haley, Supporters' Clubs Operations Manager. Looking visibly moved by the reaction her arrival prompted, she spoke passionately of plans to improve the offering for all 200 supporters' clubs – a landmark figure reached during the season about to end - to reward the loyalty shown across the globe. The pride of the football club to have reached such a significant strategic goal in the quest for global domination was evident in her words, as was the desire to nurture their continued organic growth while reaping the commercial benefits. With astronomical progress being made on and off the pitch, though, it would be churlish to criticise any objective that helped to retain a grassroots connection to the fanbase.

Coytey regaled the crowd with anecdotes of his time at Spurs in a role most fans dream of, from struggling to step one foot in front of the other through nerves having first trodden on the hallowed turf on his maiden half-time engagement to accidentally upsetting the temperamental Mido at a man of the match presentation by likening him to David Beckham – a comparison the Egyptian did not appreciate or, if we're being honest with ourselves, wholly merit.

He then made his way around the room interviewing fans as if they were half-time guests, with reflections on Amsterdam dominating his interrogations. There were loud cheers for the representative from Brazil Spurs as she expressed her pride over Lucas and a suggestion for Delhi Spurs to add the word 'Alli' into their name. The star of the show, however, was Mahmoud, representing Malaysia Spurs, who'd travelled over with my friend Amir.

'I ran through to the bedroom to wake my wife to tell her the score - she had gone to bed when we were losing 2-0,' he shared excitedly. 'And how did you react when the winning goal went in?' enquired Coytey. 'It is fasting month,' Mahmoud continued, referring to the holy month of Ramadan, 'and I was eating my morning rice. It went into the air like confetti!' he beamed, to cheers from the audience.

There was a little disappointment amongst the Yorkshire Spurs contingent when Ro's piano-playing at the Ledley King night didn't win Supporters' Club Instagram Moment of the Year. Instead, the Ghana Spurs gang singing loud and proud after beating Arsenal in the Carabao Cup won through. A UK-based relative of the African club collected the award on their behalf and I celebrated inwardly a little knowing just how much it would mean to Eric and his collective.

Before being unleashed into the inner sanctum of the greatest stadium in the world, the biggest cheer of the entire afternoon came when Paul Coyte thanked those in attendance for their support before adding an unashamedly giddy: 'See you in Madrid!'

Hearing it said out loud a mere sixty hours or so after Moura's winner still didn't entirely make sense. Even a sneak preview of the season review film to be played during the Everton match appeared to have a surreal conclusion as the little Brazilian poked home the winner and pointed to the heavens with his eyes closed – already an iconic image - as the room rang out with cheers again. For the first time since 1991, Tottenham's final league game of the season would not be their last. Pinch yourself and say it three times: Spurs are in the Champions League Final.

The party atmosphere of the following afternoon's Everton game was further boosted when Eric Dier poked us into an early lead. With fourth place all but sealed barring the kind of closing day disaster only Spurs could muster, there was one eye on trumping Chelsea into third place. Bettering the result they picked up at a tricky looking assignment against a resurgent Leicester might previously have been the all-encompassing objective in the warm spring sunshine. Instead, widespread celebrations were beginning to break out in the stands near us.

Having occupied third place courtesy of Dier's goal for most of the afternoon, a mini-implosion with just under a quarter of the game to go saw Cenk Tosun and then Theo Walcott, a player who is always afforded a warm welcome in these parts, to turn the game in visitors' favour. A welcome goal direct from a Christian Eriksen free-kick – something of a collector's item this season – gave hope of a late winner for either the Lilywhites or Foxes to catapult Tottenham back into third but it wasn't to be. With 71 points sealed, the fourth placed finish that had once been our most cherished ambition to earn a seat at Europe's top table now came tinged with disappointment; and well it might after the dramatic collapse of a seemingly plausible title tilt in the first half of the season. But as the players paraded around the pitch, all thoughts, conversation and focus switched to Madrid and the chance to reflect on the progress being made in our new surrounds.

The festivities continued into the evening with live entertainment laid on for all fans who chose to hang around. Having spent much of the afternoon singing about having their very own party when Tottenham win the cup, a common kinship between Spurs and Everton fans, two of English football's established 'big five' in the days before the Premier League and a decade or three trying to keep up with noisy neighbours, was bordering on friendship by the end of the day. With a similar bond struck with Tranmere after January's FA Cup Third Round tie, it was becoming increasingly clear that most of the nation, and a significant proportion of Merseyside, would become honorary Spurs fans on Saturday 1st June. We'd never been so popular.

Liverpool's own league campaign had been thwarted at the very last. For the ten minutes that followed Sadio Mane's opening goal, Jurgen Klopp's men sat atop the Premier League by a point. For a further sixty seconds between Glenn Murray's opener for Brighton and Sergio Aguero's equaliser on the south coast, pandemonium had ensued inside Anfield at the prospect of a first league title since 1990. A City procession towards victory confirmed what many had already suspected; Vincent Kompany's Monday night winning thunderbolt against Leicester had ultimately decided the destination of the title.

Whether the disappointment would spur on the Scouse or add

pressure to a season where they risked becoming remembered as one of the very best sides to end a season trophyless was a conundrum that Spurs fans had plenty of time to consider. With twenty days between Everton and Liverpool, the excitement was unbearable. Until the ticket details were announced, at least.

My expectation of seeing Spurs finish the season in a Champions League Final the previous September had been so low that I'd automatically assumed the fabled road to Madrid that had been touted on advertising hoardings all season must mean the 81,044 capacity Santiago Bernabéu. Instead, it would take place in the 67,829-seater Wanda Metropolitano, the recently renovated home of Atletico, meaning the chances of a ticket were 13,000 light before I'd even googled it. Next came the allocations. At 17,000 apiece, it meant that even long-standing season ticket holders disgruntled at the club's recent changes to the loyalty points scheme wouldn't even be guaranteed a ticket. Finally, the explosion of interest in flights from the UK to Madrid in late May meant that prices had rocketed, while a bed for the night in even the most unappealing of locations was averaging around the £800 mark.

A joint statement from the representative supporters' trusts on either side urged UEFA to reconsider the division of tickets between competing clubs and competition sponsors while urging corporate organisations to make their allocations available to fans. Meanwhile, Tottenham issued a statement warning that any season ticket holder who listed their seat on third party sites for profit would face a ban. And yet still, tickets were openly changing hands for thousands of pounds.

'I have a ticket,' messaged Mark Lawson. 'Bought for ridiculous money via a reseller. If it doesn't work, I should still be able to get a refund and at least I'll be in Madrid.' Stories of such desperate measures even via Australia were not uncommon.

Paul Pavlou of Yorkshire Spurs, Josh Sandhu of Punjabi Spurs and Paul Ruscoe of New Zealand Spurs among others were all gearing up to cross land and sea. With around 40,000 Spurs fans alone expected to land in the Spanish capital in the 72 hours ahead of kick-off, the atmosphere was building even by the time Arsenal were being trounced by Chelsea in the Europa League Final. The lesser of two evils at least meant the red half of North London's Champions League participation would be delayed for at least another year.

'We're heading out there on Thursday and staying a couple nights just so we don't have to share the city with some Scousers!' said Josh. 'I've got a ticket but a lot of us haven't unfortunately which is never nice.'

Meanwhile, every supporters' club had long formulated their own plans for the big match and were widely reporting sell-outs. In Kuala Lumpur, Malaysia Spurs laid on two venues, with thought going into both those who would be fasting and others who might want to enjoy the game with a beer. LA required two additional venues above and beyond The Greyhound to offer 700 places for fans to watch the Final. Meanwhile, in Canada, John McClelland was teaming up with a neighbour he'd shared the aftermath of the semi-final win with.

'We're going to have an outdoor keg party at his house,' he told me. 'I'm supplying the beer and I've also got a big box of fireworks I have left over from my daughter's birthday party!'

My own plans for the Final had begun to form several weeks earlier. Spotting an opportunity for a week away during May half term, we'd booked a cut-price return to the same French campsite we'd spent the opening weeks of the season in. The flashbacks to watching that first defeat of the season at Watford on my daughter's pink Kindle screen while the rest of the pub disinterestedly watched the All Irish Final were strong as we drove towards our temporary home for the week ahead.

With no flights to worry about and a basic bed in the Spanish capital for the Friday night secured for just 70 euros, there was 'just' a 24-hour return drive between me and Madrid. The spacious family Kia would provide a haven for the night on the way home if required; the adrenaline of a Spurs win would be enough to fly me home but the fear of the return journey following defeat loomed large. Now there was just one ingredient missing – a ticket.

That was, at least, until the spacious family Kia was ruled out through injury. With almost a fortnight to go until the big match, a loud grumble from the engine followed by furious revving and plumes of white smoke from the exhaust spelled disaster. I spent the next hour on the hard shoulder of the M62, twenty minutes away from the stage in Hull I should have been performing on, waiting for the RAC. No gig, no fee, a long tow back to Derbyshire and the main family car down and out ahead of the biggest match of our lives. It would be my wife's somewhat inferior model that would be answering the call-up. Whether it would be the Gazzaniga or Vorm to my beloved Lloris remained to be seen.

We made it to France in the end and relaxed into our week of wine and bread in the sun, but I would catch my mind wandering towards travel plans for the weekend frequently. Trains and planes were still far too expensive, even from Brittany, leaving the car winning out as the cheapest and most practical option, while admittedly being the longest and most tiring. In truth, the prospect of driving down had seemed like the only option until I began saying it out loud to sane people.

'I hear you're off to Madrid on Saturday,' said the Chelsea-supporting dad of Jacob's new friend in the caravan opposite as we rehydrated after a punishing first half of 47-aside football on the campsite football pitch. 'You're DRIVING?' was his incredulous response when I confirmed the rumour. 12 hours didn't seem ridiculous to me but then I did also have a 62-year-old father ready to jump in the car at the first sniff of a ticket from Chesterfield if I could get him one as well, so maybe it was genetic.

I think our team won 127-126 in a game that had started a week last Tuesday, as is traditional with campsite football on a holiday park. My raking cross field balls were eventually cut out bravely by a hardy 11-year-old taking one directly in the face, so I retired to the goalkeeper position for the final ten minutes; safer for everyone, not least the brave and tearful young lad himself, who I promised to buy an ice cream by way of apology if I saw him again. That touch. You never lose it.

Spurs have made me do some ridiculous things over the years. I've prematurely booked holidays I can't afford to celebrate qualifying for Europe before ending up finishing 9th. I once took my new girlfriend, now wife, to see us lose 1-0 against Grimsby after a day out in Cleethorpes. Every midweek Champions League dash to Wembley and back with work the next day. All utterly bonkers and all absolutely worthwhile. Tottenham have besotted me since I was nine years old and love makes you do silly things.

I reckon leaving my sleeping family in Brittany at the crack of dawn to drive to Madrid just to be there, whether we won or lost and with or without a ticket, especially with my somewhat patchy navigational record, was up there. COME ON YOU SPURS!

The drive down wasn't too bad. Honking at cars, coaches and campervans displaying Spurs flags and stopping off for fuel and a rest at semi-regular intervals, I had a back catalogue of hugely entertaining The Spurs Show podcasts to catch up on and the giddy excitement of a schoolboy. Passing Bordeaux, crossing the motorway border that weaves through the edges of the Pyrenees and bearing down on the myriad of lanes leading past the Alcalá Gate, one of the Spanish capital's most famous tourist attractions, the realisation of it all truly hit me when my bag landed on the tile floor beside my modest hostel bed. As I wrestled the window open to allow a little air to circulate in the 30c early evening heat of my box room accommodation, there was no going back now. Ticket or no ticket – I had arrived. First stop: the pub with my Yorkshire Spurs friends.

'I had a nightmare getting here,' Pav shouts over the din of a live band in the first Irish bar we found, before going on to tell me of almost missing the flight out of the UK after delayed trains and no taxis. He ended up unnecessarily getting a train from Reus to Barcelona and then back again, just so he could reach his connection station on the return journey. Passing right by a nudist beach, twice, everyone onboard was offered a more generous glimpse of human flesh than they were prepared for. 'It went a bit faster on the way back, so it was just a glimpse,' he laughed.

'You should just write a book about everyone's story getting here,' he added as we moved away from the noise towards the back of the bar. It was true that every fan had their own extraordinary anecdote of the long journey down.

Among them was Mark Lawson of OzSpurs, a man I had never met but Skyped with and kept in touch via Facebook. Only that morning, he had been interviewed by BBC Radio 5 Live on his astonishing commitment to the cause. You can imagine my surprise then, to see Mark himself stood having a drink in the very same Irish bar we had just wandered through to find a quiet spot. 40,000 Spurs fans in Madrid and two supporters' club chairmen were frequenting the same bar without even realising it.

As we became acquainted and reacquainted and drank and sang with the healthy mix of Liverpool fans, it was everything English fans abroad should be. The fun would continue long into the night to the tune of Sweet Caroline and the nervous anticipation when midnight passed that today really was the day.

Sleeping off the beer wasn't easy in a Spanish heatwave. While one should never wish their life away, navigating the nine hours between hostel check-out and Wanda Metropolitano check-in would be a challenge. With stories throughout the afternoon of delayed planes still on English soil with just a few hours to go before kick-off, a mix of sympathy and incredulity alongside the twisted hope that the misfortune of others might throw up a spare ticket is a guilty admission that others also later shared. Around half of the couple of hundred fans in attendance at The Spurs Show live podcast recording were ticketless as Erik Thorstvedt, Stephen Mangan and, perhaps most surprisingly, former Director of Football Damien Comolli all eased the pre-match nerves with entertaining anecdotes of their wildly different Tottenham experiences. One thing this unlikely trio had in common at least was the prediction of a Tottenham victory in a high-scoring game.

Completing a hat-trick of chance meetings, I spotted Kiwi Spurs Chairman Paul Ruscoe posing for pictures with Erik the Viking after the show. Through this remarkable network of fans, another person who would have been a stranger to me twelve months earlier soon became a friend, as he and I joined his Kiwi companion Mike in the queue for another nearby Irish bar that was rumoured to be offering an entire floor apiece and big screens for fans of both teams ahead of kick-off.

As well as being 6'5" and an extremely amiable chap on first impressions, Chair of Kiwi Spurs Mike seemed familiar. Soon enough, he confirmed why that was, having made headlines with the story of his commitment to travel before discovering his Airbnb booking was cancelled, leaving him with no Spanish accommodation. This giant of a man had planned to sleep in a hire car in a leisure centre parking lot before a friend had saved the day and offered him a sofa.

'I can't believe I'm doing this as a 45-year-old man,' he'd told the New Zealand Herald of his plight. 'We've done our research. We chose the Espace because the seats turn around,' he'd continued cheerfully.

Joining the sweaty queue just after three in the afternoon, we sang, we chatted, and we waited. We waited a little longer and then longer still. As patience began to turn to frustration and anger that the doors weren't opening, and with no communication from the bewildered owners struggling to cope with the influx of fans attempting to get into their bar following the tipping out of the fan zones, a plan B began to form in my mind – but how all of this could have been avoided had UEFA had the foresight to show the match in a controlled fan zone as had been requested by both sides.

With three hours to kick-off and all remaining hope of a late ticket gone, hotfooting it back to my car at the other side of the city via taxi seemed the best option. With a third different Irish bar out by the Bernabéu located via a small gathering of Spurs fans already parked up there and calling for back-up on Twitter before the Liverpool fans arrived, it looked like the best opportunity to watch the match in the company of Spurs fans.

On a day when you're looking for any divine intervention from above, getting an Uber driver called Moussa felt like it might be one. 'You are Carl?' he said as I opened the door. 'That's me! And you must be Moussa? There's another Moussa in Madrid who'll be lifting the European Cup tonight,' I said, gesturing towards my shirt. He smiled politely and didn't speak to me again, but I still gave him five stars a 1€ tip for luck.

By the time I made it to Paddy's Irish Bar, the ratios had changed considerably. A sea of sweaty red shirts engulfed the main bar area with two small clusters of Spurs fans at opposite ends of the pub gathered around screens smaller than my plasma at home. In that moment, away from my son and with so many friends I'd spent the weekend with settling into their seats in the stadium, it was everything I'd hoped the trip wouldn't be. A minimum requirement of watching it in the pub would be to at least feel like it was home turf.

And then something happened. Pushed back into the corners, by the draughtless entrance and being inadvertently but collectively shoved by every Scouser on a cigarette break, a sort of Dunkirk spirit formed among us. There were the two brothers who'd driven down from Sheffield via Reading to be in Madrid. The three generations of the same family, with a youthful looking grandad, enjoying the match with his son and grandson. The youngest lad was a similar age to my own son and also had Lucas Moura's name and number on the back of his shirt for good measure. There were a pair of mates who'd travelled out together in hope of a ticket and the slight hothead of the group who visibly bit his lip as a rowdy, drunk but largely good-natured Liverpool fan tried to infiltrate our corner having seemingly been ejected from his own group for generally being too irritating.

As our newly formed tribe began to chat and bond, there were more tales of long-distance travel via European outposts, near misses on club loyalty points for a seat at the match and one fan who'd sold his ticket for £10,000 that very morning and regretted it for the remainder of the day. And then the singing started. Song after song, turning our blisteringly warm little corner of Madrid into an extension of N17 for the evening. From Glory, Glory to he's one of our own; we've got Alli to our increasingly wearing version of Allez, Allez, Allez, we rolled through classics, new and old. I even discovered kinship in the form of another fan who detested 'Mauricio Pochettino, he's magic you know' – I know it's a tricky rhyme, but we *have* had five years to come up with something better…

The team news that both Harrys Kane and Winks would return to the starting line-up after lengthy injury lay-offs prompted the same debates around Spurs-biased screens across the world, not least the huge ones shipped in for a sell-out crowd at the new stadium; well, for everyone not stuck in the queue for a beer in the food market at least.

Eric Dier's omission in the holding midfield spot alongside Sissoko was certainly less controversial than semi-final hat-trick hero Lucas Moura being the man to drop out for the return of Harry Kane. While a fully fit England captain was unquestionably the first name on the teamsheet, the sluggish returns to top form following the frequently required recoveries rushed ahead of schedule were hard to ignore. It had been 53 days since what had looked to be a season-ending injury had been dealt in the clash with Fabian Delph. While only Pochettino could truly judge his match fitness, his match sharpness was unquestionably lacking. Perhaps that would be true for both teams though, following the three-week rest period. It meant, at least, that no notable injuries provided more potential game-changing options than usual with Fernando Llorente joining the little Brazilian on a crowded bench.

For the record, I sided with Poch. I might have also made a case for a third option: Dele in the deeper midfield position over Winks to incorporate all of our attacking prowess into the starting line-up and find a way to use both matchwinners; but the threat of being overrun in the middle of the park, the temptation to bring back the pressing, forward-thinking style of Winks alongside the box-to-box stamina of Sissoko and a general lack of a plan B on the bench other than Fernando if Lucas had also started was the clear argument against this option. Romance aside, the best number nine in the world starts if he's fit enough. I'm no Mauricio, though, and I'm certainly not magic.

The sensation in the moments before kick-off was hard to explain. A kind of electricity surged through my body that might just have been the combined static of numerous sweaty strangers pressed against me. I thought back to all the Champions League Finals I'd watched over the years. My very first, the mesmerising young Ajax team of 1995, watching ITV's nostalgic coverage on a small TV in my bedroom. Manchester United's treble-sealing late show in '99 that had lifted me from my own seat at the sight of an English side winning the title in such dramatic fashion. Zidane's Hampden volley in '02, Liverpool's comeback in '05 and Bayern's victory over Klopp's Dortmund in the empty living room of the first house I ever bought on the weekend we moved out. I'd ensured the telly was last to go and the Sky box was still plugged in so I could watch it with a curry on the sofa as the last rite of a much-loved home.

And what of everything that had gone before in the many years before the rebranded Champions League model? The first five all won by a team just a mile from where I was stood, including a Di Stefano penalty that had got them on their way in front of 124,000 in that very stadium when my own father was a babe in arms. Jock Stein's 1967 winners, Busby's '68 team lifting the trophy at Wembley a decade after the Munich Air Disaster. There was Cruyff-era Ajax, Cloughie's back-to-back winners, the Villa team of '82 and a smattering of great Liverpool sides through the 70s and 80s all adding to the illustrious history of a 64-year-old tournament. And now, finally, against all the odds, this was Tottenham Hotspur's long-awaited Final debut and a chance to add a new chapter to the Glory, Glory European history of the pride of London.

I'd just about finished processing all of that when the ball hit the outstretched arm of Moussa Sissoko after 23 seconds and I instinctively wondered if you could retract an Uber review.

There was disbelief at first followed by the calming assertion on view of a replay that VAR would come to our rescue again. It didn't. As the referee pointed to the spot and waved away the protests, we knew Hugo's recent penalty-saving exploits would be our saviour once more. They weren't, even though he did come close to getting something onto Salah's mid-height strike down the middle. Two minutes into the biggest night of our lives and we were already a goal down. Oh, Tottenham, my Tottenham.

Level heads were needed on the pitch and in the pub; in the stands of Madrid and North London. Better to concede in the first minute than the last, we said. We've come back from much worse than this before, we chorused. But beneath that was the same niggling frustration: why did we *always* have to make it so hard for ourselves?

As both sides toiled in the heat, chances were few and far between as neither side looked at the fluent best that had so impressively overturned semi-final deficits when the odds had seemed stacked so firmly against them. Liverpool's chances were limited to long range shots, going close from both of their marauding young fullbacks, while Christian Eriksen's snatched chance just before half-time was fittingly representative of Tottenham's paltry attacking threat up to that point.

A half-time breather in the stifling heat offered a reminder as to why the pace of the game had perhaps been so pedestrian. For two free flowing, attacking sides, the defences had dominated, with Van Dijk in particular looking imperious at the back for Liverpool.

'Why didn't it go to VAR?' was the repeated cry as the half-time replays were shown. Why Sissoko's arm was outstretched was more the mystery. It certainly wasn't in its natural position and the ball appeared to strike it after rebounding off his body. It appeared to be the correct implementation of a ridiculous rule, making the whole situation all the harder to bear. One thing was for certain: had Sissoko's stock not risen so dramatically in the preceding ten months, he surely would not have been forgiven by a fanbase who had endured, rather than enjoyed, him for the early part of his Tottenham career. That no Spurs fan would even tolerate the suggestion the Frenchman was anything more than an innocent victim in the whole sorry scenario was testament to his progress – and popularity.

A fresher looking Tottenham emerged in the second half. Awoken from the stupor of their opening minute nightmare, a foothold in the game was slowly being built that saw them begin to dominate possession and carve out chances. While Liverpool still threatened, most notably through the unlikely boot of James Milner, it was the driving runs of Son and the newly introduced Moura, replacing Winks, that caused the most problems.

With 12 minutes to go, the vision of Kane – a bystander for long periods – to find Trippier on the flank, provided a half chance via the head of Alli before a double save from Son and Moura in quick succession began to reignite hope in the stands and in the corner of our tiny pub that the breakthrough was coming. Dele would be replaced by Llorente soon after, who joined Origi on the field in the unlikely role of miracle super sub, based on earlier rounds. It would be the Belgian rather than the Spaniard who would have the game's final telling moment.

With two minutes left to play, Liverpool's matchwinner against Barcelona fired the ball low and beyond Lloris to seal a sixth European title for the Merseysiders and strangle any hope of another injury time comeback. As the pub around us erupted into celebration and song, there was good natured consolation and congratulations offered. But amidst that, it was impossible to deny that this one stung more painfully than anything that had come before.

While the emotion of Ajax had never manifested itself in tears of joy for me personally, this certainly felt closer to the surface. A few fellow fans I'd shared the rollercoaster of an evening with saw fit to console me and I realised it was probably my duty to do the same. The two brothers who'd driven down from Sheffield, and were at least a full decade my junior, were also visibly close to tears.

Realising I was now perhaps of the generation who should be offering the same words of wisdom to my new, transient friends, I began to search for the words. I'd explained it all to my son several times over, but these lads were twice his age and so, as we stood there as fully-grown men, holding back a blub while Liverpool fans celebrated around us and commiserated us sportingly with handshakes, what could I say to soften the blow? With just a handful of League Cup runners-up spots, numerous FA Cup semi-final defeats and countless near misses in the league, what could I offer from my additional years of punishment to ease their suffering?

'Bloody hell,' I started. 'It's a long way home, innit?' I concluded. It got a laugh at least. But how far we'd come.

I didn't stay to watch the trophy being lifted. It hadn't even occurred to me that each Tottenham player would be presented with a losing medal. Instead, I trudged to the car and called my son, who was too tired and upset to form much more than one-word answers. I longed to be back with him. Having abstained from the beer for 24 hours, it was time to hit the road. While Liverpool fans began their parties in the street, ours was over. Mine was over. Tottenham Hotspur Football Club's season was finally over.

As I bedded down for a few hours in a Spanish picnic area close to the French border three hours later, looking up at an impossibly starry sky, I made a mental note to cancel the appointment to get Moussa Sissoko's face tattooed on my left arse cheek. There's always next season, isn't there? A full ten months in our wonderful new stadium. We might even sign someone.

'I am so focused to stay,' said Mauricio Pochettino in the days that followed. Plenty of reason to be optimistic then. For now, though, it was time to rest and relax. Only 69 more days until the new season starts. Next year's gonna be our year. I can feel it.

MADRID 2019: SUPPORTERS FROM ACROSS THE WORLD SHARE THEIR EXPERIENCE

Sverker Otterström – Sweden Spurs

I decided directly after the return leg at Ajax that I had to go to Madrid even though I understood that it would take a miracle for me to get a ticket to the final. Me and a friend had already booked a hotel in September to be prepared so it was only the flight that needed to be booked. But I soon realised that it was not easy to get any good flights from Stockholm to Madrid, so we ended up going to Alicante and then by train to Madrid. We arrived the day before the final and had a great time with fellow members from Norway. On the day of the final we went to the fan zone which was a great experience. What an atmosphere with thousands of Spurs fans at the same place getting ready for the biggest game in the club's history! We ended up in an Irish sports bar with fans from both teams but even though there were some words exchanged, there was no trouble between the fans. For the match itself, it kind of ended after 22 seconds when Liverpool got the penalty. It felt like Spurs never got into the match after that and it would have been interesting to have seen the match with a different start.

Directly after the final there was just a feeling of emptiness and it took a couple of days before I could try to summarise the season. Overall, considering that we had no new signings and played most of the season away from home, I think that a fourth place in the league and a spot in the Champions League final was more than I could have hoped for when the season started.

For next year I just hope that the team can stay intact for most parts and we don't lose any of the key players. I think it's time to get a couple of new names in the squad to get everyone on their toes and don't think that they have a secure place in the starting XI. I don't think Spurs will change the transfer policy drastically and we might not get a super signing that costs a lot of money but perhaps some talent that Poch can develop during the coming years. In the league I hope we can manage to push for the title and hopefully get to some more cup finals!

Paddy Forte, Dublin Spurs

I've been a loyal Spurs fan through thick and thin since 1991 after watching Spurs play in the FA Cup Final. I've stuck with my Spurs no matter who the better teams were along the way. To finally see Spurs reach the final of the Champions League was more than a dream come true. There was only one place I wanted to watch it and that was the Dublin Spurs Lodge with a different kind of family and friends and the nicest group of people that I've ever met. The lodge was absolutely packed with singing Spurs fans from all over, I've never seen it so packed. The match started very badly but I never gave up hope on our mighty Spurs but on the night, it was not meant to be.

Our fans sang until the very end despite the result with all the usual group staying until very late, singing songs about our mighty Spurs and having our usual crack and banter. It's not been a bad season but there is still a lot more work to be done. Spurs just need to get out and bring in players that will make a difference. One thing is for sure - no matter what, I'll never stop supporting and singing about my team and I'll always wear my jersey with pride. If any Spurs supporter is in Dublin and wanting to watch our team play, there is only one place to watch it: The Dublin Spurs Lodge. COYS

Pat Nottage – North West Spurs

The day after Ajax, I woke tired through lack of sleep and still emotional. I had been bombarded with emails from companies offering coaches – I'd offered to arrange transport to Madrid the previous night! I rang local companies to see if anyone would be willing to help us out and managed to find one which was fortunate - many of the others were taking Liverpool fans – and so began the task of getting an itinerary together. Word got around and within a day we had filled a coach with 47 Spurs fans for this once in a lifetime experience.

For those who were staying back in the UK I'd organised a two-pub meet up to watch the match. Both pubs were taken over even before the big day itself as word spread and we were contacted on social media by Spurs fans desperate to watch it together and experience the moment as a family of fans.

On the day itself, the long journey began arriving at Dover 6am on the 31st to board the ferry into Calais and then onto Madrid, arriving just over 24 hours later at 7am. Many headed to the fan zone to soak up the atmosphere while others went to the pubs or to go watch the match in the stadium.

Both pubs were rocking with a sea of Spurs fans, with people being turned away as they were full to bursting. The match is underway, there's a penalty, they score and the mood changes. We're Spurs, we can do this, believe. In the second half, much of the same, chances not taken and we just couldn't find the back of the net. Then Liverpool score and the feeling is disappointment that it was ours for the taking.

The long trip back from Madrid was sombre but they wouldn't have missed it for the world. It's been a remarkable journey. We are Tottenham and we will be back.

India Spurs

We, the people of India, screened the final in different cities like Delhi, Mumbai, Bangalore, Kochi, etc. Some even screened in their own houses. It was an experience of a lifetime! Seeing Spurs playing in a Champions League final is something you've always dreamt of but never really thought of happening. But it happened! Everyone was quite excited to see the final, to see those dreams come true. Everyone expected Spurs to win but it was not our day. Tough luck for us. Hoping to come back stronger.

We had a pretty good season, especially the run of Champions league. We hope that Spurs will only grow and grow from where they stand right now. We are expecting some good signings to happen for us to increase the depth and quality of the squad that will help us compete in both the league and Champions League.

Syahizan Amir – Malaysia Spurs

Wow. I still can't believe we were in the final. With no stadium, no new players and such an injury plagued season. It was very nervy season. We fought every match like the finals before we reach the eventual one. We hosted around 2000 Spurs and Liverpool fans in RASTA at 3am. We were there from midnight and it was one of our biggest crowds ever, meeting lots of Spurs fans from all around the world there.

We organized lots of match viewing parties throughout the country on that day. We personally support and advise fans to organise it wherever they are. It is the fasting month, so with the game at 3am and just three days before the Eid Festival, we were surprised when most of the venues are FULL!

Most of us loved seeing the team in the final and watching with current and new Spurs fans together. The early penalty killed the game. Mane was using some dark art and deliberately flicked the ball to Sissoko's arm. If it wasn't for the penalty, we might have gone and won it. Some were questioning why Harry is playing and Lucas was on the bench. Personally, I think we have to put the trust in Pochettino. He would know what is best for the team.

It has been a crazy season with a depleted side. Losing so many games and yet reaching the Champions League final and top four? God is kind to us. I hope the club supports MoPo's vision and invests in the players we need, and I pray we can win the league or any cup to reward the players and the fans.

Vidar Edell – Norway Spurs

I really wanted to travel to Madrid and had hopes that I just might have had enough loyalty points. It turned out - no - so me and my fiancée travelled to London instead and saw the match screened at our stadium. All in all, a good experience, and I have never seen so many fans in N17 before. A full stadium, all the pubs in the area were packed, people everywhere. Considering that tens of thousands had gone down to Madrid, it really shows the magnitude of our fanbase. In the end, the match itself was a disappointment, but my day was good anyway.

The supporters' club back in Norway was involved in lots of activities with many local arrangements dotted around the country. The place many of us frequent in Oslo, called Bohemen Sportspub, was packed many hours before kick-off and reserved for Spurs fans only. There were similar arrangements in many towns and cities all over the country. There was also a number of people who went to Madrid; I think in the end only a handful had a ticket to enter the stadium, but the others made arrangements with our good friends from Spurs Sweden.

Looking at the broader picture, we have had a superb season, no doubt about it! Going forward, we must have the ambition to improve further. It looks like there will be some changes in the team and squad, and that is always potentially risky. There is conflicting information with regards to cash available, who might be going etc. Looking back, the season has shown some of the areas that must be strengthened, assuming Spurs are already on the verge of taking another massive step going forward. One of those things (which is maybe a minor issue to some) is to always

— always - make sure there is enough beer in the stadium. That has disappointed on quite a few occasions!

Paul Ruscoe – New Zealand Spurs

It's difficult to process how I feel after the event. In the days leading up to final, there was a feeling of apprehension about the fixture. If we were playing Barcelona, it would have been a free hit. But facing Liverpool meant that while we knew we had a chance, we could equally end up on the receiving end of a Chelsea-Arsenal Europa League-esque thrashing. With that came some significant pre-match anxiety.

The day itself was phenomenal, a brilliant atmosphere in the city and a few beers soon put that anxiety to bed. Until the criminal penalty decision that ultimately cost us our place in history.

The weekend however, provided me with memories I'll never forget. From meeting Erik the Viking earlier in the afternoon and reconnecting with other Spurs fans from around the world, to hearing the most inspiring and defiant rendition of 'Oh When The Spurs' at full time. Istanbul next year anyone?

Some of our members made the trip to Madrid, and I think there was a degree of apprehension amongst us all. It's amazing how terrifying the prospect of getting a social media pasting from your Scouse/Goon/Spanner/Chelski mates really is. However, despite the underwhelming final there was a sense of intense pride at what we had achieved. I'm sure many expected to feel empty at the end of the tournament. Yet one thing you'll never take from us, is that incredible feeling at the final whistle in the Nou Camp, or when the ball bounced off Llorente's arse at the Etihad, or when Lucas Moura rolled the ball into Onana's net to send us all into a frenzy.

My first reflection on the season, being somewhat pragmatic, was a sense of relief that I didn't have to book flights for the World Club Cup. Especially after hearing that it would be in

Qatar! However, what is quite apparent is that Tottenham, despite two years (give or take a few weeks) at Wembley and a self-imposed transfer ban, are not that far behind the very best in Europe.

While that won't necessarily mean another Champions League Final next year, or even in the next ten years, what it does mean is that the silverware we crave may not be far away. When Perryman came to visit us in New Zealand earlier this year, he suggested that the first trophy may not be the Champions League, and he was ultimately right. But the very fact that we were so close to lifting that cup suggests that we're ahead of the curve.

I had planned to go back to New Zealand at the end of the season, after coming home for the first year at the new ground, but may just stay another year now...

Stewart Bannister – Hong Kong Spurs

The final was tough. As soon as the game was confirmed, chances of a visit to Madrid were slim unless one took a chance on going without a match ticket. I decided that for me, I would watch the game in our local supporters' club pub. I arrived at the pub at midnight, already after having a few beverages to calm my nerves. The pub was going to close the doors at 1am, but the kick off was at 3am Hong Kong time. There was a general sense of optimism in the air, but of course the talk was about whether we play Kane or Moura. The suspect handball killed the match and it wasn't a great game, but at least Spurs came back in the second half. Not much else to say except I am still proud of our achievements in Europe this season!

Overall the fans in Hong Kong were of the same opinion as me, although some were vocal - with hindsight - at the possible bad decision not to start with Lucas Moura. Others will still argue that you should always start with your best players, but the third argument in this area is 'yeah, start with your best players if they are match fit'. This debate will continue into next season no doubt! Most fans are still proud of Tottenham's achievement in getting to the final, yet a few may be more relieved that we still qualified for the Champions League next season after such a poor finish in the Premier League.

My hopes for next season are a long-awaited trophy, a better attempt at getting into the top two or three in the League and another decent bash in Europe again. It's difficult to achieve success in all three areas but quite possible if the squad is upgraded with new player purchases and possibly a couple of lads coming through the youth or B teams. I am in big favour of applying both methods to improve the first team squad. High hopes for 2019-20 despite the likes of Liverpool and Man City also being there and I am confident that Levy will provide extra money and Pochettino will keep together that all important tight bonding of players to achieve success!

Paul Pavlou – Yorkshire Spurs

On the 26th May 2018 I invited a few friends round for a Champions League Final barbecue. We all watched Gareth Bale come off the bench and score one of the best Champions League Final goals ever. I, for one, jumped up and screamed when that goal went in! Of course, Real Madrid went on to win it and if someone told me that night that Spurs would be in next year's final, I would have laughed out loud! Fast forward 12 months and I was lucky enough to be one of the 16,000 Spurs fans to get a ticket for the Champions League Final in Madrid. The whole experience of my trip to Madrid, apart from the result, was amazing. We found an Irish Pub to have a few drinks in on the eve of the day itself, singing Spurs songs until the early hours. Listening to some of the stories of how everyone made it to Madrid was a great way to build up to the day of the Final. By hook or crook, it was a case of getting to Madrid any way possible for many fans.

On the match day we soaked up the atmosphere at the Spurs Fan Zone but essentially, we wanted to get to the stadium a couple of hours before kick-off. We got a taxi to the stadium and as the cab driver pulled up outside the Wanda Metropolitano, that's when it sunk in....the excitement, nerves and realisation all rolled into one. The game itself was obviously disappointing. I honestly thought we were going to score in the second half and if we did - who knows! After the match, we felt very deflated but very, very proud.

Only a handful of Yorkshire Spurs fans got match tickets and an army of Yorkshire Spurs watched it at the Tottenham Hotspur Stadium. One thing was very similar between these two stadiums: echoes of 'Glory, Glory Tottenham Hotspur' rang around both after the final whistle blew. The support for our team was truly amazing, even though we were all absolutely gutted at the result. Especially after that referee decision after 24 seconds....

Lots of our members also watched in various bars around Madrid and we had an area reserved in a bar up in Yorkshire. Two hundred Spurs fans turned up and took over the place – it was at capacity two hours before kick-off! The videos on social media of the bar in Leeds showed an amazing atmosphere!

Next season? Well Mauricio has said it will be a summer of change so we will have to wait and see. Looks like Christian Eriksen is on the move which is a shame, but I have no doubt there will be money to spend. I would love another good run in the Champions League, and it would be nice to win a domestic trophy. Looking forward to the fixtures coming out in a couple of weeks so we can start planning some trips down to White Hart Lane!

Ro Huntriss – Yorkshire Spurs

I was in a very difficult position on 1st June as I was bridesmaid for my best friend! When the wedding date was announced I couldn't believe my luck. There was no way that I could not have gone to the wedding, so I just had to suck it up and deal with it. I did get slight FOMO when so many of my Spurs pals were booking their flights, boats, trains, buses - anything to try to get there - but I loved following their journeys to Madrid. I had to watch the game sat on a bench in a field in Cheshire on an iPhone with one other Spurs fan and four Liverpool fans!

When we lost, it was the first time I was happy I wasn't in Madrid. I'm not sure I could have coped, so I went straight to the bar and downed a shot of tequila and the night continued in a similar fashion! I know a lot of Liverpool fans but none of them messaged me to gloat. It took me two weeks to get over it, and at that point I was able to clearly see how amazing we had done to even get to the final and what an amazing journey that was.

So many Yorkshire Spurs travelled over to Madrid. Many with tickets and many without. People just wanted to be involved, and if it wasn't for the wedding, I would have been there myself. There were lots of people who couldn't get over there so the Yorkshire Spurs got together in a bar in the centre of Leeds and it went wild! Obviously it wasn't the result we wanted but we did so well to get to that stage.

I have had some of the best days out at the football, but since the creation of Yorkshire Spurs a couple of years ago, things went up a level. Having lived in Leeds since 2005, I have never had any Spurs friends up there, but with Yorkshire Spurs I now have a family. Everybody is amazing. We are all so different. Different ages, backgrounds, jobs - but we all have this common love and passion for Spurs and it is incredible to be a part of such an amazing group of people supporting an incredible team.

Hopes for next season are new players, top four, a good Champions League performance and a bloody trophy! For me football is more than the 90 minutes on the pitch, it's about everything else that it brings with it. To put the cherry on the cake, my boyfriend is a Spurs fan – we bonded over Spurs - so me and Spurs were meant to be. My ex was an Arsenal fan. That was obviously never going to last...

Mark Lawson – OzSpurs

I was in the Pig n Whistle pub in Brisbane for an eye wateringly early 5am kick off for our Champions League semi-final, stunned we were even still in the competition in the first place, but realistically expecting to lose to Ajax and not make the final. By half time things were going to plan for us hardened Spurs pessimists - 2-0 down, playing terribly, I was in full 'this is why we are crap' mode whilst ranting with my mates over my flat white.

What happened over the next 45 minutes was beyond any Spurs experience ever. By the time the miracle winner was tucked away, I had no idea what to do with myself. I swear someone nearby started cutting huge amounts of onions up - yes that was it. And it was only 7am meaning I had to dry my eyes, stop hugging people and go to work. Impossible, really.

When I married my wife we never had a pre-nup; a lack of any significant valuables - the '91 replica kit didn't count apparently - meant there was no need. However, I had one condition - if/when Spurs get to the Cup Final, I'm going, whatever the cost. Since 2003, Spurs have managed to lose four FA Cup Semis - agonising at the time, but with hindsight it meant I'd never cashed in that promise. Whilst sitting in a work seminar one hour after the final whistle, it was head down and on the iPhone. By the end of the seminar I'd cleared it with the wife, and work, and spent a king's ransom on a solitary match ticket through a questionable but ultimately reliable agency. I still have no idea what the seminar was about.

It took four flights over two days to get to Madrid (via

Brisbane, Singapore, Dubai and Paris if you're interested). I arrived to what can only be described as the biggest Spurs party of all time. Happy smiling people everywhere, enjoying the sun, the city, and a few songs and drinks. I realised that we have no particular beef with the Scousers and got on with them as well. I was one of a good 50 or so who'd made it over from Oz. Friday night in particular was the best time - energy, excitement, anticipation, plus randomly bumping into (the author of this book) Carl in an Irish pub - what were the odds!

I'd let the club know I was coming, so when the BBC asked them for fans who they could interview with interesting stories, I was someone they suggested. The first interview was on the phone - that must have gone well, because on the morning of the game they had me and a friend come into a cafe they had converted into a radio studio. Robbie Savage was hosting. My mate and I immediately took him to task for his performance in the 1999 League Cup Final (RIP Justin Edinburgh - unbelievably sad news of his death a few days after the final) and Robbie was reasonably remorseful. It was a fun morning, the Spurs fan zone that afternoon was amazing. I'm so glad I was there to be a part of it and see it, it felt that if we could have just played a bit better it was there for the taking, but it wasn't to be...

The BBC had asked me to come back on the Sunday morning - when I went to bed on Saturday night I didn't think I could face it. I got a big welcome and a lot of sympathy. Savage told Mark Lawrenson that I had a 42-hour journey home starting that evening - did Lawro have any words of consolation to make me feel better? He was concise – 'no'.

I rate my trip to Madrid as one of the most enjoyable weekends I've had - it's the obvious thing to say but imagine if they'd won. Of course, it's Spurs, so they didn't. I'll be staying on as OzSpurs President for another year after all and visiting the new stadium for the first time over Christmas. I'll now be expecting small chocolate mints on my seat.

Anthony Al Chaer – Lebanon Spurs

The couple of nights before the big game were either sleepless or full of dreams of Spurs lifting that prestigious European trophy. All I could talk about with members of Lebanon Spurs was the expected line-up, possible scoreline and scenarios, but the gathering that the Lebanon Spurs committee were preparing kept me quite busy.

Tottenham isn't your typical Champions League finalist, so what we felt heading into that game was kind of bewildering. I personally felt torn between sheer bliss that we reached this stage and constant stress about whether Spurs would win it or not.

Lebanon is a country where fans support teams that always had a good history with winning titles, and Tottenham, for that matter, is not one of them, so getting all the Spurs fans from around the country was a difficult task in itself. I also made efforts in promoting our supporters' club via interviews with local sports journalists and spent long hours with two good friends of mine and fellow Spurs fans, Johnny and Giuseppe, constantly sending out messages in order to make sure all members received the necessary information regarding the upcoming gathering.

Fast forward to the 1st of June, the biggest day of Tottenham Hotspur Football Club's recent history. My heart was pounding hard. Nerves were kicking in. Sweat drizzling profusely. I got to the pub a couple of hours before kick-off time to make sure everything was in place before everyone arrives with my mind set on glory later that night.

As we edged closer to kick-off, the pub began to pile up – one fan after the other, which brought even more realization to me: yes, this is happening, and it's happening to my club. My Tottenham Hotspur.

This was all I wanted; there and then.

As I sat down and watched the players coming out onto the pitch, all I could hear was the commentator's voice. I noticed that the few minutes that came before the starting whistle were very quiet: no one was talking, everyone was silently thinking about what to expect. Suddenly, the whole pub started to sing and cheer. The game started, and the rest is history.

I have been constantly working these last couple of years towards an event like this. Despite the heartbreaking loss, I was glad and proud of how I managed to get such a big number of Spurs fans together. It sent shock waves throughout the footballing community in the country.

For me, the words of the great Bill Nicholson would do to perfectly portray this season: 'It is better to fail aiming high than to succeed aiming low'. Domestically, I was not totally satisfied with how it all turned out despite the lack of transfer business in the period that preceded the start of the 2018-2019 campaign. However, I do agree with what Pochettino said regarding our players. They are heroes. Real 'capeless' heroes. They worked surrounded by teams who splashed millions on new players giving them an edge when schedules became tight and matches were coming one after the other. On the European scale, I can only say that it was the best season ever. Money is nothing without passion, and that is what our players successfully proved to the world. I disagree with many Spurs fans who claim that this might be the first and last time we reach a Champions League Final because for me, we have no limit. We go to 'infinity and beyond'.

Above all, I hope that we learn from this season and build even stronger foundations for the future. The future is bright. The future is lilywhite.

2018/19 Results

Premier League

11 August 2018	Newcastle United	1–2	Tottenham Hotspur
18 August 2018	Tottenham Hotspur	3–1	Fulham
27 August 2018	Manchester United	0–3	Tottenham Hotspur
2 September 2018	Watford	2–1	Tottenham Hotspur
15 September 2018	Tottenham Hotspur	1–2	Liverpool
22 September 2018	Brighton & Hove Albion	1–2	Tottenham Hotspur
29 September 2018	Huddersfield Town	0–2	Tottenham Hotspur
6 October 2018	Tottenham Hotspur	1–0	Cardiff City
20 October 2018	West Ham United	0–1	Tottenham Hotspur
29 October 2018	Tottenham Hotspur	0–1	Manchester City
3 November 2018	Wolverhampton Wanderers	2–3	Tottenham Hotspur

10 November 2018	Crystal Palace	0–1	Tottenham Hotspur
24 November 2018	Tottenham Hotspur	3–1	Chelsea
2 December 2018	Arsenal	4–2	Tottenham Hotspur
5 December 2018	Tottenham Hotspur	3–1	Southampton
8 December 2018	Leicester City	0–2	Tottenham Hotspur
15 December 2018	Tottenham Hotspur	1–0	Burnley
23 December 2018	Everton	2–6	Tottenham Hotspur
26 December 2018	Tottenham Hotspur	5–0	Bournemouth
29 December 2018	Tottenham Hotspur Wanderers	1–3	Wolverhampton
1 January 2019	Cardiff City	0–3	Tottenham Hotspur
13 January 2019	Tottenham Hotspur	0–1	Manchester United
20 January 2019	Fulham	1–2	Tottenham Hotspur
30 January 2019	Tottenham Hotspur	2–1	Watford

2 February 2019	Tottenham Hotspur	1–0	Newcastle United
10 February 2019	Tottenham Hotspur	3–1	Leicester City
23 February 2019	Burnley	2–1	Tottenham Hotspur
27 February 2019	Chelsea	2–0	Tottenham Hotspur
2 March 2019	Tottenham Hotspur	1–1	Arsenal
9 March 2019	Southampton	2–1	Tottenham Hotspur
31 March 2019	Liverpool	2–1	Tottenham Hotspur
3 April 2019	Tottenham Hotspur	2–0	Crystal Palace
13 April 2019	Tottenham Hotspur	4–0	Huddersfield Town
20 April 2019	Manchester City	1–0	Tottenham Hotspur
23 April 2019	Tottenham Hotspur	1–0	Brighton & Hove Albion
27 April 2019	Tottenham Hotspur	0–1	West Ham United
4 May 2019	Bournemouth	1–0	Tottenham Hotspur
12 May 2019	Tottenham Hotspur	2–2	Everton

FA Cup

4 January 2019 (Third round)	Tranmere Rovers	0–7	Tottenham Hotspur
27 January 2019 (Fourth round)	Crystal Palace	2–0	Tottenham Hotspur

EFL Cup

26 September 2018 (Third round)	Tottenham Hotspur **(Tottenham win 4-2 on penalties)**	2–2	Watford
31 October 2018 (Fourth round)	West Ham United	1–3	Tottenham Hotspur
19 December 2018 (Quarter-finals)	Arsenal	0–2	Tottenham Hotspur
8 January 2019 (Semi-final first leg)	Tottenham Hotspur	1–0	Chelsea
24 January 2019 (Semi-final second leg)	Chelsea **(2–2 on aggregate, Chelsea win 4-2 on penalties)**	2–1	Tottenham Hotspur

UEFA Champions League Group Stage

18 September 2018	Internazionale	2–1	Tottenham Hotspur
3 October 2018	Tottenham Hotspur	2–4	Barcelona
24 October 2018	PSV Eindhoven	2–2	Tottenham Hotspur
6 November 2018	Tottenham Hotspur	2–1	PSV Eindhoven
28 November 2018	Tottenham Hotspur	1–0	Internazionale
11 December 2018	Barcelona	1–1	Tottenham Hotspur

UEFA Champions League Knockout Stage

13 February 2019 (Round of 16 First leg)	Tottenham Hotspur	3–0	Borussia Dortmund
5 March 2019 (Round of 16 Second leg)	Borussia Dortmund **Tottenham win 4-0 on aggregate**	0–1	Tottenham Hotspur
9 April 2019 (Quarter-finals First leg)	Tottenham Hotspur	1–0	Manchester City

17 April 2019 (Quarter-finals Second leg)	Manchester City	4–3	Tottenham Hotspur
	4-4 on aggregate, Tottenham win on away goals rule		
30 April 2019 (Semi-final First leg)	Tottenham Hotspur	0–1	Ajax
8 May 2019 (Semi-final Second leg)	Ajax	2–3	Tottenham Hotspur
	3-3 on aggregate, Tottenham win on away goals rule		
1 June 2019 (Champions League Final - Madrid, Spain)	Tottenham Hotspur	0–2	Liverpool

Final Premier League Table 2018/19

Pos	Team	Pl	W	D	L	GF	GA	GD	Pts
1	Manchester City (C)	38	32	2	4	95	23	+72	98
2	Liverpool	38	30	7	1	89	22	+67	97
3	Chelsea	38	21	9	8	63	39	+24	72
4	Tottenham Hotspur	38	23	2	13	67	39	+28	71
5	Arsenal	38	21	7	10	73	51	+22	70
6	Manchester United	38	19	9	10	65	54	+11	66
7	Wolverhampton Wanderers	38	16	9	13	47	46	+1	57
8	Everton	38	15	9	14	54	46	+8	54
9	Leicester City	38	15	7	16	51	48	+3	52
10	West Ham United	38	15	7	16	52	55	−3	52

11	Watford	38	14	8	16	52	59	−7	50
12	Crystal Palace	38	14	7	17	51	53	−2	49
13	Newcastle United	38	12	9	17	42	48	−6	45
14	Bournemouth	38	13	6	19	56	70	−14	45
15	Burnley	38	11	7	20	45	68	−23	40
16	Southampton	38	9	12	17	45	65	−20	39
17	Brighton & Hove Albion	38	9	9	20	35	60	−25	36
18	Cardiff City (R)	38	10	4	24	34	69	−35	34
19	Fulham (R)	38	7	5	26	34	81	−47	26
20	Huddersfield Town (R)	38	3	7	28	22	76	−54	16

THE HUMBLE ONE

The months that followed that heartbreaking night in June were relatively unremarkable, all considered. As the players went their separate ways for another short summer break – self-imposed due to their on-field success, this time – Mauricio Pochettino would later reveal that he locked himself in his Barcelona home for ten days. It was the instinctive response of a manager known for wearing his heart on his sleeve as he came to terms with just how close to ultimate glory he had taken his team against all the odds.

Pre-season got underway in Singapore with an encouraging start as a near full-strength squad began their International Champions Cup campaign with a last-minute winner against Juventus. Harry Kane and Lucas Moura, two men involved in the biggest selection debate since Paul Gascoigne's omission from the France '98 squad, were provider and finisher, although few could have predicted what would happen next after Moura's steal of possession inside the centre circle. The much-maligned Harry Kane, the selection of whom had remained the focus of every football debate across a quiet summer, began exorcising weeks of frustration by embarrassing the flailing Wojciech Szczęsny from the halfway line.

With the early confirmation of Tanguy Ndombele's signature in July joining future prospects Jack Clarke and Kion Etete, Tottenham's self-imposed transfer ban had also been banished. Old frustrations would rear their heads again, however, in the trying month that followed. An injured Ryan Sessegnon's arrival in a part-exchange with Josh Onomah felt unnecessarily delayed on the eve of the new season and it would take a further three weeks to eventually confirm Giovani Lo Celso's long-rumoured move on what eventually became a bizarre deadline day loan deal.

Both had all the hallmarks of transfer dealings becoming ever more drawn out; rumours of a Van der Vaart-esque coup of Paulo Dybala stemmed the criticism from the stands a little until the story came to nothing.

Going the other way would be Kieran Trippier, Vincent Janssen, Georges-Kevin Nkoudou and eventually Fernando Llorente. All had their memorable moments in a Spurs shirt – some admittedly more fleeting than others – but it felt like good business. Although, with a growing number of influential senior players rumoured to have been close to the door, surplus to requirements or refusing to sign new deals, combined with a comically naïve approach to squad depth in several positions, most notably at full-back, the much vaunted squad revamp Pochettino had called for felt more like a dallied dismantling than a painful rebuild. At least we finally had some silverware to crow about by the new season's dawn: Audi Cup Champions, you'll never sing that.

Four points from Villa at home and Man City away looked like a respectable start until a dismal 1-0 home defeat to Steve Bruce's Newcastle United shone a light on how off the pace Spurs really were. Spurned leads from commanding positions at Arsenal, Olympiakos and Leicester surrounded rare flashes of promise and began to draw unwelcome attention to the increasingly worrying inability to win away from home. Defeat on penalties at Colchester United – the aptly named Jobserve Community Stadium seeing Pochettino's ever-shortening odds for the sack race cut notably - marked a new recent low until a complete meltdown a week later during the visit of Bayern Munich saw Spurs concede seven for the first time since December 1996.

It had been a game in which they had taken an early lead and looked competitive in until the players seemingly downed tools to accept complete annihilation. I am not proud to say I made my way up the stairwell towards the exit to begin the long journey home as the 87th minute sixth from Lewandowski hit the back of the net. It would be topped by former Arsenal player Serge Gnabry's fourth of the night in injury time and would mark the moment when clichés about losing the dressing room would reach a cacophony as the reasonable minded wrestled with their conscience and a vocal but growing minority called for the head of the man who had dared us to dream just a few short months earlier.

If Bayern hadn't sealed his fate, the nature of the 3-0 defeat at Brighton a few days later surely would. A horror injury to captain Hugo Lloris in conceding the opening goal within minutes of kick-off was an indicator of things to come. It was a return to a Tottenham performance of old and was light years away from the depths found in the Champions League run that had admittedly papered over the cracks of a dismal calendar year of domestic performances. And yet Poch remained in the dugout.

There was a brief renaissance with a 5-0 home demolition of Red Star Belgrade to undo some of the damage inflicted on our Champions League campaign by Bayern. As glimpses of a return to form against the admittedly woeful Serbian SuperLiga champions emerged, a muted chorus of Mauricio's name began to echo around the stadium – a notably rare thing in recent weeks. Instead of the standard wave of acknowledgement, the Argentinian immediately turned on his heels and headed back to his seat in the dugout, almost embarrassed by the attention. "He's not hanging around much longer," I said to my mate as we watched from the lower reaches of the Park Lane and the song slowly died. That's when we knew.

By the time my son entered the field of play ahead of November's visit of Sheffield United as flagbearer - an honour arranged by Yorkshire Spurs that left him giddy with excitement pre-match after being winked at by an increasingly under-utilised Lucas Moura - Spurs felt in limbo. Fortunate to grab a point with the helpful intervention of VAR, it would prove to be the end of road for Poch, leaving Spurs languishing 14th in a congested midtable.

When the news broke on the early evening of the 19th November, it still came as a shock. A notification on the official app gave the announcement a modern feel; the website containing the statement crashing for half an hour as hundreds of thousands of global clicks all attempted to find out more felt like vintage Spurs. Eventually, we would read that it was not taken "lightly, nor in haste" and that the board was "extremely reluctant" to make the change, "made more so given the many memorable moments we have had with Mauricio and his coaching staff – but we do so in the club's best interests."

It was somehow expected and unexpected all at the same time; like finally pulling the plug on a relationship that had once promised and delivered so much but slowly fizzled out. You can't take away the memories. Better to go your separate ways and not prolong the misery. Don't just stay together for the kids.

The role would be officially vacant for just 11 hours and 59 minutes but that didn't stop the 24-hour rolling news channels going into a feeding frenzy as on-the-spot reporters quizzed dazed talking heads outside the ground, the players posted their tributes and 'experts' weighed in with their opinions. Massimiliano Allegri's name was quickly mooted with the former Juventus manager out of work. Eddie Howe was touted as an outsider in a similar mould to the coup of Pochettino from the south coast half a decade earlier. One name that seemed to stick in the throat of all but a few, however, was Jose Mourinho.

By the time he was officially announced at 6.29am on a restored website, there had barely been enough time to absorb the news of the previous evening, let alone get to grips with the fact that one of the most successful managers of all-time had taken the reins and yet still it felt like a downgrade. That wasn't entirely without foundation, of course – the former Porto, Chelsea, Inter, Real Madrid and most recently Manchester United manager had begun to look like yesterday's man by the likes of Pochettino in recent seasons. Mourinho was a proven winner though, something that neither Spurs or Pochettino could lay claim to in recent years. If Mourinho couldn't add to his career haul of 25 trophies, perhaps no-one could.

As he met the media for the first time after holding up the famous white jersey for the cameras, the Portuguese reflected on the mistakes he'd made, on how an enforced break from the game had given him time to analyse his own career to date and described himself as "humble" – before going on to boast that he'd successfully learnt to become a pundit in the intervening period.

The PR message was clear: this was a new Mourinho. A calmer, more relaxed personality, perhaps even grateful to still be considered among the elite. He'd learnt from his mistakes and he was here to rebuild – both Tottenham and his own reputation and legacy.

Later that evening I was part of a roundtable discussion of Yorkshire Spurs fans filmed for the new Amazon series All or Nothing. Despite the initial reservations, the conversation ended almost unanimously – for a variety of reasons, Pochettino's time had come. It was difficult to accept and he left on good terms, but we moved on; and it was hard to consider a better alternative in the market that Mourinho. That he'd also been linked with the soon-to-be vacant Arsenal hotseat as Woolwich persevered with Unai Emery even gave it the added bonus of helping to potentially plunge our rivals even deeper into the mire.

Mourinho's impact was immediate. A 3-2 victory at West Ham, where an emphatic 3-0 lead was almost squandered late on, was followed by falling two goals behind to Olympiakos in his first home game in charge before a 4-2 victory was sealed. 3-0 to 3-2 at home to Bournemouth pointed to the same defensive weaknesses that needed addressing but there could be no doubt Jose was getting a tune out of his misfiring stars – and the games were entertaining to boot.

A familiar transfer window of frustration in January would at least see Giovani Lo Celso made permanent and Steven Bergwijn join from PSV Eindhoven before scoring a spectacular goal on his debut to get Spurs on their way to an impressive 2-0 victory over Manchester City. That win meant Jose had brought in four more points in his 12 games in charge than his predecessor had collected in the opening dozen games of the season. An improvement? Absolutely. But lacklustre defeats at Old Trafford,

St Mary's and twice against Chelsea combined with long-term injuries to Harry Kane and Heung-Min Son gave Mourinho a B-minus on his scorecard by the end of February. Plenty of room for improvement. Must do better if Champions League qualification was to be secured for a sixth consecutive season, even with fifth place potentially enough at the expense of Manchester City.

Pochettino's departure marked the end of one of Tottenham's brightest eras. It was now up to Jose Mourinho to capitalise on that momentum and make use of the trophy cabinet. The Humble One? Time will tell. Still The Special One? Up for serious debate. One thing was for certain: it would have to be a monumental few years in the history of Tottenham Hotspur Football Club for the Portuguese to be remembered with the same fondness as his Argentinian predecessor. He really was magic, you know.

ACKNOWLEDGEMENTS

A huge thank you to each and every Spurs supporters' club who participated in this project. Your stories of unrivalled passion, devotion and inclusion were as interesting and inspiring as I'd hoped they might be when this idea first occurred to me.

Special thanks to my interviewees Paul Pavlou, Rolfe Jones, Anthony El Chaer, Sverker Otterström, Paul Ruscoe, Eric Matey, Birgir Olafsson, Charles Packard, Syahizan Amir Abd Wahab, Franz Stockebrandt, Mark Lawson, Stewart Banister, Vidar Edell, John McClelland and Josh Sandhu. It's good know I've got a sofa to sleep on in almost every corner of the globe now, complete with a Spurs duvet and pillow.

Thank you to Lynsey, Jacob, Emilia and Indiana for living with my obsession. Thank you to my own parents for supporting that same obsession from a young age.
Thank you to the mates who came along when there was a spare ticket to share the joy and misery or just listened to me bang on about this book - not least Hadders for the continual support, Jared for designing the cover and Tom for his honesty in proofreading.

Finally, thank you to Tottenham Hotspur Football Club and every player to pull on that famous lilywhite jersey for the deeply dysfunctional relationship we share. I am certain that it will continue for the rest of my life. My occasional frustration and bewilderment will only ever be surpassed by my undying love for you and everything you represent. COYS.

ABOUT THE AUTHOR

Carl Jones is a comedian and writer who, at the time of publication, retains a full head of hair that forms approximately 25% of his club set.

He lives with his wife, two children and dog - a Jack-Tsu named Indiana - in Derbyshire. He is very fond of going on holiday, going for a curry, a glass of red, a long, muddy walk and anything that involves spending time with his kids. He is, for the most part, also moderately fond of Tottenham Hotspur Football Club.

You can see him in action or find out if he's gigging near you on a very tardily updated gigs list at carljonescomedy.co.uk or ask him on Facebook (CarlJonesComedian) and Twitter (@CarlDJones)

Enjoyed this book? Tag the author with a picture of you holding your copy for a social media shout out.

Printed in Great Britain
by Amazon